The Authors—

DAVID WILKERSON is founder and co-director of TEEN CHALLENGE, an organization started when he began preaching in the streets, in borrowed churches, and in the hideouts of addicts. Today, its headquarters is in a new international complex in Brooklyn. Other centers are strategically located in the United States, Canada, and Europe. The goal of Teen Challenge is the same as that of Dave Wilkerson—to rescue today's confused youth. Few men know the "untapped generation" as this man—he has met them, counseled them, and helped them. He is also the author of the best-sellers, *The Cross and the Switchblade, Purple Violet Squish, Twelve Angels from Hell, The Little People,* and *Parents on Trial.*

DONALD WILKERSON, David's brother, and co-director of TEEN CHALLENGE, has counseled hundreds of troubled youngsters. His experience and penetrating forthright analyses of the modern social scene gives *THE UNTAPPED GENERATION* its undeniable realism. His personal contact with the actual problems of the social context, and the factual data he has enmassed have formed the authentic and documentary basis of this book.

THE UNTAPPED GENERATION

the untapped generation

by DAVID & DON WILKERSON

ZONDERVAN PUBLISHING HOUSE
GRAND RAPIDS, MICHIGAN

ACKNOWLEDGMENTS

There are several to whom we would like to express our thanks for help in writing this book. Because of the variety and type of subject matter covered we have sought the ideas, suggestions, information, and advice of friends.

We are grateful to "mom" (Ann Wilkerson, our mother) for her help on the chapter on Rebels, Runaways, and Revolutionaries; to John Benton, Associate Director of Teen Challenge and Director of the Teen Challenge home for girls (Walter Hoving Home) for his help on the materials on Prostitution; to Mary Earls, a former Teen Challenge C.U.R.E. Corps worker, for her suggestions for the chapter entitled "The Trapped Generation."

And a special "thanks" to Lester Eisenberger, pastor of the Assemblies of God Church in Yonkers, New York, and Director of Counseling at Teen Challenge. Many of the counseling techniques covered in this book are the result of Mr. Eisenberger's work at Teen Challenge and from his personal counseling. Many young people, former addicts, and troubled persons, have been affected by his counseling.

We would also like to thank our secretaries, Margaret Colao and Naomi Garcia, for the many hours of typing on the manuscript.

We are grateful to Jim Reapsome, the writer, who has taken our rough draft and put it together in the form which you will read.

DAVID and DON WILKERSON

CONTENTS

FOREWORD — *David Wilkerson*   7

THE STREETS WHERE THE LONELY WALK

1. THE UNTAPPED GENERATION — *Don Wilkerson*   23

2. TAKING AN X-RAY — *Don Wilkerson*   29
   The counselor must know God • The counselor must
   know himself • The counselor must know how to
   relate to others • The counselor must know how to
   react properly to the counselee • Answering some
   questions

3. THE CONQUEST OF INNER SPACE —
   Don Wilkerson   41
   Teen Challenge Center • Coffee Houses • Bible clubs
   and children's schools • The church and launching
   pads • Preaching and teaching

4. LIGHTING FIRES — *Don Wilkerson*   56
   The precounseling period (readiness, communication, "mooders," "conners" and sympathy seekers)
   • The counseling period (be a good listener, get the
   client to talk, pinpoint the problem, don't talk too
   much, ignite hope and spark change) • Theology
   and the counselor-counselee relationship

5. THE ADDICTED GENERATION —
   David and Don Wilkerson   85
   Tripping out with LSD • Three categories of drug
   involvement • How and why young people experiment and become dependent on drugs • The drug
   user • The drug abusers • The addict • The drug
   personality • Understanding the addict as a drug
   user and as a person • How to counsel the addict

6. GUY OR GAY? — *David and Don Wilkerson*   105
   The roots of homosexuality • Types of homosexuals
   • Developing a counseling ministry to homosexuals
   • How to counsel homosexuals

7. SOBER OR FREE? — *Don Wilkerson*   125
   Alcoholics—who are they? • Types of alcoholics
   • The roots of alcoholism • How to counsel the
   alcoholic

8. REBELS, RUNAWAYS AND REVOLUTIONARIES —
   David and Don Wilkerson   149
   The rebels • The runaways • Types of runaways •
   Types of hippies • The runaways' 'bags' • The rea-
   sons for running away • The revolutionaries • How
   to counsel rebels, runaways and revolutionaries

9. THE SEXUAL GENERATION —
   David and Don Wilkerson   180
   The premarital generation • Counseling about premarital sex • Unwed mothers • Counseling the prostitute • Types of prostitutes • How and why does
   a girl become a prostitute? • How to counsel the
   prostitute

10. THE TRAPPED GENERATION — *Don Wilkerson*   217

11. THE INTEGRATION PROBLEM — *Don Wilkerson* 233
    Why churches fear the untapped generation • How
    to integrate the untapped generation into the church
    • Guidelines for churches

CONCLUSION — *David and Don Wilkerson*   255

FOREWORD

This book was conceived in the struggles, throes and frustrations of ghetto counseling. Developed through years of trials, errors, and testings, the approaches mentioned here have proven their reliability to my brother and me.

The problems spoken of are not confined to the ghetto alone — they are consuming youth at large: a troubled generation from every social class who are seeking peace in dope, sex, perversion and ultimately in death. They are found in the large city ghettos, the upper echelons of suburbia, peaceful rural areas, and the "typical" American town. They vary from religious to secular backgrounds, from divorced and broken homes to close family relationships, from wealthy to poverty-stricken homes, from different races and intelligence levels.

We have tried to set down many of the basic tenets for hitting this generation's "vibrations" — to be "straight" in order to win them to a revolutionary life in Jesus Christ.

In the changing age in which we live, *The Untapped Generation* assumes a terrifying relevancy. These days could well be our "last chance" to reach this dissatisfied, unfulfilled yet extremely intelligent generation. Therefore it is important that our counseling make use of the most effective tools possible.

In *The Untapped Generation* these tools are revealed in a lasting tribute to the work here at Teen Challenge, and to all those working in the ghettos, small towns, rural areas and every variety of American life where youth is found.

We feel that this book will prove a valuable sourcebook to the pastor, Christian worker, and layman who find occasion to counsel *The Untapped Generation*.

DAVID WILKERSON

THE STREETS WHERE THE LONELY WALK

The streets where the party is
   Where lights blaze and glare.
The gang and the debonair from this thoroughfare,
   Amid all the gaudiness and much seeming bliss.
Loneliness stalks its prey,
   And in death finds its way.
Oh Holy Spirit, this is my prayer,
   Make me a blessing to somebody there. . . .

                                    GLADNESS JENNINGS

The streets where the lonely walk are calling to me

Every Christian worker and counselor must travel the streets where the lonely walk. And like Nehemiah of old who walked and viewed the ruin and decay of a fallen Jerusalem, the Christian worker must view the decay of humanity and the untapped generation. And again like Nehemiah, he must take it to heart: "I sat down and wept, and mourned certain days, and fasted, and prayed before the God of heaven" (Neh. 1:4).

The Christian worker must also understand the places where the lonely walk. The gay bar, the pot party, the heroin addict's shooting gallery, the scum of the local skid row or Bowery, the sexual market place where pimp, prostitute, and pick-up gather, the sex orgy den, and the teen-age gang hideout.

Come with us along a few of these lonely streets and

into some of the places where the lost and the lonely satisfy their craving.

Where the grass is not greener

First we go up three flights of stairs to the "pad" — a lower East Side Manhattan tenement house apartment. A pot party is about to take place. Inside is Mark, a twenty-one-year-old college drop-out; Frank, a nineteen-year-old runaway from New Jersey (usually only a weekend runaway); Sue, a twenty-year-old hippie runaway from Michigan in her second year in the Village; and Clarence, a twenty-five-year-old Negro musician from Harlem.

Like many similar gatherings they had not planned a "tea" party. They had just happened to meet on the street and decided to go to Mark's apartment. Pot is usually not planned among such groups; it just happens. Though the four comprised a relatively small group for the usual pot gathering, they decided to "groove" anyway. Mark's apartment was well-known by a select number of East Villagers and used frequently as an overnight crash pad. Others would have been welcome had they come.

The smell of incense filled the room. The small living room contained a couch, a non-matching chair, a bench, and a large mattress in the center of the floor — and a record player. The sound and music of The Loving Spoonfuls also filled the room. The conversation (there was much of it) ranged from "What have you been doing lately?" to more serious interaction on Vietnam, Cambodia, and other feelings about the establishment in general. Frank told about a confrontation with his father over the marijuana question and as to what he should have told his dad when asked if he was smoking pot. Sue and Clarence said, "Tell the old man," but Mark felt "What he doesn't know won't hurt him." As they continued "rapping" Mark got up, went to his bedroom, opened a dresser drawer, and pulled out a tobacco can. Hand-painted over the can were the words Acapulco Gold. Returning to the living room he opened the can and took out a "joint" which was lying on top of the loose marijuana. It was approximately two to three inches in length and about three times larger than a regular cigarette. "Wow, you really like roaches (a large pot cigarette)," commented Frank.

Soon each was puffing on the stick. Although there were other sticks in the can, only one was lit. Each inhaled carefully and deliberately, taking one or two puffs at a time. There was little talking now. As the stick burned down each smoker appeared more anxious to smoke it. They knew it got better at the end. (The resins in a marijuana cigarette build up toward the end as it burns, and the effect is greater.) Each grabbed for the end of the butt. Mark pulled a clip out of his pocket to hold the small butt, and to get the very last puff. Clarence was last. "Ahh, good to the last drop," he said.

As they continued talking at first the pace of the conversation was very slow but it soon picked up again. There was a noticeable difference in their voices — they were hoarse and high-pitched yet the words were clearly understandable. As talk continued they got deeper and deeper into each subject. However, they became noticeably more relaxed. They explored some subjects on a deep psychological level, each adding his own ideas and insights. In between there were laughter and expressions of delight. Each seemed to agree with the other's point of view. The meeting continued for about two more hours as conversation was mixed with some eating, more records and music, and some pacing back and forth through the apartment. Clarence fell asleep on the couch, Frank finally left to meet a friend, and Mark and Sue continued talking together. They all felt as if they had been to a great conference to discuss a most pertinent issue, and feeling that the matter had been settled and solved.

*   *   *

The above scene could have taken place in any number of other places. A plush upper East Side penthouse, a middle-class suburban home, a small Vermont farmhouse occupied as a hippie commune, or in a campus sorority house. Regardless of where it is, thousands of bored and lonely youth, and an ever-increasing number of middle-aged, walk into such pot gatherings hoping that the grass is greener — or browner — on the other side of the fence.

The streets where the lonely go are sometimes traveled by car. In this case we are going north of New York City to a small town just off the New York State Thruway. The place is a bar — better known as a "gay bar." At one time it was for straights, but when business became poor the proprietor started catering to non-straights (homosexuals). In such an area gay bars are not as prevalent as in a large city and thus the word spreads quickly through the gay underground. And soon *The Swan* had new clientele.

This night there were approximately twenty patrons. Two women and the rest men, perhaps all homosexuals except for a few strangers who may have been driving by and stopped for a quick drink unaware that unofficially this was exclusively for gays. Also, occasionally the bar was patronized by "fruit flies" — women who for various unknown reasons like to associate with male homosexuals.

The homosexuals themselves ranged from ages eighteen to forty-five or fifty. Some were married with families. Those who are and hold executive type jobs have traveled some distance to get here for fear of being found out if they stay in their own locality. The difference between a homosexual bar and a regular one is the conversation of the patrons. At a regular bar the talk is usually lengthy and the interaction between groups of twos, threes, or fours is generally involved. Not so with the "gay" crowd. There is much milling around or standing alone, and the conversations are short. What talk there is is very superficial — and cheap. Also there is much waiting. What they are waiting for no one knows. It is as if some lost friend is about to come or that long-looked-for lover who is going to make them live happily ever after — is going to come prancing in. Homosexuals are always looking for that ideal sexual object. Often they play cat and mouse games with each other, fearful of making contact, not knowing if they do approach someone whether they will be accepted or rejected. Homosexuals have the same problem in asking for a date as young men have inviting a girl out — there is always the fear of being turned down.

One might think by evening's end in the bar that all

would pair off and go away together. This is not always the case. Some sit all evening and go out as they came in — alone. Others do make contact.

The gay bar, although unknown to the mass majority of American people, is one of the most lonely places on the face of the earth.

Where the society is "high"

The place is a walk-in basement apartment of a Brooklyn brownstone house. Rachel, a thirty-three-year-old drug addict prostitute, lives there with her nine-month-old baby boy. The dark, musty-smelling, dingy four-room apartment is also the temporary shelter for approximately a dozen or two male and female addicts who use the living room as a "shooting gallery." A shooting gallery is any place occupied by a number of addicts where they inject the drugs into their arms.

It is 10 p.m. as we enter. The baby is sleeping. Five addicts have gathered, each bringing his own "stuff" (heroin). The regulars have hidden their set of works (needle, eye dropper, etc.) in a corner of the room. Others take theirs out of their pockets. One addict has no works so he will share another's. Pabo, the oldest of the group, lays his "instruments of death" on the floor. The cooker, a small bottle cap, has a hair clip fit around it to serve as a handle. Placing the eye dropper and needle in front of him he takes his home-made eye dropper holder — the edge of a dollar bill approximately 1/4" in width — and rolls it around the top of the needle and fits it into the eye dropper. The wet dollar bill edge serves as a sponge to secure the dropper and needle snugly together. Next he opens the five-dollar bag of heroin, licks his finger, then touches the heroin lightly. He tastes it to test its strength. He is asking himself, "Is it good stuff; is it garbage, or is it pure heroin?" If the latter is the case, this could be his last shot. Most heroin is only 2 to 5 percent potent.

Occasionally, either by accident or design, pushers will sell stronger heroin and the result can be an OD (overdose). It is a quiet way of doing away with somebody. Pabo is assured this bag is safe. Now he puts it in the cooker, carefully scraping it to be assured that every bit is used. Then taking the eye dropper and needle he places it in a glass of water, fills up the dropper, then shoots the water into the cooker. Next he puts a match under it to heat and dissolve the white powder in the water. Taking the needle again, he draws the substance out of the cooker and up into the dropper.

Anticipation is written over his face. Quickly he removes his belt and wraps it around his left arm, making a tourniquet. Now he is pumping his arm — the veins slowly puff up. Balancing his left arm on his left leg he takes the needle in his right hand and slowly injects it into the vein. With the thumb and first finger of his right hand he squeezes the rubber part of the eye dropper. Slowly the heroin goes into his arm. But suddenly he stops and pulls the needle out. He has missed. Papo's veins are very bad. He has been on drugs thirteen years, since he was twenty years of age. It is not uncommon for him to take two or three minutes to find a good vein. Again, he drills. Smack — "It's a hit," he says out loud. Quickly the heroin enters his bloodstream, warms his body, and once again he is "up, up, and away."

Now he feels like a new man. Taking a piece of brown wrapping paper, he puts his works inside and rolls them up and puts them back in his hiding place.

While the others complete the same ritual, he sits down in a chair to "goof" (experience the dreamy world of the heroin high). In two hours the heaviness of his high will taper off somewhat and he will go home to his wife (a non-drug user) and go to sleep. Tomorrow he will go through the same routine three times. In the morning when he wakes up, about 3 o'clock in the afternoon, and late in the evening. He will do it, that is, unless he gets "busted" (arrested) or takes an OD. Or he will stop if he finally makes up his mind to listen to the pleading of his wife and go to Teen Challenge. If he is fortunate enough to remain alive and does not find a positive cure — he will continue to be a member of the "high" society — and live on those streets where the lonely walk.

Where "groupies" group

The small basement discotheque vibrates with the pulsating sounds of electric rock. Spotlights — all of them white — hang from the ceiling and flash off and on in split-second timing and seem as though they are timed to do so with each beat of the music. The rhythm and beat of the rock sound, the loudness of the amplifiers, and the effect of the split-second flashing of the white spot lights bouncing off from black walls produces a simulated drug trip. A rock group calling themselves The Grass Stains, provides the entertainment. The smoke in the small room is heavy and so is the odor which is sweet-smelling. It is marijuana. About fifteen young people are dancing. The rest, about twenty-five of them, sit at tables talking, listening, smoking.

Dottie, a close friend of the lead guitarist, sits off to the side at a table. The music, as it always does with her, blows her mind — a little. When she smokes pot in such an atmosphere she quickly gets stoned. Since she has plans with Mike, the guitarist, after the show, she trips out on the music and passes up the grass.

*　　*　　*

Dottie is a rock-away, which is an offshoot of the runaway generation. The rock-aways follow the various rock 'n' roll musical groups around the country getting high on the music and pot, or both. In the summer the rock-aways go to the out-of-town rock festivals and in the winter make the rounds of the rock concerts, discotheques, hippie coffee houses, or wherever the acid rock groups perform. Dottie, besides having been a rock-away for two years, has recently become a member of the "groupies" — a special group which has come about as a result of the whole rock scene. The phenomena and the popularity of rock 'n' roll music and its almost addictive influence over teenagers has created the groupies. The object of the average groupie member is to have sexual intercourse with as many members of as many of the rock groups as possible. The excitement and romantic aura that surround the life style of the young and hip members of rock 'n' roll groups lures the sexually promiscuous girl into such a group sex bag. Some girls even play the "group conquest" game which means she tries to "make it" with every member of a particular rock 'n' roll group (going to bed with each of them). Groupie activity may also include going on a traveling tour with the group, sharing motel or hotel room and bed or beds, or to become an "old lady" — the mistress of one particular member of a group. Some rock groups have an "old lady" for the whole group, she is known as a "mother groupie."

Dottie is a non-touring groupie, which means she does not go on tour but instead is "in" with about four different performing groups. When one comes to town she goes to the performance and afterwards participates in her own groupie performance — sex. She is eighteen years of age, a high school graduate who lives at home, when she is there. On this particular night she is dressed in long pants, and is wearing a bra-less blouse. Shining purple eye make-up is spread heavily on her eyelids and around her eye sockets. Black mascara covers long, artificial eye lashes — she has no other make-up on. Her hair is brown and plain. When she first tried to break into the groupie scene, she wore her hair Afro style although she is white. She did this simply to be noticed. Once she got to know some fellows she didn't wear it that way any longer.

Her first affair took place when she started hanging out in the lobbies of the hotels where the rock groups would stay. The activities in hotel suites of rock stars on tour resemble an orgy, especially on the last night after a several-night stand. One night Dottie overheard several members of a group talk about a group gathering that was about to take place in one of the suites, so she decided to crash it. They allowed her in. She let two members use her sexually that night and thereafter became friendly with Mike. Every time he came to town she was his "old lady." Only she didn't tell him that she was the "old lady" for three other members of three other groups. She only hoped they all didn't come to town at once.

Where a man can meet God

John sat in my office looking up with innocence written all over his face. "I don't know anything about that case, Brother Don. Honest, I don't. I am innocent." A detective had just called Randy Larson, the dean of our Teen Challenge Center, and told him he found out from John's mother that he was at Teen Challenge. The detective stated that he was on his way to arrest John for a charge being held against him for receiving stolen goods. We asked the detective if rather than coming over to arrest John, he could come and turn himself in. Having John arrested within the premises of Teen Challenge would not set too well with the other young men in the program who usually have great resentments against the police. As we further questioned John he insisted that he was not guilty. "Really, I don't know what this is all about," he said most convincingly. I finally convinced John that it would be best for him to go turn himself in and if he was innocent, I said, "God will get you out of this situation."

Another staff worker drove him to Manhattan. Once before the detective, John continued to insist that he was innocent. He spoke of the change in his life and gave the detective a rundown on the Teen Challenge program. After hearing the full story the detective, a narcotics agent, said, "Wait here. I'll be right back," and disappeared. When he returned, he told John that he had spoken to his supervisor and that the case would be dismissed. They shook hands and John and the staff worker walked downstairs to get into the car to return to Teen Challenge. As John was opening the door he looked at the staff worker and asked, "Should I tell the man the truth?"

"What do you mean?" asked the surprised staff worker.

"I'm guilty," answered John. "I really do know what that case is all about. I lied to the man. I don't know why I did. But the Lord is convicting me now. I know I can't go back to Teen Challenge and live a lie. Let's go back up and tell him the truth."

Slowly they walked back upstairs and found the detective again. "What's the matter?" he asked. As John made his confession, the gentleman became visibly upset. He began pacing up and down the floor. Angrily looking at John he said, "What are you trying to do to me? Do you know something? I just got assigned to the detective squad and you're one of my first cases. I don't know what my supervisor is going to say. You're going to make me look awful bad." Finally after pacing the floor trying to figure out how to handle John's confession, he went back to find his supervisor. When the two returned the supervisor came over to John and said, "Let me shake your hand. I admire you for doing this. You restored my faith in humanity. I've never seen anything like this before. I respect you for the courage you had in coming back to confess this. We'll have to process this case and you'll have to go to court, but in the meantime you can go back with these people until we call for you. I wish you a lot of luck."

John walked out of the office proud of himself that he had faced this important crisis in his new Christian life. He knew now that Christ had really changed his life. It had only been a few weeks since John's conversion. This was not to be the last crisis that John faced in his new-found faith. He had been an addict for many years and his steps from the needle to the cross are not easy ones. But this was his biggest crisis and the fact that God had given him the strength to face it gave him hope for the future.

John is 26 years of age, white, from a European background. He is single, received his high school diploma in a penal institution, and also learned a trade there. In counseling sessions, when asked why he came to Teen Challenge, he simply answered, "I want to face life without drugs. I'm sick and tired of jail. I want to live a decent life."

John's trouble started in the second grade when he began to play hooky. Through subsequent years, his parents were called to school but he was always able to talk his way out of it. When he was twelve he said he began to drink. "In my neighborhood the fifteen-year-olds were drinking. It was the thing to do. It so happened I hung around the older fellows. They let me drink with them because they thought it was funny." At eighteen he was sentenced to a house of detention for larceny and unlawful entry. After serving twenty-one months he was released on parole as a craftsman's helper at $60.00 per week. He felt his employer took advantage of him in paying this small amount but he was reminded that it was this job that got him out of prison. This caused him to have a considerable amount of resentment. Then he was picked up by his parole officer while he was on the job. At the time he was high on pills. He was returned to the penal institution where he remained until he was twenty-one. Then he started using heroin, cocaine, speed, and even experimented with LSD. The latter experience he said, "was a good trip but I didn't take any more because I was afraid I would blow my mind." When he finally became hooked on heroin, he spent time in two different hospitals trying to kick his habit. But both times he was back on drugs in a few days after his release.

John was introduced to Teen Challenge one day when he heard some fellows talking about it on a street corner. Two of the fellows were former users he had known. He asked one, "You look pretty good. You must have just gotten out of jail. How long was your rap?"

"I haven't been in jail, man. But I was arrested. The big Man got me — God. I went to a program and there I accepted Jesus Christ into my life. You are looking at the result." John went away from that street corner thinking that it was incredible that these two fellows had been cured. Later a woman gave him a tract from Teen Challenge but he didn't read it. He said, "I put it in my pocket. I remembered thinking that something must be going on. First I met those fellows who had been cured and now a strange woman gives me a tract. I felt afraid, yet glad that God was after me."

A few months later when his drug habit was getting bigger and bigger, and getting the money together was becoming more and more difficult, he pulled the tract out of his pocket and called Teen Challenge. He was told to come for an interview and was accepted. "I split (left) after the second day. The religion was not for me. All that praying and Bible reading. It was too much for me," John stated. But after staying on the streets, shooting drugs for a week, he came back to Teen Challenge again. This time he stayed for one day. Then he split again. This time he said, "I stayed on the streets a day and a half, then called Randy and asked if I could come back again. God must have really been on my side 'cause Randy let me in for the third time, and when you split like I did usually that just doesn't happen. When I returned I still felt strange in the chapel services, but for some reason I started to feel good inside. You know, it's like they say. When they feed you God in the morning, Jesus Christ in the afternoon, and the Holy Ghost at night — you start getting 'hooked.' The Spirit revealed Himself to me one day, and I don't remember just when it was but suddenly one day I knew that I was different. I just knew I was converted." From this time on John said, "This place was simply beautiful."

John's parents were glad that he was off drugs, but they weren't happy about his being at Teen Challenge. He had come from a good section of the city, and his father had a supervisory job in a good establishment. He has two brothers, one older and one younger. John states that he got along well with his father, but there are other indications from the counseling sessions that give a different relationship. His father never disciplined him, and all discipline was handled by his mother with whom he got along very well. His relationship with his siblings was poor.

His parents are devout Roman Catholics and consider Teen Challenge strictly a Protestant organization. John told them, "Would you rather have a dead Catholic drug addict or an alive Protestant?" Later John stated, "Actually no one ever spoke to me about what religion Teen Challenge believed. I see now that it was not a church but the Bible and Christ that was most important."

THE UNTAPPED GENERATION

1

THE UNTAPPED GENERATION

During a Sunday evening service an alcoholic drifted into a church in New York's Bowery district. He staggered to the front and sank into a pew. It wasn't long before he leaned over and dozed off, then suddenly he popped upright.

Much to the speaker's consternation, the drunk's unsteadiness soon distracted the congregation. No amount of preaching could overcome the man's bobbing and weaving in the front row. Finally, the speaker, a Teen Challenge staff man, ended the service and went to the alcoholic's side.

At that moment a deacon also arrived and admonished the Teen Challenge staffer, "Don't waste your time. Get the bum out of here!"

Was it a waste of time? The fellow from Teen Challenge didn't think so. Just a week before, outside the same church, he had stopped to talk with an alcoholic who was doing a little panhandling. The upshot of that conversation was a new man in Christ. After a period of time at Teen Challenge Inn he had been converted, reunited with his family, and started on a new job.

What made the difference in attitudes? The one Christian saw the alcoholic as a bum to be disposed of; the other saw him as a potential member of Christ's kingdom, part of the church's untapped resources. Perhaps the deacon was guilty of what I call the sin of the Jericho Road.

Remember the story of the Good Samaritan and the man who was robbed and beaten on the road to Jericho? The priest and Levite passed by the unfortunate victim. They saw his bleeding wounds and heard his groans of agony, but they didn't really see him as a man who needed their help.

It is possible for Christians today, seeing and hearing the awful effects of sin in the lives of people, to pass by on the other side.

Do we have an eye to see the potential in the untapped generation? I recall the time I was traveling through an African game preserve. The underbrush was thick and it was hard to see any animals. But by careful observation I was able to point out some of the monkeys, lions and zebras to others in our party who couldn't see them.

That's something of the way it is when you look at the youth of today, when you peer into the juvenile jungles of our society. Some Christians have an eye for the game and some don't. In the parable Jesus told, the Good Samaritan had an eye that penetrated the surface. He saw the possibilities of rescue.

Whether the church reaches the so-called unreachables among young people depends on whether or not Christians have an eye to see them and reach them for who and what they really are. Are they attractions or distractions? Blessings or burdens? Are Christians willing to work with them, love them, pray with them, accept them and counsel them until they become blessings?

What do you see walking the streets, sleeping in gutters, shooting heroin? Immoral vagrants? Disobedient children? Unclean loafers? Yes, all that, but what else? Do you see the possibility of chosen vessels for the Lord Jesus among them? Is there among today's street people a future soul-winner, a man of God, a great evangelist, a teacher of the Word of God?

At the 1969 U.S. Congress on Evangelism at Minneapolis I gave a seven-minute response to Leighton Ford's paper on "The Church in an Age of Revolution." I asked the 6,000 delegates from a hundred different denominations how they would feel if a smelly, unkempt hippie came into their church and sat on the front pew. Little did I know then that two nights later something like that would actually happen at the Congress.

During a musical program two hippies came into the auditorium and sat on the floor at the front. When asked to leave by the ushers, they refused and so they were picked up and removed bodily. The audience booed. Later on the speaker for the evening remarked, "I must get this off my chest. We've just thrown out of this auditorium the two people who look more like Jesus Christ than anyone else here."

While the crowd cheered his statement, the two hippies were escorted back into the auditorium. The delegates stood and applauded. Then the speaker said to the hippies, "I'm talking about phonies in the church, and I'm sure you'll catch on real quickly."

Jesus said, "Ye have not because ye ask not." It is also true, "ye have not because ye *want not.*" The church has already lost too many young people because it doesn't *want* to be bothered with them. By its actions the church shows that often it caters only to preferred types of people. Former addicts and former homosexuals, for example, aren't welcome.

Such an attitude denies the fundamental nature of the church. "Surely you know that the unjust will never come into possession of the kingdom of God. Make no mistake: no fornicator or idolater, none who are guilty either of adultery or of homosexual perversion, no thieves or grabbers or drunkards or slanderers or swindlers, will possess the kingdom of God. *Such were some of you.* But you have been through the purifying waters; you have been dedicated to God and justified through the name of the Lord Jesus and the Spirit of our God" (1 Cor. 6:9-11, NEB, italics mine).

What a crowd made up the church at Corinth! Former thieves, adulterers, homosexuals, alcoholics, slanderers and swindlers — hardly a desirable group.

Of course, you can say, "And look at all the problems they caused." But who is to say the problems would have been any less, or any different, with a sophisticated, refined church? Unfortunately, today, the church prefers to have its pews filled with nice middle-class people.

The issue is not whether Christians should reach up-and-outers *or* down-and-outers. We must not go after one group to the exclusion of the other. The Lord Jesus Christ came to give His life as a ransom for *all:* the pretty and the ugly, the refined and the uncultured, the good kids and the bad ones.

Some types that we wouldn't go out of our way to help, He deliberately sought out. Take the woman of Samaria whom He encountered at the well, for example. Jesus crossed ethnic lines and social barriers to talk with her. She had had five husbands and was not married to the man she was then living with. Yet Jesus took time to sit down and talk with this outcast, one who definitely was not "our kind."

Remember the crook, Zacchaeus? He was hidden in a tree, trying to get a glimpse of Jesus as He passed by. But Jesus looked up and saw him. Even more astonishingly, He invited Himself to stay with the man who had milked the Jews out of their money for many years. That was the day salvation came to this unlikely candidate for church membership.

Or, there was that skeptic Nathanael. When told about Jesus, he replied sarcastically, "Can anything good come from Nazareth?" We might have rejected him on those grounds, but not the Lord Jesus. He called Nathanael to Himself and said, "There is nothing false in him." Jesus saw the real Nathanael through the facade of his skepticism.

Christians are often deceived by appearances. They are impressed by how bad the young generation looks and assume that this hard appearance means hardness of heart. This is a definite hindrance in reaching the untapped generation for Christ. We cannot assume anything by appearance, either hardness or indifference.

One night I was speaking at a street meeting in Brooklyn. A young fellow right in front began to put on a little show of his own. He told jokes, did tricks on his bicycle, and generally disrupted things. He was having a good time entertaining himself and the audience.

Then I spoke up and said, "Friends, you notice the young man making all the noise. Out of all who are here, he's the one who is the most insecure and the one who needs this message. That's why he's making all the racket."

I looked right at him. "Young fellow, you're not fooling anyone. *You* are the chicken. *You* are the fearful one. Why don't you stop and listen? You need help," I said.

He stopped his antics and started to listen. After the meeting, he was one of the first to ask for prayer and help. He told me, "You cut me down, preacher, and you were right. I was afraid. I just put up a big front, but the only one I'm fooling is myself. I need God. Pray for me."

The challenge of the untapped generation is all around us, not just in the slums and ghettos. Young people are in trouble everywhere, the posh suburbs just as well as anywhere else. Most Christians feel inferior when it comes to working with addicts, prostitutes, and homosexuals. They think they can only work with middle-class people, housewives, businessmen. Somehow the church must break down this emotional barrier; new approaches must be found; practical training must be given.

The purpose of this book is to help Christians reach, counsel and rehabilitate the forgotten, the overlooked, the forsaken among us. You will find hints and guidelines here that will give you the know-how and confidence you need to work intelligently and compassionately with young people with all kinds of problems.

Much of our problem is fear of addicts and alcoholics. I had to learn to overcome fear when I first started to work with Teen Challenge. I was afraid to go out on the streets and talk with gang leaders, addicts and militants. This preconceived fear was a barrier to my witness for Christ.

But I soon found out that apart from drugs, apart from the pull of the gang, these fellows were lonely and insecure. Most of all, they wanted love and attention. I did not have to be afraid of them.

Of course, you learn not to take unnecessary risks. Addicts in pursuit of narcotics and gang members heated up for a rumble can be dangerous. You have to find the right kind of atmosphere and setting for counseling.

Further, we do not assume that these young fellows are not interested in what we have to say. Many of them put on a front; they appear to be hard, tough, indifferent. They try hard to maintain the image they have constructed for themselves. Our job is to penetrate that facade and find the real person underneath. The counselor must probe through layers of habits, attitudes and characteristics to reach the youth's mind, heart and will.

The same thing must be done in what seems like an untroubled suburban situation. I often make the mistake of looking at the faces in congregations and thinking that these people seem to be happy and well-adjusted. Later, I find out that the neatly dressed business man is an alcoholic; the innocent-looking housewife is on pep pills; the sharp teen-age girl is getting ready to run away from home.

The Christian worker has to be a spiritual detective, wherever he is, to catch the signs of need.

One night a group of drug addicts stood outside a church. Inside, the Christians were singing enthusiastically. Soon the addicts started to dance around the street to the tune of the hymn. One of them said, "You know, those people inside have something to sing about. We're out here dancing and we have nothing to dance about."

The Now Generation, the youth of America, are dancing to Satan's beat and lyric: drugs, sex, the Playboy philosophy. They are dancing, but deep inside many of them know they have nothing to dance about.

At the same time, Christians in the church do have something glorious to sing about. What we must do is build a bridge, or a pipeline, and get what's inside the church plugged into the needs of people outside.

Too often those inside wait for those outside to come into the church. This rarely happens. Instead, the Christians must go to those outside, those who are lost, those who have no hope without Jesus Christ. The "outs" may never come in, but the "ins" can go out.

2

CHAPTER 2

TAKING AN X-RAY

The most important person in counseling is the counselor. I say to all our new staff counselors, "The most important thing you'll learn here at Teen Challenge is how much *you* need to change."

One of our staff was asked, "How's Billy doing?"

He replied, "He's doing all right. I think he's making some real progress, but I think I'm making more progress."

Billy was teaching the counselor lessons about himself and his own need to grow and adjust to the situation.

Before entering a counseling ministry, and during the process of counseling, the counselor must diagnose himself. He may need to make personal and spiritual adjustments; he may need additional maturity; he may need to resolve emotional conflicts.

One of the most difficult things to do is to tell someone they are not prepared for working with addicts and distressed people on an in-patient basis. A person may be well-trained theologically and academically, yet lack personal qualities necessary for working on a one-to-one basis with troubled souls. They may love, and have a burden to reach those in need, but they do not know how to relate to them.

What are the special spiritual demands on a counselor?

Carrying the burden and weight of another person's problems; personally confronting problems in depth; discerning the problem and presenting the answer; trying in faith to lift a person out of his distress and despair. A counselor must have the spiritual resources to bear up under this strain. If the counselor is in a "live-in" situation, the problems and resulting tensions are compounded.

If the counselor is not able to carry this load, he can unintentionally do more harm than good. As will be pointed out in a later chapter, the counselee is usually a person who needs someone of strength to look to for guidance and confidence. If he is let down, he may never recover from the experience.

One of our counselors was asked to drive some resident clients to a camp where we were holding a spiritual retreat for them. "Will you drive some of the fellows in your car?" we asked him.

"No," he answered curtly, "I want to get them off my back."

The supervisor replied, "They should be on your heart, not on your back."

If the counselor does not have a strong enough heart for the task, he cannot carry them. He will always feel as though they are on his back. The weak, the weary, the wounded cannot only break a counselor's back; they can get on his nerves. Many a Christian worker in the field of rehabilitation has broken under the strain of the ministry. It is one thing to say you have a burden to work with people in trouble; it is another thing to have the qualities necessary to fulfill that burden. Few who either emotionally or spiritually respond to the need for counselors, realize what it takes to qualify.

Some may feel that if God has called them to this work, He will equip them to do the work. It is better to say, "If God has called me to work with the addicted generation, I will — with His help — prepare myself and try to learn everything that is necessary to fulfill His call."

What are some of the qualities necessary to be a good counselor?

1. *The counselor must know God.*

A minister came to me and asked, "I want to help. What do I have to do to get started?"

I said, "Be convinced of your own personal relationship to Jesus Christ. You have to know where you stand with God."

Unfortunately, he had great doubts about the fundamentals of Christianity as they applied to him. He had a seminary training; he was a well-educated man; he was sincere; he was willing to help in any way he could. Yet he was not qualified. He did not know God. Deep inside he was aware of his doubts, but he hoped by working with addicts and others whom he felt were less fortunate than himself, he might find some answers to his doubts.

Many qualities are necessary to be an effective Christian counselor, but the foundation stone upon which all other qualities are built is a vital and growing relationship with Jesus Christ as Savior and Lord.

A young college graduate asked me, "I have a degree in sociology. Would you hold that against me if I were accepted in the work of Teen Challenge?"

"No," I said, "as long as you were first of all trusting in Christ, rather than trusting in your training and in your technical knowledge."

Her education and training would be great assets, if used properly and kept in the right perspective. On the other hand, it is possible to look for answers in secular training rather than trust in God.

2. *The counselor must know himself.*

The counselor must have insights into his emotional needs, as well as his spiritual needs. Self-understanding is important. The counselor must know his weaknesses, and not let them hinder the counseling process. His own feelings, attitudes, even his prejudices, can throw a smokescreen up between himself and the counselee. If the counselor knows what his weaknesses are, and if he asks the Lord to help him overcome them, they need not be a hindrance.

A counselor must ask himself, "Why do I want to help someone? What are my motives? Am I trying to work out some personal hang-up? Am I trying to fulfill a personal need only?"

Everyone needs to be needed. Christian ministers and

workers do not have a sense of fulfillment unless they are helping others; that's why they feel they have been called by God to Christian service. Yet the counseling process can be used simply to serve one's own needs and not primarily those of others. A counselor can be using it as a tool to work out his own feelings of frustration, or rejection by his peers, or other personal reasons.

A certain counselor kept questioning a client about his sexual life. Although this was not the real problem of the counselee, it was the real problem of the counselor. He was using the counseling sessions as an X-ray to diagnose his own problem. He was projecting his problem — a major one — on the counselee, even though it was only the counselee's minor problem.

A noted psychiatrist warned counselors, "You have to be careful you're not writing a contract in which you want something back from him [the client]." The counselor must not have, without his being aware of it, a need to be needed, a need to cure someone, to be important to someone.

3. *The counselor must know how to relate to others.*

He must not only *have* love, he must know how to share it. A person may be sincere, well-adjusted and compassionate, yet not have the ability to properly relate his love to others. Tom Skinner calls this process "fleshing out Christianity." The old cliche applies here: "It is easier to preach sermons than to live them."

How do you show love? How do you relate to others who don't want you to relate to them? How do you relate to those who want you to relate to them, but don't know how to accept your love? The greatest obstacle the counselor must overcome is bridging the problem gap. How do you bridge the gap between the person with a problem and the one trying to help?

The counselor, especially if he's a clergyman or someone closely identified with the church, will have the hardest time bridging this gap. He will be viewed as giving advice from his pulpit position as a professional.

The counselor must talk across the table, shoulder to shoulder, not with an "I'm up here, you're down there" attitude. The counselor's interest, sincerity and love must be conveyed — not through his ministerial position, or with religious jargon — but with a soft voice and simple words. Often a counselor will talk *at* the needy person, rather than *with* him.

Counseling must not be done from a superior position. The counselee must be accepted as a person of worth. He must not be given the impression that he is inferior.

The counselor-counselee gap can originate in the mind and attitude of either. On one hand, the counselor can be so dignified, so aloof, so unable to relate that he is the cause of the barrier; on the other, the counselee may feel that because of his problems he isn't worth listening to.

Regardless of who creates the barrier, the counselor must learn to break through it and relate to the counselee. One of the greatest comments that can be given to a counselor is, "You're coming through, preacher."

Role changing is important in knowing how to relate. The minister must move from his preaching role to that of a friend. The parent must change from his role as an adult to that of a companion of youth. The teacher must change from the role of instructor in the classroom to that of a concerned Christian friend outside the institution.

Some people find security in remaining in their one role. They seek respect, or demand it because of their position, but they do not earn the respect of others by relating to them as a friend on a man-to-man basis.

When clients come to live at Teen Challenge, there is a certain amount of respect they give me and I can request it because I am the director. If that is the only right I have to be heard, if that is the only basis on which I can ask for a hearing, then I have become glued to my director's role; I have created a wall of dignity, professionalism and position around me. I may never get through to my clients.

In my book, *The Gutter and the Ghetto,* I wrote of my experience coming from Bible college to the streets of New York. I did not know how to relate. I was comfortable in the pulpit within the confines of the church, but I was like a fish out of water on the streets. I had to learn to be accepted for who I was — apart from the church and apart from the fact that I was a preacher. I had to learn to accept each individual for what he was — alienated from God, the church, and myself.

There is another extreme to be avoided in relating to people. It is possible to go too far. This is the opposite of the "I'm up here, you're down there" attitude. It is the counselor's loss of respect, dignity and leadership, caused by his going too far in trying to identify with a client or prospective client. There is a difference between being accepted and being so aggressive the counselor turns off the client. The outsiders, the sinners, run away from zealous Christians who force themselves on them. In trying to break down alienation, the counselor can make the gap wider.

A certain counselor made the mistake of developing the attitude, "I'm one of you fellows. I'm with you." He felt he had to get into their clique. But they didn't want him to become a member of their gang. The moment he went too far, he lost their respect.

In our resident program, counselors are warned against developing a buddy-buddy relationship with clients. It is a matter of learning how to identify, how to relate without getting so close that the counselee no longer sees the counselor as a counselor, but just as a buddy. The counselor must win the client as a friend before he can lead him to Christ, but no progress has been made if he has *only* gained a friend.

Too many well-meaning counselors, or those who are trying to play the counseling role, have been fooled by clients who were friendly to them, but did not actually make any progress toward changing. There comes a time in the counseling process when the counselor must say and do things he would hesitate doing to someone he considered a close friend. This is the reason identification must be maintained, but not at the expense of losing the proper working relationship between counselor and counselee.

In the close relationships that develop between counselor and client, many disheartening things have resulted. Male counselors have been emotionally, romantically, even sexually involved with a female client. Even in a man to man or woman to woman situation, there can be an emotional involvement that blinds the counselor to the counselee's real problem.

A further problem is overdependence of the client on the counselor. The client needs a shoulder to cry on, but not a crutch to lean on. The counselor can become the client's substitute savior. As long as the counselor is around to lean on, the client can function; when the counselor is removed, the client goes to pieces.

The counselor must know when to maintain close identification and when to remove himself. Clients must not be spoiled. Counselors must not have pets or special cases.

In learning how to relate to a counselee, the counselor must come off as a person sincerely interested in his client. He must not appear to be counseling out of a sense of duty or obligation.

A counselor can act as though people with their problems are an intrusion of his privacy. If a client suspects the counselor is serving out of a sense of duty, and not because he has a real and actual interest in the client, the client will withdraw from the relationship.

We have a saying in our Teen Challenge resident treatment program, "Are you serving from the schedule or from the heart?" The counselor's duties must not appear to the client to be just a job. Drug addicts can spot a phony. They are keenly aware of the difference between those who are interested in them as persons and those interested in them as addicts.

Counselors must not use clients for their own ends. Some counselors simply want to gain some experience. Others are looking for a story, for some excitement and glamor, or just for a good case history. They may be totally unaware of the individual's inner feelings and struggles. Such counselors may throw scripture at a client and show him a superficial love. This kind of counselor will only try to keep his client on the hook until he gets his story and his own ends are met. This kind of exploitation has been the pattern of many counselors in the past. If the client senses that the counselor, too, is only using him, it can be an experience from which he will never recover.

4. *The counselor must know how to react properly to the counselee.*

It is possible for a counselor to be able to relate and to get inside his client, but not be able to react properly. An X-ray of a person's physical, psychological and spiritual make-up can help the counselor formulate a right reaction. There are reasons why people act the way they do. Behavior is not a matter of chance. We've all heard the familiar cop-out, "Well, that's just the way I am. That's just me." The counselor's task is to find out *why* a person acts the way he does, in order to try and change that pattern of behavior.

Developing a right attitude toward the person being counseled and accepting him as a person of worth is important. This means accepting him with all his sins, hangups and problems. I have seen counselors spend much time trying to win someone, trying to relate to him, but when they got inside the person they were quick to judge him. They reacted in a way that prevented them from properly understanding their client.

What are some improper reactions to clients?

1. "This person doesn't want help." This may be true, or it may just appear to be true. In most cases it is a matter of trying to understand the client's reactions. He may show the opposite actions and attitudes from the average person. He may be hostile just to see how the counselor reacts to his hostility. He may act indifferently as a cover-up. All of his actions may be deliberately calculated to test the counselor's reactions.

Rather than deciding the client doesn't want help, the counselor might better say, "He does not know how to accept help." Everyone wants help. It may be a matter of not wanting your kind of help. Or the client may not see that the kind of help the counselor is offering him is the kind of help he needs.

2. "He is just no good." I've driven guests down the streets of New York where groups of men have been standing on street corners in the ghetto, and someone has remarked, "Look at those lazy bums; they just sponge off the taxpayers' money." There are spongers, but there are also young people who stand on street corners because no one has given them reason to do anything else. No one has tried to understand their lack of motivation. There are reasons why men stand on street corners and wait for their welfare checks, why they drink, and why the young men wait for the narcotics pushers. These reasons have nothing to do with laziness, the taste for alcohol or drugs, or the fact that they are "no good." If a counselor has such an

attitude, it will affect his approach to the individual and his problem.

3. "I think he's a nut." Some people do have mental disorders. Often a client will ask me, "Do you think I'm crazy?" Or, they will comment, "I know there's something wrong with me." The counselor must react in a way that will ignore the client's feelings about mental disorders, but at the same time he must keep in mind the seriousness of the person's problem. He might be a mental case, but he should not be treated any less cordially because he is.

Answering Some Questions

The following questions are related to the material above. These are some of the questions most often asked by those wanting advice on how to deal with the untapped generation.

1. Is it necessary to have been an addict to reach one? If you have been a runaway, rebel or hippie are you better able to reach others with the same problem? If you are a middle-class white, can you effectively work with blacks in the ghettos?

It is not experience alone that qualifies a person to work with those in trouble and distress. Training and experience are necessary. Training in understanding a person's spiritual, emotional and psychological needs is most important. There are many so-called experts in the fields of drug addiction, juvenile delinquency and other related problems who can tell you all about drugs, addiction and misbehavior of all kinds, but they are not qualified to work with the individuals afflicted by those maladies.

Former alcoholics, drug addicts, prostitutes and homosexuals often have an advantage over others who have not had such problems, in that they can understand the feelings, attitudes, weaknesses and hopelessness of those who have problems. But unless they have the ability to counsel, to relate to people in need, and to react properly to those with such problems, their understanding alone will not qualify them to be successful counselors. Often former addicts do not have the maturity and spiritual depth to stick with persons involved in problems.

In a residence program converted addicts, if properly utilized, can be of great service. They can detect problems in the new cases that other counselors cannot. The convert-counselor can detect insincerity more quickly. He cannot easily be fooled. He knows the ropes. The counselor who has never been an addict is often too soft, too trusting and more easily fooled.

Convert-counselors should not be used as such until they have had sufficient time to develop in their Christian walk. While a counselor who is a recent convert may be able to immediately relate to a new client, he may not know how to react. That's because he may be struggling in his own spiritual life. The new client will listen to the recent convert who has had his same problem. But when the going gets rough, if the recent convert-counselor reacts improperly, all his good relating will go down the drain.

The convert from drug addiction, alcoholism and so on must take time to get Bible training and to prove his Christian testimony. However, any Christian worker, regardless of his background, can overcome the counselor-counselee gap.

2. How do you bridge the cultural, social, ethical and religious gap between the counselor (especially one raised in a middle-class Christian atmosphere) and the client?

My own background could not have been more opposite to that of those with whom I work. This is true of many who want to reach the untapped generation. Bridging this gap is possible, but difficult.

The first step is to get the picture. The counselor must get out where the sinners are. The first thing we do with new staff workers is get them on the streets, out into the neighborhoods and communities where all the trouble starts. No counselor can be effective until he has been exposed to the scene. He must see the sights, hear the sounds, smell the odors of the ghetto, the gutter, the skid row, the hang-outs. How do you do this?

If you are a pastor, take a day or night and go into the problem areas of your town. Find someone from that section to take you on a tour. Call the police department and ask if you can ride in a cruiser on a night tour. See humanity at its worst. Meet the people, talk with the children, the teens, the parents. Get into the homes, the apartments. See how the other half, the have nots live. Let some of the atmosphere soak in.

Go through the flophouses, visit the jails — go everywhere or anywhere so that you can develop the full image of their distress and difficulties. See addicts and their addictions. See the gay bars where the queens hold sway. Watch the hustlers make their contacts for the prostitutes. Such a tour does not turn a person into a qualified worker or counselor, but it's a place to start.

Assuming the counselor knows God, that he knows his own weaknesses and has submitted them to the Lord, and that he is seeking to counsel for the sake of others and for the glory of God and not for his own ends, here are some other characteristics he should possess to make a go of it. He should:

1. Not be given to anger.
2. Be able to accept criticism.
3. Not be given to prejudice (racial, religious, social).
4. Not be subject to moods of depression.
5. Have a sense of humor (ability to laugh at himself).
6. Not be given to over-optimism.
7. Not be given to pessimism.

3

CHAPTER 3

THE CONQUEST OF INNER SPACE

The counselor must determine his goal. What result does he hope to achieve? Jesus said, "According to your faith, be it unto you." The same may be said for the counselor and counseling. What he thinks, or believes he will accomplish, that he most likely will achieve. As a Christian, the counselor must see what the ultimate will of God is for an individual life, and let this be the goal he hopes to help his client obtain. Anything less might be commendable, but still not be the attainment of his goal.

To accomplish his highest purpose, the counselor must understand the crux of everyone's problem. The problem is basically one of the heart. The Scriptures say, "Keep thy heart with all diligence; for out of it are the issues of life" Prov. 4:23). Also, "Out of a man's heart, come evil thoughts, acts of fornication, of theft, murder, adultery, ruthless greed, and malice; fraud, indecency, envy, slander, arrogance, and folly" (Mark 7:21, 22, NEB).

This is what makes the Christian counselor's approach to all problems different than the non-Christian counselor's approach. The Christian sees all problems as starting with the heart. The problem of the heart is sin. The non-Christian counselor may give it other psychological names, but

Christ calls it sin; as sin it must be dealt with. If the counselee's problem is viewed in this context and properly dealt with, there will always be the potential for success.

Sin has various manifestations. Sometimes a person's problem is not only caused by his own sin, but by the sins of others inflicted upon him. Regardless, the basic problem is still individual and personal sin. The outward manifestations of sin might be drug use, alcohol consumption, sexual perversion, delinquent behavior, violence, etc. But these are only the signs of deeper problems. Underneath may lie rebellion, bitterness, hate, anger, fear, loneliness, depression, etc. The outward acts of misbehavior are only the top of the iceberg.

I do not believe man is fully qualified to counsel until he views a person's problem morally and spiritually. State and federal institutions have failed in criminal rehabilitation and in the rehabilitation of the addict because they do not provide for dealing with spiritual needs. I believe in the separation of church and state, organizationally and institutionally, but you cannot separate a person's bodily and mental needs from his spiritual needs. Therefore, every institution should provide the opportunity for a spiritual ministry.

If there is a religious worker on the staff, he is seldom on the same level with the psychiatrist, the psychologist, the social worker, or the vocational therapist. A person's religious therapy is left up to him; other forms of therapy are not. Other therapy is a regular and required part of the so-called treatment. The chaplain may be there. But when he is, he is shoved so much into the corner that he cannot instill faith into his clients. The relegation of religion and God to the lower rungs of the treatment ladder results in the failure to get to the core of the patient's problem and need.

Teen Challenge has been successful because we deal with individuals as sinners who can be delivered by the power of God through Jesus Christ. We have learned that drug addicts are not sinners because they are addicts, but *they are addicts because they are sinners.* We have been accused of oversimplifying the problem. But the results speak for themselves: approximately 70% of those who graduate from Teen Challenge remain clean from drugs and continue to live a productive Christian life. No other program or organization can make such claims. We have found the key. Christ can conquer the inner space of the heart. Since "out of the heart are the issues of life," treating the heart first, or along with treating the body, makes sense. The way to solving a man's mental, social and physical needs is through his heart.

The counselor must aim for the heart. He must seek to lead his client to the knowledge of Jesus Christ as personal Savior. Christ has power to conquer and defeat the sin nature of the heart, the nature that causes the specific acts of sin. If the counselor does not aim to do this, there cannot be total success. In many cases there will be complete failure, or at best, only limited success.

There are multitudes of ideas about the problem and its solution. When one person talks about "helping someone," he may have one goal in mind, while the next person may have an entirely different concept. New programs appear every day with new approaches.

The problem of drug addiction puts this into focus for us. There are various approaches to this problem. At one time the medical profession was thought to hold the key to a cure. One doctor stated, "It's a medical problem and the laymen should stay out of the field of drug addiction treatment." It was felt that the addict's problem simply was drugs, so the answer was to get rid of the drugs in the body and the addict would be cured. However, it was soon discovered that addicts left the hospital only to shoot up dope within hours, even minutes. The hospital became a place for the addict to get rid of his physical dependence on drugs. He knew he would not find a permanent cure. Drugs were taken out of his body, but his craving remained. Furthermore, the reason why he used drugs was not found.

Psychiatrists have attempted to deal with the drug problem too. They take into account the emotional, psychological and sociological factors that contribute to the use of drugs in the first place. This approach has produced only fractional results. The psychiatrist can diagnose but he can't deliver. He can analyze but he can't provide the inner strength and motivation needed to overcome the problem. A problem that has been effectively analyzed and brought out in full view of the afflicted person, without the hope for change, is double trouble.

One fellow told me, "The psychiatrist told me about problems I never knew I had before. So when I came out of the hospital, I left with all the problems I carried in with me, plus all the new ones I picked up from the head shrinker. I ended up with twice as many hang-ups, and still no solution to my situation. I went deeper into drug addiction as a result."

I have seen this happen all too often. The despair is immeasurable for the addict who has been made aware of what is wrong with him, but is bereft of the influence of hope, faith and love! Such despair adds to his addiction and plunges him into deeper anti-social acts and self-reflecting behavior.

Another fellow said that after many counseling sessions with a psychiatrist who had helped pinpoint some deep-rooted feelings of hatred toward his brother, he finally came to realize that such feelings did indeed exist. "What should I do?" he asked the analyst. The answer was simple: "Start trying to find some love for him and show it whenever you get the opportunity." The young man returned later to talk to his psychiatrist. "I've got another problem now," he complained. "Where do I get that love I need to show my brother? I know I need it, but where do I find it?" One problem had led to a further one.

His dilemma serves to illustrate a point. Unless the person in need finds something outside himself, or finds some outer force to enter into him and provide the strength to overcome his problem, then the psychiatric approach is more harmful than helpful. Many come out of the counseling session confused and confronted with knowledge about themselves and their problems that they are totally incapable of doing anything about.

*　　*　　*

Another popular method of treatment for addicts and alcoholics is the self-help method used by various non-professional groups. There has been some measure of success with this approach. The key to it is addicts or alcoholics helping others who are hooked. Each has a chance to talk about his problem. Some treatment programs use a group therapy method known as "encounter sessions." In these they "tell it like it is" about each other. No holds are barred. Everyone's attitudes, feelings and behavior are scrutinized by the rest of the group. No one is allowed to hide or play the phony role. Each person is brought face to face with himself and with the truth about what he must do to recover. A certain standard of behavior is maintained, such as total abstinence from drugs (for addicts) and alcoholic beverages (for the alcoholic). Certain other disciplines are also strictly enforced.

This approach incorporates some good elements, but it has loopholes. No inner controls are provided. There is no acknowledgment of God; the standard of moral behavior is left open to question; since each group establishes its own. What if a small group within the larger group should vote a different standard? What happens when the addict is away from the group?

Sometimes leaders exert undue influence on the group. Such was the case with the Synanon group in California. The leader started viewing himself as the messiah of the addicts; everything revolved around him. The treatment program turned into a cult of leader worship.

What can be learned from these groups is that the addict needs to find a relationship with a higher being to find a standard of behavior to pattern his life after, and a motivating force to give him the strength to make the difficult journey out of the deep hole of addiction, depression and perversion.

The most important element is left out of the counseling in all of these programs. The counselee is not led to the conquest of inner space. Each program denies the dynamics of a spiritual encounter with supernatural power. The psychiatrist or counselor becomes a substitute god or savior, rather than the agent to lead the one in need to the God and the Savior. The patient-helping-patient approach means they are using one another as priests and lords. The client must always have the support of the group; otherwise, he is left alone to work out his problems and face the obstacles involved.

If the counselor cannot present a way of life that enables his client to be born anew from above, then at best he is only going to lessen his miseries. A girl who was under treatment by a psychiatrist was asked if she was doing any better since her visits with him. "Well," she said, "I'm not better, but I'm less sad." If the counselor knows God, and if he can present the truth about the Conqueror of the ages, Jesus Christ, there is every hope of a lasting recovery for the client.

The conquest of inner space must go by various routes. The journey inside man, to deliver light and life through Christ and by the Holy Spirit, must be done in various stages and through such routes as the physical, psychological and sociological aspects of the client's problem.

When I said that the counselor's goal and highest task is to lead his client to a saving knowledge of Jesus Christ, I did not mean that we are to bypass his physical or material needs. Spiritually speaking, the way to a man's heart may be through his stomach, or pocketbook, or family. The client's temporal needs dare not be neglected. We must not be so concerned with souls that we forget lives. There is a balance and we must find it and minister accordingly.

I am greatly concerned about those who relegate the mission of the church to feeding the hungry, aiding the poor, binding up wounds of the body — involvement in temporal needs — and then call it quits. Such social involvement is commendable. The Christian humanitarian with a social conscience is often hard to find — especially in evangelical circles. The Bible backs up the social activist. It speaks of giving "cups of cold water" in Christ's name. Jesus warned, "When I was hungry you gave me nothing to eat, when thirsty nothing to drink . . . when ill and in prison you did not come to my help" (Matt. 25:42, 43, NEB). The world suffers today because the church often failed to see this as part of its mission.

However, the Christian counselor dare not limit his calling to meeting social needs. Does the man to whom you've given the cup of cold water have the living water in his soul? Will you leave him with a full stomach but an empty heart? Does the one you have visited in prison know about the One who broke the prison bars of sin and death? If I had to choose, I would rather go to heaven on an empty stomach than to hell on a guaranteed annual income. This is not to say I oppose or approve of guaranteed wages; it is to say something about priorities.

A drug addict told me, "I went to a minister to ask for

help. He gave me five dollars and sent me on my way. I could understand that he might not know how to treat an addict, but he could have at least prayed for me. He didn't even tell me about Jesus." I wish my liberal, social activist friends would hear and heed this message. Perhaps this word is written to them.

We have had many come to Teen Challenge and say, "I want to help. I want to work with addicts." The sad part is that they have not been rehabilitated themselves. They do not know how to pray. They do not know how to lead a soul to Christ. They would gladly wipe the sweat off a brow, carry cups of cold water, or soup, but they do not know how to minister to the heart. In the absence of a mission to save souls, they have taken up the cause of saving lives. Again, I admire and commend such a commitment. Its only fault is it does not go far enough. It is a commitment more to earth than to heaven; more to the body than to the soul.

Perhaps one reason our liberal friends have forsaken the Gospel to "wait on tables," so to speak, is because some evangelicals bathe themselves in the sunshine of God's love, while millions of people are suffering the bitter pains of human existence. I believe in the rehabilitation of men's bodies, minds, marriages and work habits just as strongly as I believe in the salvation of their souls. The evangelical can be so hung up on reaching men for Christ that he fails to see that the man he is trying to reach might be out of a job, need an education, and be the object of discrimination.

Man's spiritual and material needs are not two different bags; they are one bag and the counselor has to get into that bag by whatever means he can. We cannot compartmentalize man and his needs. The secular world acts as if the soul does not exist; the sacred world acts as if the body does not exist.

One man, commenting on the strong evangelical approach taken by Teen Challenge, said, "I'd rather give a drug addict two slices of bread than a gospel tract." It so happens that we give them a tract along with the two slices of bread.

Sherwood Wirt in his book, *The Social Conscience of the Evangelical,* said:

Why does the move toward social involvement seem to require a rejection of Biblical Christianity, why must the one accompany the other? What is there in the present age that seems to make it mandatory for a man to move from orthodoxy to atheism before he can be taken seriously in his quest for the good of humanity?

Some people who are concerned to affirm social change are also inexplicably denying the reality of spiritual change in persons. . . .

Jesus never for a moment believed that his kingdom would be rung in simply by an improvement in the external conditions of human life. . . .

When a man becomes a believer he does not retreat from his responsibilities as a member of society.[1]

Bill Milliken in *Tough Love* wrote:

We have to change our cities. We need to replace rotten buildings. We must bring education to ghetto people. But if we aren't giving equal rights to their hearts, if we aren't giving them ourselves as well, the problem will never be solved. Nice, big, new houses don't answer the cry of the hurt heart. Any look at the statistics on the number of alcoholics behind expensive suburban doors will show that. Better clothes, better homes, better schools don't give the complete answer. People want more than material things, they want more than eight hours of your day, or a job, or analysis. They want your heart. But we have to give our hearts with no strings attached. We can't say, "I'll love you if you'll come my way, if you'll believe what I believe. If you follow Christ, then I'll love you." We must remember He loved even those who did not love Him.[2]

We must meet people in need where they are. If they are socially or materially well off, and their need is basically spiritual, then the counselor can get down to the business of conquering inner space. But if the client has immediate external needs, then the counselor must begin there. If he is destitute, we must minister to his destitution. If he is hungry, we must feed him. If he is in prison, we must visit him. And we must not turn him off, regardless of the circumstances of his destitution. We cannot ignore someone because "it's their own fault." We dare not take the attitude, "Well, he made his bed; now let him lie in it." It is not ours to judge or condemn his failures.

[1] Sherwood Wirt, *The Social Conscience of the Evangelical* (New York, Harper & Row, 1968) pp. 8, 24, 41.

[2] Bill Milliken with Char Meredith, *Tough Love* (Old Tappan, New Jersey, Revell, 1968) p. 149.

A young man came to us in dire physical straits. Among other things, he suffered from hepatitis, a common problem among drug addicts contracted by using a dirty needle when injecting a shot of heroin into their veins. We helped him get admitted into the hospital, which turned out to be a difficult project in spite of his apparent suffering. Later he returned to Teen Challenge to enter the rehabilitation program. But while he was in the hospital various staff members visited him, took him slippers, newspapers, candy, reading material, and other things. The fact that he was being treated kindly even before he had come to Teen Challenge, and even before he had accepted Christ, was more than he could understand. He said, "I've never had anyone do anything like that for me — ever — in my whole life. You people were total strangers, and you treated me like an old friend."

Another young man, after being at Teen Challenge for two months, stated, "What really touched me was when this white fellow came to my room and when he saw that I was not feeling well asked if I wanted a back rub. Here I was, a dirty, greasy dope addict, and this fellow was soothing my back with rubbing alcohol."

Such simple acts of kindness are often the wedges into a man's soul. Even the most simple deeds can mean so much. Sherry, a girl who had just come out of prison, was greatly affected one day when a counselor came to her room while she was making her bed and assisted her in this chore and chatted with her. Sherry said, "She didn't preach or counsel with me, she just treated me nice, and this impressed me so very much."

Sometimes a person's external problems are serious. They may be pressures that weigh on the individual or they may be road blocks hindering him from finding the spiritual help he wants and needs. Providing assistance may mean the counselor has to give up a day of his time to help the counselee take care of some business. It may mean a difficult confrontation with a parole officer, with an alcoholic's wife, or with a drug addict's family, or convincing the loan company not to press charges until the person is rehabilitated enough to assume his personal debts again. It can also mean a personal financial investment in this person's soul. At Teen Challenge it has sometimes meant arranging child care for a girl addict's baby.

Whatever the external problem, we must use this as the point of contact to get through to the client. These are the routes we must travel to conquer inner space. You may have to go via the stomach, the pocketbook, the mind, or various other routes, whatever is necessary to get to the heart. Whatever is necessary, as Bill Milliken comments, to "earn the right to present Christ."

This point of contact is the launching pad; that's where we launch our conquest of inner space. In some cases, if you are a minister or in another position where you are recognized as a counselor, the client will come to you. Your office becomes the launching pad. By his coming, you already have the point of contact. (The psychiatrist's couch is another example of the launching pad.) But few who need counseling will come to the church or the minister. The counselor will have to establish his own launching pad. He will have to meet the person on his level, amid the external elements of the client's problem.

This is where social assistance serves its highest purpose. This is where the church must get into the mainstream of human need. By any and all means, the counselor will have to get out where the sinners are and get involved with all their problems.

I am mentioning here only a few examples of launching pads; there are many more.

1. *Teen Challenge Center.* This is our residence for addicts, alcoholics, and other habit-bound persons. In the home a bed, food, shelter, clothing, recreational and educational facilities are provided. Medical treatment is also provided whenever necessary. Whether the client accepts the spiritual cure or not, he is still given this material aid. What if he continues to refuse the spiritual cure? He is allowed to remain, as long as he keeps the rules and regulations of the home. (Only a small percentage are dismissed.) However, it is not easy for one to remain in a Christian atmosphere, living under biblical ideals and principles, without accepting Christ. Those who refuse to accept usually leave on their own. However, no one is left out in the cold. Those who leave are referred to other

agencies where they can receive treatment without the religious element.

2. *Coffee houses.* These are points of contact with hippies, runaways, tourists, students, and anyone who wants to talk. The program is the person. As the advertising circulars state, "Come for a unique experience in religious conversation." But always more than religion is talked about: politics, war, sex, the church, whatever. Everyone who comes in has his or her own "bag." Each has his own philosophy of life. Conversation must begin on the person's level. The counselor must show an interest in that person as an individual. He must show an interest in his interests. He must listen long and carefully. By listening in sincerity and showing a genuine interest in the humanity of that person, the counselor earns the right to talk and to present Christ. It is not always easy. But listening must come before preaching. Human interest must come before heavenly interest.

Coffee houses all over the world have become excellent launching pads for Christians to carry on a limited form of counseling. Often the Christian can only touch on the spiritual problems of the one to whom he is witnessing. However, the counselor can do a little probing and thereby make his witness and counsel more relevant to that person's particular need. At other times the Christian witnessing purely on a spiritual and biblical level may be helping the person with some psychological, emotional, or fleshly problem — although without being aware of it. Regardless of how far the counselor is able to get on the journey to deliver the message of the Gospel to inner space, the coffee house situation is an excellent launching pad.

3. *Bible clubs and children's schools.* Christians in each locality must evaluate their own situations and establish points of contact accordingly. Different approaches are necessary for different situations. In order to reach the ghetto child in the inner city, Teen Challenge has used the school approach. The schools, called New Start Schools, are patterned after the government's anti-poverty Head Start schools. Conducted by Vista-type volunteers, these schools are staffed by qualified teachers. The Gospel is presented to ghetto children who will become the addicts, alcoholics and muggers of the future, unless they receive

now the instruction and counsel of God's Word from compassionate Christians.

For the teens there are small group Bible clubs. A full round of activity, both sacred and secular, is conducted. The Gospel is presented to lead the teens to Christ and to make disciples out of them. Most of these teens already have been involved in delinquent behavior. Patterns have already been established. Slowly but surely, they are traveling on the road to addiction and other problems. Others can still be reached. Inner space can be conquered. The club and its activities are the points of contact. If the worker knows in what direction he needs to go with each youngster, the point of contact can lead to conversion. Again, the goal must always be kept in mind.

At the same time, the counselor cannot forget that he is ministering to the whole person. He must always be aware of the struggle for survival the teenager may be going through in his home, school and community. If this is kept in mind, the counselor will understand the lack of interest or understanding the teenager may have in responding to the goals of the counselor and the organization, and his lack of response to the love of God.

Another effective method is to have staff live in the community and become fused with the people. This has been a good way to earn the right to be heard. This method has been used with good results by Bill Milliken and his Young Life group in their work in the ghettos of the Lower East Side of Manhattan. This I am convinced is *the* most effective method of reaching inner city youth, and conquering inner space amid the slums, garbage, vices, poverty and frustrations of the outer space of the ghetto. (See chapter 11.)

4. *The church and launching pads.* The reason I have chosen to list the church last is not because I view it as the least effective point of contact. I do so to stress its importance and to show how it has been an unnoticed center for counseling and rehabilitation. Many problems are solved within the church, although unnoticed by the pastor and the people. Many have been rehabilitated through a dramatic conversion experience and through the follow-up of a minister in Bible teaching sessions, in private counseling, and in small group situations which, though not particularly

structured as such, still result in a therapeutic, problem-solving ministry.

The church has been under severe attack for its failure to solve many of the problems in our society, and rightly so. When we decry the corruption in our society, we must always come back to the church and its failure to be a strong influence in stemming the tide of immorality and iniquity. But I fear that while the church is being attacked, we fail to notice the good that it is doing. If we think things are bad, they would be much worse if the doors of the churches were closed.

Long before special programs such as Teen Challenge and others were established to conduct specialized ministries, the church in various degrees was reaching the same type of individuals and preventing addictions. I think of many alcoholics who have been made "new creatures in Christ Jesus" by going down the sawdust trail, by making a decision in a gospel crusade. I met a man in Canada who, while sick and in misery from an alcohol binge, heard a gospel preacher on the radio. That started him on his search for God. Through a further point of contact with a Pentecostal church, he now enjoys, after fifteen years, freedom from alcoholism. This same story can be repeated over and over, in church after church. In days gone by it was common for people with severe problems to come into the church and find an answer simply by receiving the Gospel and being helped by the follow-up program of the church.

The church is and ought to be a "Society for the Prevention of ————." The blank stands for whatever the situation calls for. It has been the prevention of divorces, broken homes, suicides and addictions of various forms. It has also been the prevention of poverty, prejudice, perversion and a number of other problems. True, it must do more of the same, but let us not forget the prevention it has already provided for multitudes of people who find refuge and help within its walls.

It must also be pointed out that opportunities for the conquest of inner space are often lost in the church. Tragically, many potential points of contact are missed. For various reasons good contacts are unnoticed, ignored and unwanted. The addict or the troubled soul cannot make a point of contact, or be launched into the kingdom because he is different socially, economically, racially. He cannot find counsel or refuge in God's house because *he doesn't fit into the pattern of the type of sinner that church is looking for.* He may be an "unrespectable" sinner, whereas that church has developed a ministry to "respectable" sinners. Perhaps inwardly the members say, "Get the bum out of here," or, "he's the wrong kind of bum. He doesn't fit into our counseling category."

Consequently, many people like this attend church, sit regularly in the services, and never have a point of contact established with them. Furthermore, some of them who do outwardly seem to fit the ideal of that church may have serious problems, but they are never given the opportunity to reveal their problems, to talk about them, to receive counsel for them. Many of these same people come to the altar, have a prayer said over them, and are sent on their way still fighting battles for which they have no answers — and for which they may think there *are* no answers.

My brother Dave established an effective method in his crusade ministry by counseling every young person who comes forward. Even when there are several hundred, he takes time to let each young person make a confession of faith, briefly relate a problem, or request prayer. Each one is given a brief word of counsel by my brother and afterward he prays with them. Then the one who has made a decision is assigned to a personal worker who gives further scriptural counsel.

The altar has always been one of the best points of contact and launching pads for lost and troubled souls. They should not be shoved through the altar as if it were an assembly line. I have made it a practice, no matter how many or how few come to the altar where I am the speaker, to ask each one why he has come to the altar and what he would like me to pray about. Use the altar service as an opportunity for counsel and guidance. It is often the only place where certain people will open up to relate problems and listen to advice.

5. *Preaching and teaching.* Through preaching and teaching a minister or Christian worker can establish an indirect point of contact by presenting the Gospel as it relates to

particular problems. When I speak in church, often young people will come afterward to confess drug use, promiscuity, homosexuality, and other problems they would not dare to mention to others. They do so, perhaps because they know I am only there for a day or evening and then I'm gone, but also because they know I will not be shocked by their problem and will understand the difficulty they are having, because of my experience in working with people who have similar problems. Any pastor or Christian worker who is in a place of leadership can establish similar points of contact and counseling launching pads. For example, a pastor might speak on the dangers of drug use and the Christian approach to the problem. This will open the door for young people in the church to come and talk about their temptation with drugs. Or the pastor might speak about homosexuality, presenting not only the scriptural warnings against it, but also expressing a compassion toward those who might be involved in it. Such speaking will in time bring out of hiding those who have such problems.

4

LIGHTING FIRES

Counseling has been described as a dynamic relationship between two people who are approaching a well-defined problem with consideration for each other so that the less mature or more troubled person is aided to a self-determined resolution of his difficulties. The outcome from counseling should be that the client should make some constructive helpful action on his own behalf.

How do you get the counselee to do something? How do you light the fires within him that will produce hope, action and change, so that the one who has been doing wrong will begin constructive action that will lead him toward recovery and healing?

One of our Teen Challenge counselors came to me, concerned about the progress and attitude of one of our resident clients. "He's got to do something," the counselor stated firmly. "No," I said, "you've got to do something. The problem is yours and ours as much as it is Freddy's at this point."

"What do you mean?" he asked.

"We have to ask the Lord to show us how we can spark the right action in him," I said. This is the counselor's great challenge—lighting fires, sparking that ray of hope within the troubled person so he will begin to take constructive action for himself.

When someone walks out of our treatment program, we must ask ourselves, "Did we fail to light the fire?" A match must have a sulphur tip before it can spark into a flame; in the same way, the counselee has to be lightable. He must have an underlying desire to be changed. If he has that desire, if he is ready, we must ask ourselves, "Did we fail to scratch the surface of his desire and spark him toward a new life? Did we fail to understand his problem, so we could show him the way out of darkness and into light? Did we fail to get him to do something?"

Gregory was another one who thought about going out the door. I had taken a strong interest in him for a number of reasons. To begin with, Gregory was a Negro who had come to us during the time of some of the worst riots in the Bedford-Stuyvesant area, where he had been living. Since this section is just a few blocks from our Center, I felt that if Gregory could find a solution to his problems at Teen Challenge, then others from that neighborhood might be encouraged to come to us too. We had done a lot of praying for Gregory, knowing that his short stay with us had not yet been productive. It was unfortunate that at the time he was with us there happened to be several boys at the Center from the deep South, one of whom had made things rather difficult for Gregory.

All our efforts seemed to have been in vain, though, for one day Gregory came to me and said, "I can't make it here. I haven't made any progress here and I don't feel the Lord has done anything for me. It's time for me to go." I knew Gregory had sincerely been trying.

"Give God one more chance," I said. "If you go into the chapel with me and pray, I guarantee you that God will do something for you."

As soon as we got to the chapel, I prayed for Gregory, asking God to come to his rescue at that very moment. Gregory didn't stir, didn't say a word. I thought to myself, *Don, now you've really put God on the spot. You promised Gregory that something would happen.* I closed my eyes and prayed a little longer. Still, Gregory did not react in any way at all. I began to think that perhaps I had overstepped my bounds by insisting that God would take hold of him. Then I looked at Gregory and I saw the tears rolling down his face. . . . He began to sob. Then he began to pray out loud. When he arose, he told me, "I feel that the Lord has touched me." During the remainder of his days at the Center, it was evident that the Lord had touched Gregory and it was a pleasure to watch him grow in Christian stature.[1]

Many clients the counselor deals with will have been in other treatment programs, and will have spent time with other counselors. They may come to you having suffered the bitter disappointment of past failures. They have sincerely tried to change, but in the end found themselves worse than before. They may have been told by other counselors, "You don't want help." One of our clients had been told by a social worker in a previous program he had been enrolled in, "The only way you'll get out of your trouble is if, when you leave this place, you run in front of a truck and get killed."

The client may not have had any motivation, or little motivation, in past attempts to find help. In most cases the fault, however, lies at the doorstep of the programs in which the client was involved. The client found no one to light his fire. He found no power to connect with his own will to produce true and effective willpower. The difference between the counselor-counselee relationships developed by Christian counselors and non-Christian counselors is that with the Christian there is a Third Party present in all his conversations and sessions with his client. The Christian counselor allows the power of God and the power of the Holy Spirit to help the client believe change is possible, and to show him that God will supply the power to get behind his desires and his will to help him to do all the "somethings" necessary for full recovery.

From the moment the counselor-client relationship develops, the counselor must look for the opportunity to strike a chord of hope — to light the fire — in the client. As the client reacts to the counseling sessions, the counselor must find that "something" somewhere during the course of the exchanges, to signal him to throw out the challenge to the client.

Have you ever struck a match that wouldn't light? You may have kept striking it and striking it, but it just wouldn't light. Then finally you gave it that one last effort and out came the flame. Counseling is similar to this simple ex-

[1] Don Wilkerson and Herm Weiskopf, The Gutter and the Ghetto (Waco, Texas, Word, 1969) pp. 82-83.

perience. The counselor must keep trying to rub the counselee the right way. He must keep the counseling process flowing along until the client reveals the true nature of his problem, which may be just the point where contact can be made and the fire lit.

In reasoning with one client I tried to convince him that Christ would free him from the misery-go-round of arrests, jail terms, hospital visits, and the daily hassle (the addict's life routine of stealing, purchasing drugs, injecting the needle, etc.) of the drug addiction life. He was not interested in spiritual things so I sought his response on a human and social level. He could not see himself as a Christian. "Do you want to be a dirty dope fiend the rest of your life?" was the theme of my counseling. This however didn't arouse his interest. There was no response — I wasn't making contact — no flame or even a flicker was evident.

The next time we were together I began on a new line of counseling. "Christ will make a man out of you," I said. Then he told me that he had a daughter. I further explained how God would give him the power to be physically and spiritually cleansed from dope and sin so he could get a good job, support his daughter, and assume his role as a father. This he very much wanted to do. He began to take a new interest. When I explained Teen Challenge has a job training program he was even more interested. A spark had been lit. In further counseling I kept feeding this flame of his interest in rehabilitation based on his desire to improve himself.

What was the difference in his reaction to the two lines of reasoning? We hadn't rubbed him the right way. The first way we hadn't reached the level of his real interest and need. When fear of suffering from drugs did not spark an interest, a challenge to a better and fuller life did.

Sometimes a person's problem may not be only spiritual. It may be a serious emotional one. We find in some counselees who respond spiritually yet are having difficulty that perhaps something in their mind is "bugging" them. One young man feared he could no longer behave fully as a man sexually. (Years of drug addiction help make the addict incapable of functioning normally sexually.) When he was able to express freely his fears, he was reassured by the example of others who had been drug addicts yet after their conversion had gone on to live a happy married life, that he could do the same. He felt relieved and was able to grow faster spiritually from that point on.

"This program just isn't working for me," an alcoholic client said one day. "Nothing is happening to me. I still feel the same as I always have," he further bemoaned. He was in my office with coat in hand ready to terminate our counseling relationship. "Do me and yourself a favor before you go. Go downstairs in the chapel and tell God what you just told me," I suggested. At first he hesitated, then said he would. About an hour later I ran into him. "I'm not leaving," he said. "God just told me to be patient and to wait on Him. I'm going to do it." He learned his first lesson in "doing something." He found that God does help those who help themselves.

One young man walked out of the Teen Challenge center having made up his mind to return to drugs. While standing waiting for a subway to take him back to the pusher and the cooker, he felt the spark and flame of God's love well up within his soul. He felt free from the craving of drugs. As the subway train pulled in, he walked out of the station and back to the center and got on his knees to thank God for revealing Himself. After eight years the flame still burns.

Sometimes a fire is lit in a client, and it looks as if he has begun to do something to seek change. Then the light quickly goes out. Perhaps the fire was lit on the wrong surface. Perhaps the counselor struck only the top level of the problem. There usually are several levels to a person's problem; the fires of change must be lit on the right level. The right level is the roughest level. It's the most difficult level for the counselor to talk about and to expose, but the lowest, roughest level of the client's problem provides the best surface and opportunity to spark change. When Jesus spoke to the woman at the well, He began on the surface level, her need for water. Then He got to the core of her problem, her five husbands, which symbolized her thirst for living water. Had Jesus not reached that level of her problem, she would have gone away still carrying that secret and that problem — only to face it again without help.

So the counselor's great task is to challenge, to motivate, to get the client moving in the direction of a cure.
This is not easy when the person feels he has no reason
to change, no strength to change, and when he is addicted to drugs or alcohol.

Our problem at Teen Challenge is that although our
home is full of clients, often they have a very low level
of motivation. Their bodies are present with us, but their
thoughts and desires have nothing to do with God or a
new life. Referring to this problem one day ,in chapel, I
asked them, "How many of you are present this morning?" They looked at me quizzically. "Some of you are
here," I said, "but many of you are not. You're walking
the streets of Harlem looking for the pusher, or you're
up on a roof preparing a set of works to shoot it up.
Maybe someone else is in bed with a prostitute." That got
their attention. "Bring your mind into chapel," I continued.

The point is, how does the preacher, the Christian witness, and especially the counselor, capture the mind, heart
and will of those who may be different, unwilling and
rebellious prospects? Every case deserves a chance. No
one is beyond reach. There is nothing or no one "too
hard for the Lord." Many people with whom we have dealt
seemed at the outset impossible to reach. Without the
hope of the Gospel, without faith in the power of God
to change and transform people like this we would never
have tried to light the fires.

The counselor must have faith, dedication, patience and
compassion to keep trying to light the fire, and once it
is lit, to keep throwing coals on it. Some clients have worn
out more than one preacher, Christian worker and counselor. I have seen many once zealous Christians give up
on "impossible" cases. Policemen, doctors, social workers
and others in various professions have thrown up their
hands in despair and have become indifferent to the needs
of the addicted generation. "I think we should do what
Hitler did and build furnaces to put them in," one policeman told me as I was walking the streets making contact
with drug addicts. As sorry as I feel for the addict, I feel
more sorry for that policeman and others who have no
hope for the hopeless. Perhaps some are incurable, but
only from the standpoint that they do not want to be

cured. However, the counselor must maintain a positive conviction that every client is curable.

Suppose you are now ready to light the fire. You have made contact with a prospective client. What steps do you take? This book does not deal primarily with making the initial contact; it is primarily about how you help your client find "newness of life." We shall discuss the steps toward that end under three headings: (1) the precounseling period; (2) the counseling period; (3) the postcounseling period.

The Precounseling Period

1. *Determine readiness.* Is the client ready for the kind of help you have to offer? Some are ready for recovery; others must go through a process of precounseling to be made ready. Many Christian workers and counselors are ready, but their prospects are not. You can be too eager and thus scare off your would-be client.

Some of the signs the counselor should look for and question regarding a client's action, to determine readiness, are the following: Does he appear interested in help only to please someone else? Does he appear to want *only* temporary assistance? Is he looking *only* for material aid? Does he appear to be in a "tight spot" because of a pending trial, jumping bail, being AWOL from the service, or neglecting child support? Is he a traveling hippie, runaway vagrant, or a traveling alcoholic mission tourist? If any of these signs apear, chances are this client is not ready.

Readiness can also be measured by positive signs. Is the client willing to be inconvenienced to obtain help? An alcoholic called me and wanted an interview. "I'm real desperate," he said. "Can you come tomorrow (Wednesday) at 10 o'clock for an interview?" I asked. "Can we make that Friday instead?" was his reply. It was apparent he was not that desperate for help. The counselor should ask himself, "Is the client ready to accept a plan for recovery?" The client may question, express doubts and fears, and be somewhat resistant, but is there a basic willingness to at least try? Most of all, is there a basic spiritual desire to commit his life to God?

The counselor may also set up various appointments with the client. If the client keeps them, he is showing readiness. A pastor called me and asked, "An alcoholic is coming to my church. How do I know if he is really sincere? I've been stung so many times by these fellows, so I want to be sure," he questioned me. I suggested that he have the gentleman attend various church services, and that the pastor request him to attend private counseling and prayer sessions at other times. After one month he called me back to say that the client had done all of this, what should he do next? We invited him to come to Teen Challenge where he became established in his faith. Later he returned home and is now a faithful member of the same church. The pastor had waited for the client to turn from a nibbler into one who took a solid bite.

Don't play the "ready or not, here I come" game. Another version is "ready or not, you're going to have to seek help." That game is played mostly by parents, husbands and wives, and relatives of the person who needs help.

Some counselors are the way I am when it comes to fishing. As soon as I get a nibble, I yank up my line and I lose the fish. I have not learned to let the fish nibble the bait long enough so I can set the hook. The counselor may think he is getting a hook in the prospect's jaw, only to find out there was no real bite. The prospect may have been only nibbling, asking a question or two. There is a difference between "nibblers" and real "biters." One is a prospect, the other is a client. One is still in the pre-counseling stage, the other is ready to be counseled.

We get many nibblers at Teen Challenge. They come to us shopping around for a cure. They are not at the point of desperation and are not really motivated to find a cure. They feel they can be choosy at this stage of their problem. They listen to our offer. Some even think it's a sales pitch. They want to know if it's easy or hard to be cured by our methods. How long does it take? Do you give a "money back if not satisfied" type of guarantee?

The nibblers often talk like they want help. They may be courteous, acknowledge God and make promises. From all outward appearances, they seem ready. "I'm sure he wants help" is often what ministers, parents and new counselors say when they bring someone to us for help. Experience, however, tells us that most likely this person is not ready for help — yet. But it's hard for the inexperienced counselor to detect this. "I thought it was just terrible when you turned down this one fellow," a staff counselor recalled as he reflected on his early days of becoming a fisher of men. "I thought for sure this fellow really wanted help. It's not Christian to turn him away. But then I learned that I was ready to help him, but he wasn't ready for my help. It was a valuable lesson I had to learn, but it wasn't easy."

Parents sometimes bring a son or daughter to me and say, "Talk him into staying at your place." Or they will say, "Tell her what she's doing to herself." Sometimes they will come with the pronouncement, "My son must stay. I insist." One father told his son, "You stay here or I'll kill you."

Such action on the part of parents or relatives only creates a wider division between them and their children, and makes their children more determined not to seek help or accept it. They hope to spite and punish loved ones by their refusal. In the same way, the counselor can widen the gap between himself and his prospect by over-eagerness, by forcing the counseling, and by not knowing when the person is ready.

2. *Keep the lines of communication open.* Often the counselor will get angry when the prospect does not respond. The anger may be prompted by the counselor's feeling of rejection and by frustration over his seeming inability to get through. Such anger shuts the door to future relationships. The door must never be shut completely. It should always be kept open, even if only a crack.

At Teen Challenge we tell those who are not ready, "Whenever you make up your mind you want help, we'll be ready to offer it." No matter what the circumstance of their rejection, we try to maintain a Christ-like spirit toward them, so they will know that at some future time they will be welcome.

There are reasons for a prospect's refusal of initial offers of help. He may be embarrassed. Perhaps he was high, drunk, or in a state of deep anxiety, and did things for which he was later sorry. If those who dealt with him during this difficult and tense moment acted in anger or hostility, the lines of communication could be permanently damaged. Jesus said we are to forgive "seventy times seven." That does not mean the church, the Christian worker, or counselor must be a doormat for a prospective client to walk on, but it does mean that the counselor has to deal with the situation with TLC (tender loving care).

The father who says to his teenager, "Get out of the house and don't come back until you change," is not an example of keeping the lines of communication open. Parents of rebellious and addicted children must try to maintain some form of communication with them. Even when drastic measures have to be taken, the action should be done with the most possible kindness and understanding. This is easier said than done. How can you be understanding and kind when you have to commit your child or relative to a correctional institution? It can be done; I have seen it happen. The family keeps in contact and expresses an interest in the child during the correction period. Committal sometimes must be made for the protection of the child, society, and other members of the family. When family, parents and friends refuse to visit, write, or call during this period, this cuts the line of communication.

A former addict recalled his early days of drug addiction, when he would come home high on drugs. His mother would always scream, cry, lecture, and plead. Sometimes he would listen, sometimes he would ignore her. One night he came home and his mother looked at him and said nothing. It happened the next night, and the next, and the next. He became very depressed and finally one night he went to his room and cried. He thought his mother didn't love him anymore because she didn't yell at him and lecture him anymore. He felt secure as long as his mother said something about his addiction. When she stopped saying something, he felt he had lost contact with her.

I don't advocate such measures to keep in contact. There are better ways to maintain those lines of communication. The counselor should let the prospect know that the door to his home, office, church, youth center, and his heart will always have a welcome sign hanging outside it.

3. *Don't give up.* The moment of readiness may come at any moment, at the most unexpected time, and often

through the most unusual circumstances. Don't give up hope. If the counselor gives up, the moment of readiness will go by unnoticed. The counselor's faith, patience and compassion will be tested to the breaking point, but he must not give up.

The Jerry McCauley Mission in New York City is named after a converted alcoholic who, while on New York City's Bowery, went to a mission altar eighteen times and made a profession of faith and a start toward a cure. Eighteen times he went back to the bottle. Some people gave up on him, but others did not, and finally the nineteenth time he made it. Later he started a mission to help others. He made it because someone didn't give up.

The continual resistance, hostility and failure on the part of a prospect can throw the counselor off course. He can become indifferent, hardened and blind to the evidence which may later appear to show that the prospect had changed and was ready to be helped.

What do you do about someone who abuses your kindness and interest? What do you do about someone who is "conning" (deceiving) you? The counselor must not allow a prospect to take advantage of him. He may have to tell the prospect outright that he feels he is not being honest. This may break down the relationship, but it does not mean the case is forever lost. If the counselor does not give up, the prospect may change his attitude later and come back seeking help on the right terms.

Not giving up means the counselor must be *available*. The cliche, "Where were you when I needed you the most?" applies here. Circumstances can change overnight, especially for the prospect who is addicted to certain habits. On the other hand, it may take months or years for a prospective client to be ready. Regardless, the counselor must not give up and he must be available and accessible. Those who are addicted to serious habits live dangerous lives; they run the risk of getting into trouble at any time. This works against them on one hand, but it works in their favor on the other, in that their trouble can wake them up to their need for help and provide the proper degree of motivation toward seeking it. The counselor and Christian worker must be there when that person wakes up to his need.

4. *Strike when the iron is hot.* Keeping the lines of communication open, not giving up, and being available are important in the precounseling period because the counselor is then ready to light the fire and to strike when the iron is hot. Here, too, it is important to determine when the client is ready to move out of the precounseling stage and into the counseling stage. The purpose of the precounseling period is only to set the stage for the all-important process of getting the client to "do something." During the precounseling period what the counselor does is most important, but in the counseling period the most important thing is the client's action in taking concrete steps to help himself.

5. *Let the Holy Spirit prepare the prospect.* The counselor can hinder matters by being more ready than the prospect and by doing too much. Certain measures must be left to the Holy Spirit. The Spirit leads into all truth and convicts of sin. Don't try to do what only the Holy Spirit can do.

I asked a young man in our Teen Challenge program why he came to us. "Because my parents made me," he said. He was honest, but his answer showed he was not ready. Because he was with us against his will, he resisted counsel and became even more belligerent.

I recall a new convert witnessing at our Greenwich Village coffee house. One of his friends, whom he was trying to win to Christ, did not appear interested. Finally the new convert grabbed him by the front of his shirt and said, "Look, buddy, don't get smart with me. You need Jesus Christ and you better accept Him, if you know what's good for you."

That is not what Jesus meant when He said, "Compel them to come in"! Many honest and sincere personal workers use the wrong methods and thus turn off prospective clients. There comes a time for "do or die" tactics, when the counselor feels his prospect is the hottest he will ever get, but this must be done prayerfully and by the leading of the Holy Spirit. No one should be badgered into the kingdom of God or into accepting counseling. Badgering is certain to meet with failure; conviction is done by the Holy Spirit and is met with success.

6. *Be alert to "mooders," "conners," and sympathy seekers.*

a. "Mooders." Two staff workers came to me quite upset. They said they were disturbed because "every time we bring a drug addict or alcoholic off the streets, they are turned down by the staff. They are told to come back the next day, and when the next day comes, they are no longer in the same mood for help."

"You've answered your own complaint," I said. "You said the next day they were no longer in the mood for help. If they really wanted help, don't you think they would have showed up?"

There are those who for various reasons go through moods when they want help, but when their mood changes, they no longer respond. The "mooders" are those who on certain occasions, either when under the influence of drugs or alcohol, or when depressed, say they want help, but when their mood passes, they no longer are motivated to find help. It was only a mood and nothing more. The mood that motivated them in the first place must be strong and deep enough to make them really want to quit their habit and get away from their problem. They have to stay in the mood long enough to do something.

We have devised methods to test "mooders." We call these methods the "mood testers." In the case of an addict, we may ask him to come back the next day or call the next day. Depending on the case, the counselor can do other things to test the "mooder."

A young, attractive airline stewardess came to one of our services and sought counsel. One of our staff girls spoke with her. The stewardess expressed a desire to serve the Lord, but the counselor could only go so far with her; she did not seem to want to go any further in the counseling process. Later, I found out why. She was in a state of temporary spiritual openness. She had been carrying on a secret affair with a married pilot, who had just informed her that their relationship would have to stop. She came to us during the shock and depression brought on by this experience. She was in the mood for love — spiritual love and the counsel of others. Her interest, however, was a rebound from the bump the pilot had given her. Perhaps that was the thing she needed to draw her to Christ. Or, it could have been just a mood, and she might have gone on to another lover to fulfill her needs.

b. "Conners." They turn on the tears, tell the sad story, or tell the counselor just about anything they think the counselor wants to hear. Their purpose may be to get a free meal, a bed to sleep in temporarily, money, or just a little attention. A key phrase counselors should look for to spot "conners" is: "I need a place to stay." Chances are he is a touring panhandler who frequents mission after mission preying on the compassion of the Christian for three hots (meals) and a cot (bed). Another thing to watch for is someone who comes seeking your help on Tuesday and on Thursday informs you he must appear in court on a criminal charge and would like you to go with him. Nine times out of ten it is all part of a plan to make it look good before the judge. In another case a young man came to the altar for prayer. When I asked him why he had come forward he said, "Do you think Jesus can get me a new pair of shoes?" The "conner" is different than the "mooder." The "mooder" usually is sincere during his mood. The "mooder" does want help when he says so. The "conner," on the other hand, knows just what he is doing and usually plans what he is doing. He plays it cool and slick. The experienced counselor learns to pick out the "conners." But in the process of gaining the experience, the counselor may lose time, money and effort.

c. Sympathy seekers. These people do not want help, only attention and sympathy. They will do anything to gain attention, and after they get it, they go on to someone else. They will take the counselor down the road of their sorrows and miseries, delighting in them. They may even be proud of their failures. They are happier when they are sad. They find security in their hopelessness because their problems have become their identity and they fear losing that identity. They can be helped, if they want to be and if they are willing to admit that their problem is that they enjoy their difficulties.

My brother Dave found a teen-aged addict living in the basement of a tenement house. The young fellow took care of the furnace and in return slept on a bed in the basement. He was a greasy, dirty, skinny dope addict. My brother was so moved by his condition that he compelled him to come to Teen Challenge for help. He stayed overnight and then left. Later my brother went to visit him and asked him why he had left. The boy replied, "Preacher, you did a mean thing to me."

"What do you mean?" Dave asked. "Why do you say that?"

"Preacher, you took me out of that basement; you took away my security. I don't know how to live where you live."

Not only was this boy hooked on drugs, but he was also hooked to his misery. Perhaps something he had done in his past made him feel he deserved to be in that condition, and somehow he felt he was working out his sins by being in that state. He found happiness in his misery.

The Counseling Period

Once the counselor has determined that his client is ready, the counseling process can begin. Some who counsel are unaware of any techniques or procedures to follow and thus they stumble along doing more harm than good. Others, who may have had no training but who look to the Lord for insights into themselves and their clients, and look to the Holy Spirit for guidance, use the right techniques even though they are not aware of it.

The Lord has revealed many things to us in the Teen Challenge work. He has shown us how to do the right things, even though we were untrained. The Holy Spirit gave wisdom, discernment, and knowledge when they were needed. But we have made mistakes out of ignorance. The fact that some of our clients became converts, in some cases, was not because of our counsel but in spite of it. God overruled our mistakes. We were sincere, but sincerity is no substitute for truth and for proper training.

The counselor should seek all the technical training he can get. This does not mean training is a substitute for trust in the Lord and the guidance of the Holy Spirit. The counselor must know by the wisdom of the Holy Spirit when and how to apply any training he may have. At the same time, he must realize that only the Holy Spirit can, in the final analysis, provide the solution to problems. This is the unique difference between the Christian and the secular counselor. The secular counselor looks at a client's needs from a psychological and emotional perspective. The Christian views the problem also from a divine perspective. In many cases, the solution to the problem will be through the meeting of the client's spiritual needs. If the spiritual need is met, and the client still has problems, then the counselor's knowledge of emotional and psychological needs may be just the key to getting to the root of the problem. This is why the Christian counselor should be the most qualified to deal with the needs of the untapped generation.

What are the important procedures to follow during the counseling period?

1. *Be a good listener.* A counselor is usually noted first for his ability to talk to his client, but listening is more important than speaking. In normal conversation few people really know how to listen. Jesus said He knew many people who listened but did not really hear. The great sin of the church is that it looks, but does not see; it listens, but does not hear.

Listening is done on several levels. The first level is when we listen for just the words that are being said. What is heard is taken at face value. The second level of listening is when the hearer concentrates on the words he hears and tries to understand the deepest significance behind them. That is listening with thought. The third, and most important, level of listening is to listen with the ears, the mind and the heart. While the client is talking, try to get into his mind.

A popular song talks about the "rivers of the mind" and the "back roads of the mind." While the client is speaking, the counselor slowly walks with him along the "back roads of his mind," trying to understand the deepest and fullest meaning of what the client is saying. Sometimes the words of the client are misleading; they are detours around the real problem. The counselor must try to find this out, and learn the feelings, attitudes and needs of the client that are *behind* his words.

Bill Milliken in *Tough Love* says, "It's so easy just to listen at the first level. We strip off the first layer of the onion, and then we don't want to smell any more, we don't want our eyes to water any more, we don't want to feel any more deeply. Therefore, we condition ourselves to listening only superficially to what people have to say. What happens then? We miss what they are really trying to tell us. We come up with the wrong medicine, the wrong answer. We give answers to questions that aren't even being asked."[2]

The counselor should not be shocked by anything he hears. If the one being counseled is a close friend or relative, the counselor should not make judgments or exclamations of surprise, such as, "John, oh no, how could you do that?" Or, "John, no, not you, don't you know that's wrong?" At this point such judgment and expressions of shock will cause the client to withdraw. He will be afraid to relate any more of his problem, feeling the counselor will not understand.

Proper listening helps build a bridge between the counselor and counselee. If the counselee senses that the counselor is listening (third level) and is trying to go hand in hand with him through his problem, confidence and trust will begin to build up between the two.

In the counseling process there is the "marriage of problem-solving." That is when the two — counselor and counselee — become one. The counselor walks with the client into "the deepest chambers of his soul."

Some professional counselors call this empathy. It is "feeling into." It is derived from the Greek word "pathos," which means a deep feeling akin to suffering. It is identifying with the sufferer and his problem. It is trying to enter into the person's problem as if it were your own. Empathy is the key process in counseling.

When a client was sent to the office of our director of counseling, Lester Eisenberger, he went most reluctantly. The client felt the counselor was only doing a job and had no real interest in him. As the young man sat in the office, he answered all the routine questions as to his name, address, and other personal data. In the course of such questioning the client mentioned that he had polio. Mr. Eisenberger then asked the client how he had contracted polio, how it affected him physically, (the client walked with a limp), and how he felt about his problem. From

[2] Bill Milliken, *Tough Love* (Old Tappan, New Jersey, Revell, 1968) p. 125.

that point on the client became very open and talked free-ly. When he left the counseling session the client said, "You really are interested in me." Had the counselor not been listening, he would not have been able to empathize with him. As soon as the counselor heard the client mention polio, he left what he was doing to travel with him into the back roads of his mind, allowing him to explore his polio problem which, as it turned out, had created a severe emotional hangup.

One psychiatrist described this process as becoming so identified with the other person and his problem that the counselor "gets rid of himself." If the merging process is successful, both the counselor and the counselee are changed. Rollo May in his book, *The Art of Counseling*, says, "We might even, in fact, judge the merit of a particu-lar conversation by asking how much it has taken us out of ourselves."[3]

It is also through the listening process that the Christian counselor gets what we call a "burden" for his client. This is the marriage, or falling in love — in a spiritual sense — of the counselor and the counselee. When this has been accomplished, the process can go on to the solution of the problem.

2. *Get the client to talk.* It would seem that getting the client to talk should be listed first, but it is listed second for good reason. Getting the client to talk is not usually a problem, but getting him to talk about the right things is. That is why listening is most important. The counselor must be a good listener, on the deepest level, so that he can pick out certain key phrases and themes that are com-ing through — and then try to get the client to talk about those themes.

Much territory might have to be covered before you get to the client's real problem. The counselor will have to do a great deal of listening — and let the client do a great deal of talking until "the real client stands up" and says, "This is me; this is my problem." In this process the client will take the counselor down the rivers of his mind — back into various tributaries and detours, getting stuck (if the

[3] Rollo R. May, *The Art of Counseling* (Nashville, Tennessee, Abingdon Press, 1967) p. 79.

counselor lets him), in a lot of muddy nonessentials. The counselor will have to pick out the important things and bring the client back into the main river of the problem and keep rowing along that course.

Tony came to me and said he felt like leaving Teen Challenge because he couldn't read. "I'm very embarrassed about this," he said. We prayed and then I said, "Is there anything else bothering you, Tony?" I had the feeling he hadn't come out with the real problem. Then he related another problem, but I didn't react or say much to him about it. Again, I had the feeling he hadn't come clean. Finally, he admitted having difficulty adjusting to other people who were different from him. He had been running away from the normal adjustments of life, be it family, friends, or the people on the job. In the process of talking it out, he also realized that others were getting used to him as well, and that he hadn't done his best to help them get adjusted. It took time, but after a few detours Tony had finally admitted what was really bothering him.

When the real problem is coming out, the client may not want to talk about it. It may be painful for him to do so. The counselor should carefully and tactfully get the client to talk about his painful experience. It must come out. Like a surgeon with his knife, the counselor will be cutting into the client's very being — but it is a hurt that will heal. And it will only heal by going through the painful experience of talking about it.

3. *Pinpoint the problem.* A counselor asked a new client, "What's your problem, young man?" To which he answered, "That's why I came to you. I want you to tell me what my problem is."

The purpose of the counseling session is not so much to tell the client what his problem is, but to guide him along so he will talk himself into a corner, and come to see his problem for himself. It takes time for the problem to emerge and come to the surface. The counselor and counselee will have to discover it together. The client may be "hung up" on the symptoms of his problem and still not know the cause.

Don't react too quickly. I've had clients leave my office, and after they were gone I felt that somehow we had not arrived at the real problem. The counselor may react too quickly to a surface problem or a symptom and keep the client hung upon a major aspect of his total problem. Much time can be wasted by majoring in minors.

One client, Paul, pointed out his difficulty in relating to another Christian who was trying to help him. "What he did to me was not right. How can he be a Christian and do that?" Paul complained. I proceeded to "get to the bottom of this" by hastily defending Paul before the fellow Christian worker. When the worker told his side of the story, it revealed that Paul was having a serious problem in learning to relate to other people. "Paul," I said, "you told me what he did to you, but you didn't tell me why." As it turned out the Christian worker had handled the situation properly. The client had lured me into his favorite game of pin-pointing his own problem and getting someone to defend him. He lived a life of majoring in minors, and I was letting him play the game at my expense. After this we began to deal in majors — his difficulty in accepting authority and listening to the advice of others.

Majoring in minors is also done by dealing with symptoms rather than causes. A young teenager who may have a habit of marijuana smoking, or another who is being influenced by friends to do harmful deeds cannot be told to just "keep away from old friends" or to change schools, neighborhoods, churches, or whatever. What must be dealt with is why he is so easily influenced. What can be done to provide him with the inner resources to stand up against the crowd?

However, serious problems can be missed by the counselor's brushing off a statement of a problem. Reuben came to me and said, "Brother Don, everyone keeps telling me I talk in my sleep and blaspheme Christ."

"Come on, Reuben," I said, "don't pay any attention to what others are saying. They're just trying to get you all upset."

But my quick reaction turned out to be wrong. He *was* blaspheming in his sleep. His subconscious mind was being revealed in his sleep. It was a serious problem and it needed to be dealt with.

Often in a family situation children will come to parents, or young people in the church will come to a minister, and relate what may seem to be an outrageous problem. They appear to be exaggerating; it's something you think Mary could never do. But in reality it's true and very serious.

If a client's problem is overstated or evaded, the client must work through the counseling process until he arrives at his real problem and pinpoints it. If the problem is understated, then the counselor must keep probing, that is, by allowing the client to talk until the more serious problem is pinpointed.

In pinpointing the problem the counselor must determine if the problem is physical, psychological, emotional or spiritual. It may be all of these. All problems are spiritual in nature, but are they only spiritual? Is a person's emotional conflict due to a spiritual emptiness? The girl who goes out with any fellow who will have her and gives her body to him — is she expressing only a spiritual need, or has she been emotionally and psychologically damaged from something done in childhood? The young man who uses drugs — is it because he rebelled against God and the teaching of Christ that he got into the wrong crowd and out of curiosity used "stuff," or has he suffered from emotional conflicts brought on by a broken home and mistreatment from parents? Moreover, has he suffered brain damage from extensive use of drugs?

The non-Christian counselor denies the existence of the spiritual needs in the client, but the Christian counselor can be just as wrong by denying the existence of physical, psychological and emotional problems. The counselor must understand that whatever seriously affects one part of a person will also affect another part. Emotional and spiritual problems are twin brothers. Man is a whole being; the whole being must be kept in mind during the counseling process.

What should the counselor do if he feels the problem is physical or mental? What should be done about referrals? No referral should be made until an effort is made to minister to the spiritual needs of the client. Ministers who turn clients over to a doctor or psychiatrist should not leave them in the hands of someone who is not providing ministry to the soul. This kind of cooperation is possible; more of it needs to be done in solving multiple problems.

Referral may not even be necessary. If the counselor leads

his client to a conversion experience with Jesus Christ, the total problem may be solved. The solving of the spiritual need may lead to the solution of the emotional need; the solving of the emotional need may be the solution to the physical need. Some churches are full of people who would have needed hospitalization, psychiatric sessions, or even confinement in another type of institution, but for the grace of God and the power of God to heal the total man. Through the ministry of physical healing, many side effects brought on by that physical problem have been solved.

This does not mean referrals should not be made. Some counselors and ministers feel that to refer someone is an admission of failure and a lack of faith. Healing comes through many forms and the counselor must not deny a client medical or other professional assistance. Again, if this assistance is provided not as a substitute for ministry to the soul but along with it, then the counselor should feel safe in making referrals.

4. *Don't talk too much.* Most counselors have difficulty withholding advice and solutions. It seems strange to tell a counselor not to counsel, but this is vital to the counseling process. The counselor will be tempted to pick up something the client says and go into a long, wordy, perhaps biblical explanation filled with religious jargon and nice-sounding solutions. There is a time for the counselor to give advice, but only after he works with the client through a session or several sessions, and only after he is sure everything has come to the surface.

It is helpful for the counselor to restate some of the client's problem, or to lead him in one direction and away from what appears to be a detour. The client may come to a brick wall; he may be at the core of his problem and have difficulty getting everything out. The counselor can help the client clarify, modify or redefine certain things to aid in his "coming out" process.

Don't cut the client off. An example of talking too much, too soon, is to say to him, "Oh, I know just what your problem is. What you need to do is...." The untrained Christian counselor may brush off the person with, "All you need to do is get right with God." That may be true, but the person may never see his need for getting right with God until and unless he sees what his problem is, and why he needs to get right with God.

Edward came to my office with a problem. "I listen to jazz music all the time and go to dirty movies. I do this rather than read my Bible." He had presented his problem to several counselors. They had immediately gone into a sermon about the evils of jazz and movies. He was dealt with on that basis only. When he came to me, I asked him, "What are the reasons you do these things?" It was evident that the things he was doing were only symptoms of a deeper problem. After several sessions the real Edward stood up. He had had several homosexual experiences in the past, and now that he had completed our residence program and was out working, the problem had come up again. Jazz and movies were a smokescreen for his real problem. Those who had been dealing with him had talked too soon and too much.

Try to get the client to answer his own problem. Through the counseling process the client should arrive at the conclusions the counselor desires, without the counselor's having to state them. When the client asks a question, it is good to say, "What do you think?" A client may reply, "What do you think I should do?" In many cases the client knows what he should do and is trying to avoid it. He can be questioned in return, "But what do *you* think you should do?" In this way the counselor has a chance to find out whether the client would accept his advice before he gives it.

While talking with our trained resident counselor, Lester Eisenberger, I asked him about a particular case. "What did you tell Bob?" "I didn't say anything," Mr. Eisenberger answered. "Why didn't you tell him that what he was doing is wrong?" I asked. His answer was simple: "I can tell him what's wrong, but at this point he is not ready to accept it; so what good will it do for me to tell him? He has to arrive at this conclusion himself. I think with a few more sessions together he'll reach that point."

Many counselors arrive at conclusions the counselee himself has not reached. I've given, in counseling sessions, what I felt was an excellent diagnosis and answer to a certain client's problem. I felt pleased with myself for having given such an answer and counsel. The only problem was, my client didn't come to the same understanding of his problem that I had.

It might be that the client is looking for quick, simple answers; to give them to him would be a disservice. The desire to tell people how they should handle their problem is not an acceptable substitute for allowing the troubled to pour out their feelings.

5. *Involve the client in his own cure.* A common mistake of rehabilitation programs is to try to perform a cure regardless of the motivation, attitude and cooperation of the client. One of the mistakes we made in developing the Teen Challenge program was that while we were treating clients, we smothered them with our love, but we were not preparing them for the outside world. We were not getting to the root of their problems. Like many parents, we spoiled and babied them along, being overly protective, pacifying and sustaining them on our faith and prayer. We picked them up and accepted them at any time, under any circumstances, and in any condition. They were allowed to remain almost without any restrictions. They came into our program carried along by our zeal and enthusiasm. They were given constant attention, often were pleaded with, begged and coaxed to remain when they wanted to leave. Some would stay for a time just because we asked them to. However, at night many did run off. We soon realized we were running a hotel, not a rescue station.

Our biggest mistake was in not allowing the addict or prospective client to involve himself in his cure by proving, to one degree or another, that he really wanted to receive help and overcome his problem. We therefore began to make some changes, so the person could show signs of wanting help. Screening was done more carefully, and other measures were taken.

Many addicts and alcoholics who came to us had in previous situations been given this same royal treatment. Everything had been done for them. They were given free drugs; they were never allowed to suffer pain. Every comfort for the body was provided. Nothing was done to give them a chance to exert their own efforts toward a cure. They expected this same treatment when they came to us. They called up and said, "I'll join your program if you drive over and pick me up." They had developed an "I'm doing you a favor by coming" attitude.

To overcome our mistake, we first made it harder for a person to enter our treatment program. We set up tests to determine a degree of motivation. If we met someone on the street who expressed a desire to be treated, we set up appointments for him to fulfill. If he came, we felt he had passed one small test. When addicted persons are involved, passing this small test is an accomplishment. Even for other more sophisticated people, keeping an appointment with a pastor, Christian worker, even a friend, can be a difficult thing. The counselor should not run after a client. If there is no response, he should keep the lines of communication open, but other than that, he should make the prospective client come to him. This enables the person to express by an outward act that he wants inward help.

One young man who came to Teen Challenge said, "You don't know how hard it was for me to knock on that door. I walked up the block, looked at the door, then passed on. I walked around the block several times before I had the courage to knock." That simple act, which most people can do without giving it a second thought, is a difficult task for a distressed and troubled person. But if he is to overcome other difficult tasks, he must begin as soon as possible to tackle the immediate ones. Forcing or trying to persuade a prospective client into a counseling session or relationship is to deny that person the right to express his own will. Such denial robs him of his most precious asset — self-expression and self-determination. For one who feels robbed of self-respect and self-expression anyway, this is a tragic denial.

6. *Ignite hope and spark change.* Talking too much can be a mistake, but not talking enough or at the right time can also be a mistake. The right moment and place during the counseling process must be found, when the counselor begins talking, advising, and counseling. It must not come too soon or too late.

After the counselor has listened, interpreted and pinpointed the problem, he must begin to speak words of hope and instruction to help the counselee "begin to do something" to help himself. This is the real moment of lighting the fire. The counselee must turn hope and desire for a change into action. Someone has said, "Feed your faith, and your doubts and fears will be starved to death." The counselor's task is that of feeding faith, igniting hope, and sparking action in the counselee. The difficulties he faces will dampen his hope; the flame will flicker; it may even go out temporarily or completely. The counselor may have to "relight" the client many times over.

One great difficulty of counseling with those who are weak, struggling, and slow to progress, will be the visible disappointment and anger the counselor may display before the counselee. The temptation will be to terminate the relationship. "I can't do anything else for you, Andrew," I said to one counselee. "I'm sorry to disappoint you. Please forgive me," he apologized as he saw my disappointment. Then realizing what I was doing to him — reinforcing his despair rather than helping him out of it — I went into forward gear in my counseling. "But God can still forgive you. He hasn't given up on you." After I put my arm around him, we went down on our knees. I asked him to pray and slowly he began to confess his weakness and to pour his soul out to the Lord. When we finished he was ready, as he said, "to go out and give it another try." A dying flame had been re-ignited.

The counselor must never lose his faith in himself or in God. Also, he must not lose faith in the one he is counseling. This does not mean the counselor should fool himself by thinking that progress is being made when it is not. Being realistic is important, but not at the sacrifice of faith and hope. The counselor must by faith see the "evidence of things not yet seen" in the counselee. He must keep throwing on coals of fire to keep hope alive, so that his client's "becoming" progress will continue.

This is the importance of the Christian counselor. When the non-Christian counselor exhausts every means of endeavor, all hope is lost. The Christian counselor has a further hope. He has God on his side. As long as the counselor and counselee believe God is alive, hope for a solution still exists. The counseling process may seem to be at a dead-end, but as long as God and faith are alive, there is hope.

A word of caution. The counselor should not make promises to his counselee. Statements such as this should be avoided: "Give me a few sessions with you and everything is going to be all right." Or, "God is going to come down and take your whole problem away." Or, "Let's just pray about this; God is going to work everything out."

There comes a time for expressions of faith in God and His Word, but positive faith must be arrived at by the counselee, not just the counselor. Likewise, the counselor should not tell the person he is making progress when he is not. He should be honest, yet positive about the future.

Theology and the Counselor-Counselee Relationship

The counselor and the client must understand the place that God, faith, and salvation have in the counseling process. Proper understanding can mean a solution; improper understanding can mean a failure.

The client may be looking to God and the counseling session to remove the reasons for his distress and trouble by some magic or automatic force, rather than learning how he can by faith in God cope with the circumstances surrounding his problem. He must not run away from his troubles, but face them squarely and, by so doing, overcome them.

The client must be shown that God wants to give him the resources to face life, and that He works in and through his circumstances to find a cure. He cannot run away from himself or from his problem, but he can run "through the fire and not be burned." Salvation is an escape from sin, not from life. Christ saves from sin, but the client must realize he still has to be "in the world."

The proper theology of counseling is to help the client not to be confused about God's part in his recovery. God works in and through the client, but with his cooperation.

The counselor must have faith that God can change his client; and he must try to spark that same faith in his client. Faith is that spark; it is not the end result. When the Bible says, "All things are possible if you believe," it does not mean one can just believe and immediately the problem is removed. It means that faith and belief make it possible to achieve the end result.

Harold Hass in *Pastoral Counseling With People in Distress* says:

Man's essential problem is his alienation from God, which results from sin. Man's sinful nature and his sinful behavior have separated him from God and worked havoc among men. Ultimately sin is at the bottom of all of man's physical and mental distress. It is also what prevents him from reaching his full potential as a human being. To alleviate distress at its source, the breach with God must be healed. To free man to be all the Creator intended him to be, that is, to realise his full potential, the results of sin must be remedied. The pastor's (counselor's) unique function is to be about the business of mending this break by means of the gospel of Jesus Christ.[4]

The problem of the client does not end, nor does a solution begin, until Jesus Christ is accepted as personal Savior. It may take much counseling before this decision is reached, or it may come at the beginning of the contact. Regardless of when the decision is made, only through this new birth experience is the person able to be healed. Everything before this is preparative counseling or "sowing the seed." When conversion takes place, a whole new dimension is added to the counseling process. The counselor through the power of the Holy Spirit is the agent to light the fire; Christ is the fire.

[4] Harold J. Hass, *Pastoral Counseling With People in Distress* (St. Louis, Mo., Concordia Publishing House, 1970), pp. 55, 56.

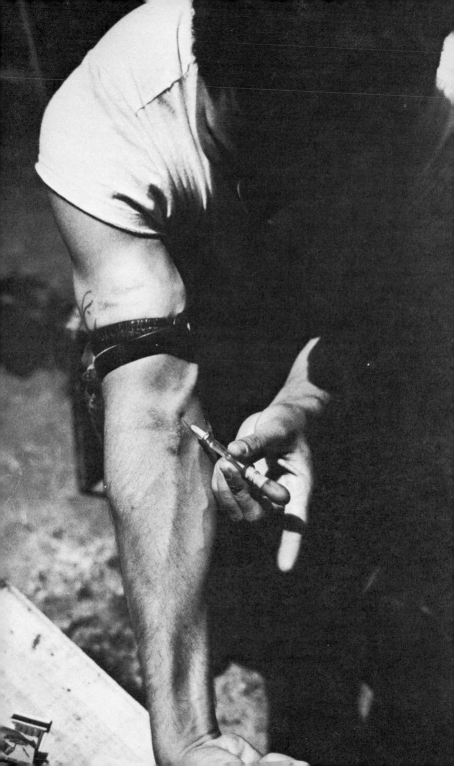

5

THE ADDICTED GENERATION

Tripping Out With LSD

"It's a groovy experience. Nobody can psych you out once you reach this utopia. You're immortal. You think you are God and can judge, or fly, or float, or condemn or all four. You're in a purple haze where red stars and blue moons cover your feet. At the same time tunnels begin to form. As they take shape, they loom larger and larger and whirl madly.

"Suddenly there are hundreds of them — dark, black, empty tunnels. You fall to your knees as they rush at you, pounding you into the red stars and blue moons.

"Then you're plunging head over heels through the tunnels, past snakes and cows and frogs with bloodshot eyes. You fall and fall. It feels like only minutes and yet eternities too. Then you see flames . . . waiting for you, surrounding you. They begin to burn. *There is no escape!*"

*   *   *

"Isn't it true that drug addicts are mainly people of low intelligence, and that only certain kinds of personalities are addiction prone?" a high school student asked me.

"That is a tragic misconception," I answered. "While it is true that certain people may have more reasons to turn to drugs to fill a need in their lives, the drug addict population is made up of a wide cross-section of society. What you must understand is that anyone and everyone is a potential drug user and thus a potential drug addict."

If we have heard it once, we have heard it a hundred times from young people: "I am different. I can take drugs, but I can always leave drugs when I want to." Sadly enough, many who take drugs just to experiment, find later that they cannot stop taking them. Many are sincere in their desire only to experiment, or to take drugs for kicks. However, they find out that they are unable to make the proper judgment regarding further use of other more potent drugs, once they are in a drug atmosphere. The result is that the "now" generation is turning into the addicted generation.

Because of this rise in addiction, the church is going to have to find a new kind of youth worker. In addition to a Christian education director and a youth director, the church must enlist and train a full-time youth worker who can converse with those caught in the web of drug addiction. Some of the strongest churches in the country are facing the problem of drugs among youth from the best homes in the church. A book I have in my library, written in 1965 for pastors interested in counseling drug addicts, states: "Few ministers in the suburban churches will have occasion to counsel an addict." That statement was accurate at the time it was written. But it must now be said that this is no longer true. In the last few years drug use and drug addiction have spread like a cancer into the tree-lined suburbs, those islands of what was thought to be safety and isolation from the problems of the inner city. Parents who moved out and bought homes at great financial risk to hide their children from drugs and other related problems, now find they must face the very same difficulties they sought to escape.

In the face of this rising tide of addiction, what basic facts does the Christian worker need to know?

Three Categories of Drug Involvement

The counselor will meet three different groups of young people involved in the drug scene: (1) users; (2) abusers; (3) addicts. These three groups are distinct yet closely related. The counselor must not mistakenly treat the user as an addict, nor should he treat the addict as a user. There is a difference between drug use, drug abuse, and drug addiction. Yet, the difference is often a very thin line. It is important to know where one type of drug involvement begins and ends, and where the second type takes up.

The drug user and the drug addict may be compared with the social drinker and the alcoholic. And the drug abuser may be compared with the problem drinker. The drug user uses the drug, but the drug uses the drug addict. The user can control the amount of drugs he takes, the addict cannot control himself or the drug. The user is an experimenter, the abuser is one who finds he has an ever-increasing need to experience the high or the euphoria it gives him, and the addict is one who seeks total escape from reality.

Addiction has been defined as a state of periodic or chronic intoxication produced by the repeated consumption of a drug and involves tolerance, psychological dependence, usually physical dependence, and an overwhelming compulsion to continue using the drug which detrimentally affects both the individual and society. The World Health Organization (WHO) recently recommended that the term addiction be replaced by a single and more general term — "drug dependence." They described drug dependence as "a state arising from repeated administration of a drug on a periodic or continuous basis."

Programs to help the users, abusers and addicts are more effective if they deal with each group separately. Mixing users and abusers with addicts may result in the addicts' influencing the others; users and abusers often look up to addicts and go on to more serious drugs to prove they know "where it's at" in the hard drug scene. Younger drug users learn about other drugs and the "tricks of the trade" from the more experienced. Addicts are proud of their drug knowledge and will show it off to others, in order to compete with their drug addict peers.

However, once the addict experiences a genuine conversion to Christ, he can have a most effective influence on the users and abusers, and on those who have never tried drugs but are facing the temptation to do so. Youngsters will listen to one who has been there. In Teen Challenge work we see the effectiveness of converted addicts who give their testimonies at high school assembly programs and relate the problems they encountered through drugs.

The whole drug scene is often glamorously painted as an innocent "in" way of life. Many young people feel they are being left out if they do not indulge. Drug use has become fashionable. One of the reasons why accurate figures on drug usage — especially marijuana — are hard to obtain is because many kids claim to have used it when they have not. This is because they think "everybody is doing it." Teens get a one-sided view. They are told about the supposed harmlessness and the nonaddictive aspects of pot, and about the mild high it causes. They are told that it is no worse than a cocktail. That side is only the street side of the story, the party atmosphere side of the drug question.

Young people need to hear and see the darker side. They need to be told the facts about what drugs will do and will not do. They can't be scared into staying off drugs, however.

After one school assembly, a young girl came to our group and said to us, "Thanks for coming. You told us about one side of the drug problem that the other kids never tell us. Now I'm in a better position to make the right decision about whether I will use drugs or not."

A student at the University of North Dakota told one of our Teen Challenge converts, "You said you smoked marijuana and then went on to heroin, but all I read refutes this. Research seems to contradict you." Mario, the converted drug addict, answered: "You read about marijuana in the paper, but I experienced it; that's the difference."

The high school and college marijuana users represent the type of drug user who emerged in our society in the mid-nineteen sixties. He is not an addict in terms of physical addiction. Some outgrow such drug use. Others do not. Unfortunately, wherever marijuana is found there are also hard drugs. In a very short time a marijuana user can turn to more frequent use of drugs and become an abuser. The abuser can become an addict almost overnight.

Young people who think that they will never become hooked on drugs often are sincere. But once drugs go into the body and mind, will-power, reason, good sense, and sound judgment all go out. We tell young people, "I believe you when you tell me you don't plan on getting hooked. But when you take drugs, you are in a certain atmosphere (the atmosphere of drug use has become just as important as the drug being used) and you become a different person in that atmosphere than you were when you first walked through the door."

A further danger is that a person does not know just how he is going to react to a drug. For example, when using marijuana the reaction can be different on any occasion. The initial effect of pot is often nil. First-time smokers usually get sick, some report no effect after several uses, some no effect even after ten times. However, eventually, the user will begin to experience mild sensations and perhaps get stoned. The effects come on slowly and smoothly. But after repeated use, and if the dosage happens to be stronger, the effect can be frightening. Marijuana is smoked, sniffed, or ingested. The mental effects include a feeling of euphoria, a dreamy sensation, or exultation. One user said, "I felt like the world had stopped and I had gotten off — I was in the twilight zone." In this state there is a free-flowing of ideas (good or bad, or both): senses of time, distance, vision, and hearing are heightened. Hallucinations may result from large doses. Some users are talkative, some giggle, some act silly, others become boisterous, moody, and drowsy. When such effects occur in an atmosphere of rock music, psychedelic lights and the gaity of a crowd the net result may be a stoned young lady or man who has no ability to resist other drugs or large doses of the same drug.

The step up or down from the marijuana culture may never happen, yet it does more often than the user will admit and more often than any authority will ever be able to know. When other drug usage takes place, it may be LSD (acid), a stimulant such as amphetamine, or meth-amphetamine (speed), a depressant or sedative (goof balls), or the direction may lead to heroin (horse).

The depressants cause intoxication similar to that experienced by the alcoholic. The abuser also exhibits slurred speech, his reactions are sluggish, he may be emotionally erratic and easily moved to tears or even laughter. Or he may become very angry. One client became upset with me when I refused to interview him because he was "goofing" so bad. "I'm not high," he kept insisting. He became very disruptive and created a scene in front of others. Then he started to laugh.

Those on stimulants become talkative, excitable, and noticeably restless. One young man said, "When I take 'ups' (a stimulant drug) I like to walk and walk and walk." Others experience insomnia, heavy perspiration, or tremors of the hands.

The LSD user experiences changes in perception, thought, mood, and activity. Time seems to slow down or even stop. There is also sometimes a sense of being detached from one's body. One user said, "I kept feeling like my fingers were falling off." The user may experience a free-flow of weird or bizarre ideas — including feelings of persecution. Trivial events take on unusual significance and importance. "A button can appear to be the most important image you have ever seen," said another LSD tripster. After a number of hours the effects of LSD begin to wear off. Sometimes fatigue, tension, and recurrent hallucinations (flashbacks) may continue long after ingestion of the drug. Psychological changes brought on by the drug may continue for indefinite periods.

The counselor who meets on an individual basis with those involved in drugs will have to determine the extent of the person's drug problem. (If the person is only a user, that may not pose too great a problem in the counseling process.) If abuse or addiction are involved, then the counselor's task is to help the person to overcome both the addiction to the drugs and the reasons for it. The addict will first need help and strength to get clean from the drug, physically, and then to face up to the problem of overcoming the emotional and spiritual needs that led to his addiction.

How and Why Young People Experiment and Become Dependent on Drugs

1. *The curious.* Some young people are always curious about something that is mysterious, adventurous, dangerous, and illegal. But while curiosity is given as an excuse for having started a habit, it is often later found out that some character defect perpetuated the drug-taking.

2. *The weak-willed.* Some young people seek a simple, quick, magical solution to the problems of life and to their own character defects. Such young people need little urging to get them started and they find it difficult to put down the habit once it has been fixed. These include the severely inadequate, immature, and the lost and depressed.

3. *The social addict, or the social give-ins.* These are young people who take drugs because it is the sociable thing to do. In their clique, everyone is doing it. Not to do so would mean to be left out. Taking drugs is a prerequisite for belonging to some groups.

4. *The sense seekers.* These are made up of the more artistic types who are seeking break-throughs or a renewal of their creative power. They perpetually seek to spring free of their ordinary way of seeing or sensing the world around them.

Some users claim to have understood themselves better after taking the mind-expansion drugs. One boy said, "My mind opened up — I found out a lot of things about myself I didn't know — but I didn't like what I found. And I have no ability to do anything about the things I learned."

5. *The escapers.* These are young people seeking escape from boredom, responsibility, frustration and anxiety. Many are affluent youths who have become bored with blessings. They don't know how to get high on life. They cannot accept responsibilities or the difficulties that make a young person grow. Life turns them *in,* not *on.*

6. *The accidental drug user.* This is a young person who has been turned on to drugs by a friend, relative, or some older person. The young person taking the drug did not really know what he was getting involved in, and accidentally got hooked.

One fellow related, "My best friend gave me a marijuana joint. Although I knew it was dangerous, I trusted him and so I thought everything would be all right. I had a pleasant drug experience and so started smoking from time to time with him until I woke up one day and found myself hooked." Although in the latter case, the young man was not completely naive to the drug scene, he nevertheless became accidentally involved because he trusted a friend.

7. *The persuaded addict.* Related to the social and the

accidental user are those who have been persuaded to indulge. A husband persuades his wife; a boyfriend turns on his girlfriend. The user may go along because of some misguided sense of love, or — in the case of some girls — because of some idea that if she were involved, she would be able to help her man with his drug problem.

8. *The prescription addict.* Some get involved in drug addiction through physical problems for which the doctor prescribed a certain drug. However, they find that while the drug alleviates their physical problem, it creates a worse one in that they develop a psychological dependence of which they are unaware. Prescription addicts are often people who started their drug use under extreme stress.

9. *Stone heads.* This is the type of young person who has found absolutely no meaning or value in life. He has come to the conclusion that anything is better than what he has experienced. He will take anything and everything, perhaps even a combination of drugs and alcohol.

10. *The religious seekers.* A growing number of young people use drugs as a religious sacrament. They seek personal insights or religious experiences. More frequently, they use psychedelic drugs (LSD and others). They are searching and believe that these drugs open up new levels of spiritual understanding.

With an estimated 250,000 addicts in the United States, there is of course a great challenge for the Christian to direct his efforts to this group. But there is perhaps an even greater challenge to reach the users and abusers who number in the millions. Some young people can be reached through their drug problem. The counselor who is able to address himself to the counselee's drug use, and then go beyond that to get into his mind and heart, can develop an effective ministry to the addicted and to the preaddicted generation.

The Drug User

The users primarily are made up of marijuana smokers, the so-called "soft drug" takers. Included in this group are young and old from all walks of life: the teens, the young adults, students, musicians, doctors, lawyers, businessmen, actors, as well as the more commonly known users, such as the hippies, the runaways, and the inner city teen-age gang members and delinquents. There are no "typical" marijuana smokers.

In dealing with this type of person, focus should not be put entirely on the drug. The pot generation has made up its mind about the so-called harmlessness of their "thing." No argument based on facts or experience will convince them otherwise. There are definite and real dangers in marijuana use — apart from any other drug — but its effects have not been studied long enough to present the necessary proof. Even if this proof were available, it might not do any good — as witness the warnings about cigarettes and cancer.

The more serious aspect of marijuana is the person using it. For young people, marijuana has become a symbol of rebellion. The problem is not the pot, but the person. Parents and many authorities make a mistake by focusing too much attention on the drug and trying to prove its dangers, without dealing with the rebellion or other issues and problems that young people face. Marijuana is only a symptom; causes, not symptoms, need to be dealt with. The cause may be a serious personality disorder, or it may be just the severe growing pains of adolescence.

Threats, and scare tactics will not work with a pot rebel. This is not to minimize the problem. Marijuana is dangerous. It is dangerous because it is a drug and it can lead to the use of other drugs. The counselor should be aware of the hazards of marijuana, but he also should know the difference between it and hard drugs. However, he should not spend his time trying to convince the counselee of the risks involved. When the facts are pointed out, it should not be in an emotional frenzy, but in a calm, convincing manner.

The counselee, on the other hand, may seek to lure the counselor into the great debate on marijuana with such statements as: "It's not any different than alcohol," "It ought to be legalized; alcohol is legal." or "Prohibition never worked." or "Getting high is a way of life; why aren't young people entitled to a high?" Another excuse is, "It's my body; I can do with it what I want; no one has the right to stop me."

These statements and questions can and should be faced, but only after talking about the more important issues.

In most cases of drug use, there are difficulties of young people relating to their parents; there are broken homes; there is a lack of discipline; and many other problems that have been common to all generations.

And then there are the problems young people have in making adjustments to life with all of its hang-ups and hardships. Those who have found a way (and *the* Way) to face up to these adjustments do not need the thrill of a cop-out through drugs. Through their faith in God and their faith in Christ, they have found the strength and the ability to grow, to mature, and to attack life — not run from it. If the drug user can be made to see that the use of drugs is a testimony to his immaturity and inner weakness, he may be able to see a deeper reason why he uses drugs. Most users will not admit to themselves that there is anything more to their use of drugs than the desire to get high or to have a kick. This craving is a greater danger to them than the drug. Marijuana, unlike heroin and other drugs does not build a tolerance or physical craving, but the need or desire to turn to some harder drugs may become stronger.

Drug use is both a "high" (pleasure) and an escape. The pleasure may be good for your feelings, but it is not good for your life as a whole. Marijuana smokers must be brought to see that they are *copping out,* not *coping with* life.

Copping out comes in many forms. The marijuana smokers may actually represent the smallest group in our society who are on an escape route. Some escape through harmful means, such as alcohol. Others do it through legitimate means. But the overriding desire to escape is nonetheless harmful to their personalities. There are those who escape from life by changing from job to job; those who go from social involvement to social involvement, from one romantic and sexual association to another. There are a multitude of things that the average American does to relieve his frustration and find escape from life's difficulties. It is all part of the same thing — hiding from life's realities and trials, rather than facing them head on.

The greatest danger of marijuana may not be in what it does, but in what *it does not do* for the individual. It makes promises, but it cannot fulfill them. It may make the user think pleasant thoughts, but it's like putting the gearshift of your car in neutral — the mind is disengaged. It is not in drive. The user does not go forward. If the drug user can be made to see the loss of values, the destruction of character, or the weakness of his personality, he may be able to view his smoking pot as having an adverse effect on his total being, and thus be ready for help and to seek change.

The Drug Abusers

Drug users become drug abusers. Copping out can become a way of life. The more youth turn *away from* rather than *toward* life and its problems, the more they get used to escaping and the more it's necessary. Drug abuse comes as a result of both the effect of the drug upon the mind and body, and the deterioration of the personality.

Users never intend to become abusers. But slowly and subtly the process takes place. Before they know it, it happens. When it happens, it is a blow to their egos and a frank revelation to themselves that there is something wrong with them. This shattering revelation usually means they need more drugs to alleviate the pain of this knowledge.

The drug abuser is in the process of becoming addicted. Most likely he will not see his involvement in drugs as a serious problem. Users and abusers see only the "high" side of drug consumption. All too often the abuser is at a phase of his drug-taking cycle when he is deriving satisfaction, euphoria, and release of tension from the chemical he is using. He is feeling no pain; what more can you as a counselor offer him? The symptom is pleasant, the cure much less so. The low side, the side effects of his drug use that bring misery and suffering may not have appeared yet. Therefore, it is difficult for him to be motivated enough to examine himself and his reason for using drugs.

The abuser (who could be termed the pre-addict) usually withdraws from family and society, and will not come out of his seclusion unless the counselor makes contact with him. The counselor will have to work with him along the lines suggested in Chapter 4 under the heading of precounseling. The Christian counselor's greatest task is to make contact and keep contact alive. Methods for making contact should be developed as launching pads.

From the launching pad the counselor can work with the abuser until the counselor-counselee relationship develops.

Users and abusers are saying by their drug-taking: "Please, help me." But they do not know they are saying this. Not until they see that drugs do not give answers, but instead rob them, will they be ready for help.

The Addict

Usually, the problems caused by drug-taking prepare the taker for rehabilitation: criminal arrest, sickness, physical weariness, family and home conflict, jail and hospital confinement, social stigma, the misery-go-round of hustling for the money to support his daily habit. Apart from the above reasons, addicts usually do not want help. Rarely will they submit to counsel or rehabilitation in the early stages of their drug use or addiction cycle. Jesus said, "They that are whole need not a physician" (or counselor). The addict views his drug use as a cure and not as a problem. If the addict is on mind expansion drugs, he will have a feeling of superiority and wisdom. Not until he has had a few bad trips (they all do, eventually), and not until he suffers the related miseries of addiction, will he be a good candidate for counsel and rehabilitation. Therefore, don't play the "ready or not, here I come" game with the addict.

What can be done for the user, abuser or addict who has not been motivated to seek help? In some cases, nothing can be done but to wait for the situation to get worse. When it gets worse, we may be able to help that person. The challenge and task of the counselor will be to watch and wait. The lines of communication (chapter 4) must be kept open. Periodic visits into the drug world are one way of keeping the lines open. Through the counselor's Christian witness, the addict may recognize his spiritual need, and seek help. Through an experience with Christ his need for drugs will be alleviated. The best response we have found has been from those who have been motivated to seek a change in their life because of the conviction of the Holy Spirit.

On one occasion I was speaking at a church near London. A young man came to the altar, drawn by the Holy Spirit because he recognized his spiritual poverty. He had been on his way to London's Soho district to trip out on LSD. After making his decision, he turned to the Christian counselor who had prayed with him and said, "I just discovered something. Now I don't have to go to Soho and shoot LSD. Now I have accepted Christ." He had come to Christ, not to get away from drugs, but because the Word of God convicted him of his need for a Savior. But through his experience with Christ the need for drugs was removed.

One young girl addict who was converted said: "Well, this is just like getting high." That is not to suggest that receiving Christ is just a good feeling. Certainly Christ is more than a feeling; He is a way of life — but a way of life that is accompanied by good feelings of joy and peace. The Christian has his periods of euphoria that are far more powerful than a shot of dope.

One converted addict, who was tempted to return to drugs, said that after he took a shot of heroin he got the shock of his life when he found that he could not get high. He said, "Once you have felt the fullness of God's power, dope no longer has the same effect on you." Such Bible promises as, "I have come that they might have life and that they might have it more abundantly" (John 10:10), and "Oh, taste and see that the Lord is good" (Psalm 34:8), and "In thy presence is fulness of joy" (Psalm 16:11) have an appeal to the drug generation.

The Drug Personality

Much has been said about the addictive personality, or those who are prone to become drug addicts. However, no one type of person becomes a drug addict. There are certain types who are fertile ground for drug addiction, but it is not the personality alone that causes drug use. Many young people with so-called addictive personalities are not addicted, and will not become dependent on drugs. They number in the millions. Once a person becomes physically and psychologically addicted — regardless of age, race, or social and economic background — he reacts to the drug craving like other addicts. Addicts develop similar behavior patterns: dishonesty, deceptiveness, lying, stealing, and various criminal acts, in addition to not trusting other people. However, these patterns are usually brought on by the drug. Most addicts did not steal or commit crimes before their drug addiction.

Apart from the drugs, addicts are persons with individual problems and personalities. Each one must be dealt with according to his particular needs. A fifteen-year-old and a thirty-year-old may behave similarly on the streets and in their activities in the drug world, but in counseling and rehabilitation they must be dealt with on the basis of the particular personality.

Understanding the Addict as a Drug User and as a Person

It is difficult to counsel the addict while he is in his drug world and under the influence of narcotics. Contact, and Christian witness can be done while the addict is high or sick, but it is best that *counseling* should not be done when an addict is in such a condition. When high the addict is another person. Judgments about his reactions cannot accurately be made when he is in such a state of mind. He may make promises while under the influence of the drug, tell lies, talk incessantly about meaningless problems, and relate other feelings that have been brought on by the drug.

There are exceptions, of course. One addict told me, "Look, I'm high, but I know what you are saying and I know what I am saying." However, it is still a good rule not to go into extensive counseling when the addict is under the influence of the drug. It takes a trained and experienced counselor to know just how much the drug is affecting the user. Many ministers and other workers have been fooled because they passed judgment on an addict's decision made while he was under the influence of a particular drug.

The opposite condition from the above is when the addict has not had any drugs for a period of time, and is suffering withdrawal. He may not want to talk to you because he is getting low or sick, and only has a shot of dope on his mind. He may be irritable and hostile as a result. He also could be dangerous if he gets real sick and becomes desperate. He may act sincere and make promises of rehabilitation, but only to build up the counselor for a "con" job. He may ask for money, or for some consideration that is part of fulfilling his need for drugs.

It is not advisable to try to lead an addict to a decision for Christ while he is under the influence of drugs. It never hurts to pray for him, but it is best not to have him pray for himself, unless it appears that the Spirit of God is moving upon him, which can happen.

However, when the addict is low or sick, (if he is open and ready for it), it is a good time to minister to him from the Word of God and to pray for him and with him. In our rehabilitation program at Teen Challenge, we find the withdrawal period an excellent time to reach the addict. If he is motivated, and if he is willing to submit to the withdrawal, he will become very sick. In his pain and suffering, he can be led to look to God for help and strength. We have seen many cases in which supernatural healing took place. Through His healing touch on their bodies, they have found that God does have power. Through this discovery they commit their lives to Christ. We have found that when an addict does not have pills, drugs, or any form of medication, it forces the issue with him. He has to do something to help him through the withdrawal. He usually does one of two things: he either runs away or he runs toward God and asks for His help.

Some would question the medical and theological soundness of this method, but it works for us. No addict at Teen Challenge has ever died during withdrawal. The pain does not leave them with any physical damage. We carefully supervise the withdrawal. If any complications arise, we immediately send the person to a clinic or hospital. A registered nurse is also in residence at Teen Challenge. The spiritual benefits of withdrawal through prayer far outweigh the physical hazards that accompany "cold turkey." As we tell the addicts, "What is five or ten days of physical suffering, compared to a whole new life you have waiting for you after your withdrawal is over?" The nights are long and the days are cold, but any addict who has gone through it and has experienced freedom from drugs and the new life in Christ will tell you, "It was worth it!"

We are not opposed to other methods of withdrawal. "Cold turkey" withdrawal happens to be a method that works for us. We recommend it to others.

The following is a brief outline of the important steps to take in counseling the hard-core, physically and psychologically addicted person. The addict, as opposed to the abuser and user, is one who has become physically and or psychologically hooked. The use of drugs has disrupted his normal pattern of living and behavior.

1. *Establish the fact that the person is hooked (addicted).* If the person is physically hooked, this might not be difficult to establish. However, he may be in the early stages of his addiction. Some addicts will wait until they are "strung out," using five or ten bags of heroin a day, before they will admit they are hooked. The drug addict will delay this admission as long as he possibly can.

In the booklet, *A Positive Cure for Drug Addiction,* which we distribute to addicts on the streets and elsewhere, there is a section entitled "The Teen Challenge Message to Drug Addicts." It lists five steps to a cure. The first step is "admit you are hooked." The addict is told: (a) It doesn't matter whether you take off once a day or ten times a day, you are hooked, so admit it. (b) Quit talking about a big habit or a little habit. You are either hooked or you're not hooked, so be honest.

2. *Find out what kind of help or cure the addict wants.* The addict may want only temporary help, such as a physical cure (withdrawal). Perhaps he is a mooder, or a conner, who only wants attention and not the permanent cure. He must be told that there is no simple, painless cure. There are no sympathetic drugs or substitutes that can pull him out. He must be convinced that hospitals cannot help him on a permanent basis. A doctor can pacify him with some pills; a psychiatrist can tell him why he is on drugs; but neither can cure him.

He must also realize that places where group therapy is used as the only means to a cure cannot give him what it takes to stay clean when he is out on his own in a real crisis. If he thinks that other forms of therapy might work for him, he will not be ready for you and for a spiritual program.

3. *Be honest with him about the difficulties he faces on the road to recovery.* He must be desperate and willing to

fight for his cure. Instilling faith, confidence, and hope in the addict regarding the possibilities of a cure must be done honestly, objectively, and without being overly optimistic. He will want the quickest and shortest route to recovery — one that has no pain, no sacrifice, and no cost. He is used to quick answers to all his problems and to all pain—a shot of dope. He finds it difficult to have to wait for something and to fight for his answers.

Telling him that God will take care of everything might lead him to think he doesn't have to do anything for himself. He must realize that he can't be cured in three weeks or three months. It will take him at least one full year before he is able to assume all the normal responsibilities of life and be on his own.

In our *Positive Cure for Drug Addiction* booklet, step number two is "quit looking for an easy way out." We tell the addict "Don't expect to be trusted or babied. You can't fool experienced people in the field of narcotics, so quit working angles.... If you run around making connections, you can work for a cure. Get up off your seat and quit acting like a baby."

4. *Through prayer lead him to a personal experience with Jesus Christ.* The addict is also a sinner. Use the same methods leading him to Christ as you would with anyone else. Get him on his knees before God in prayer. Pray with him and pray for him, and teach him to pray.

Quoting from *A Positive Cure for Drug Addiction:* "You must have faith in God. When you connect with a pusher, how do you know he is not giving you rat poison instead of H? You shoot it up without testing it under a microscope, because you must have faith that it is junk. If you can trust a pusher, why can't you trust in God? He never lets you down. You must come to Him like a little child and ask for His help. He has never turned anyone down who is sincere."

The addict may be reluctant to accept Christ because of the possibility of returning to drugs and thus not being able to follow the Lord. Some addicts, like others with serious difficulties, will want to work on their problem first and then give their lives to Christ. They must be made to see that the way to overcome their problem is *through Christ.*

5. *Help him face his fears.* The fear of failure is stronger in an addict than in any other individual. He has sensed failure from the early stages of his life. He has probably failed at various attempts at rehabilitation. He is afraid to start again, and of perhaps having to face the pain of failure. He must see that through Christ he can make it. He must realize that it is "not I, but Christ liveth in me" (Gal. 2:20).

The new convert must realize he is not operating under his own will power alone; he is under 'new management, not in the hands of man, but of God. His faith will have to rise above his fears.

The convert also has fears of his past. The guilt from previous sins often haunts him. The teaching of the Word of God, plus personal prayer, will give him the assurance of sins forgiven, that there is "no condemnation to them which are in Christ Jesus" (Rom. 8:1). Help feed his faith so that his doubts and fears will starve to death.

6. *Help him find meaningful activity.* For many addicts, the only work they have known is that of working angles. Normal work — household chores, handy work, cleaning up — is difficult for them to adjust to. Such work is not only important as a sign to show the addict that his life has changed; it is essential to his recovery because it keeps him busy and occupied so that the devil cannot play with his mind. Whatever work he is assigned to do, it should not be just busy work, but meaningful work in which he feels he is helping someone else or helping himself.

The counselor will have to keep challenging and pushing the addict. He must try to understand the mental and emotional stresses the addict has lived under which have caused physical inactivity. Laziness starts with the mind. It takes the addict time to get used to using his body and keeping his mind on what his body is supposed to be doing.

Those who are making successful recoveries will soon learn the beauty and satisfaction that comes from seeing a job well done. Little things they could never bother about before — doing dishes, mopping floors — for the first time in their lives can become meaningful. Some of our converts volunteer for additional work besides that which is assigned to them, because they get a sense of satisfaction. They sense that they are working for the Lord, and are helping to carry their own work load.

Spiritual activity, when not balanced off with work and recreation, may be harmful.

7. *Help him start planning for his future.* The addict has always lived for today; the only planning for tomorrow he ever did was to plan for tomorrow's dope fix. Through his conversion, help him to see that his future is not only in heaven, but also on earth. Encourage him to start planning his life all over again.

Some addicts started on drugs at an early age and thus they never had any ambitions. Some have never worked one day in their lives. According to their age and ability, help them to arrive at some practical goal for their future. Addicts who got involved in drugs later in life may already have a talent or skill. Some may want to return to jobs they had before addiction started.

Beware of the converted addict's grandiose attitude about the type of work he plans to do. Suggest that he start with something small, yet meaningful. When he handles that, he can go on to greater things.

In *A Positive Cure for Drug Addiction* there are two important paragraphs regarding this:

"If you have no plans for your life, and if you are sure you can't help others, then mark down on a piece of paper five things you think you would like to do or be. Spend a few weeks investigating what is involved in each of these five things, then choose the one that appeals to you most. You must choose a goal. . . . Know what you want to do, then go after it.

"You must learn to love the things you once hated, and to hate the things you once loved. You can do the right things now because God gives you the power to do them."

How the Teen Challenge Center Environment Helps the Addict to Overcome His Addiction

If the drug addict is going to learn to grow — emotionally, mentally, and spiritually — he must be taught how to live apart and free from drugs or alcohol. He must also learn how to function without anti-social behavior, without anger, hostility, immaturity, or in whichever way he previously reacted to reality. The addict must learn how to do this in a setting that to some degree is patterned after a home. It must resemble a normal situation. He must be in this environment of his own free will, and he must have the freedom to leave whenever he wants to. But he must also know there are consequences if he does choose to leave.

At Teen Challenge the addict learns behavior by: (1) the example of other Christians; (2) the teaching of Christian behavior through the Word of God; (3) direct confrontation of anti-social, unchristian behavior through rules and regulations based on Christian concepts; (4) personal prayer through which the Holy Spirit reveals what Christ-like living is.

The result is that the addict is taught how to live and act. This teaching was the missing link in the addict's treatment in jails, hospitals, or other confinement programs. In other programs he was told why he must change but not how. He was told what he was, but not what he could be. At Teen Challenge, while he is learning *how* to live, he is also learning the *why*. The why without the how is failure. The why with the how is success.

Because at Teen Challenge we have chosen an old, tested, and proven method — the Christian faith — we have found the key to successfully rehabilitating the addict.

6

GUY OR GAY?

We were walking through a certain section of New York City when a fellow minister pointed to a person in front of us and asked, "Is that a guy or a gal? It's hard to tell, you know, nowadays."

"It's neither," I replied.

"What do you mean?" he asked with a puzzled look on his face.

"That's what is called a 'gay,'" I said, further confusing him. I went on to explain the term "gay" which was not familiar to him.

"Gay" is the street terminology for a homosexual. There are various types of homosexuals, but gay is usually used to describe those who are obviously effeminate, flagrant, and who act and dress the part of the homosexual. The other kinds of homosexuals hide the identifiable characteristics usually associated with the "homos."

The gays are becoming a prominent, activist minority group in our society. They are making their presence felt around the world. They are organized and open about their demands.

In large cities a whole gay world exists. There are gay bars, clubs, restaurants, theaters, movie houses and bookstores. There are beaches, vacation resorts, bowling leagues, computer dating services, campus fraternities and health clubs catering to homosexuals. There are apartment houses for homosexuals and even gay churches.

Homosexuals are found in all walks of life. Many famous stars of stage, screen, radio and television are notoriously "queers"; so are some top sports figures. A psychiatrist revealed that one of his homosexual patients was a world champion boxer. A substantial number of outstanding writers, artists, doctors, lawyers and business executives are known to be homosexuals. There is an unofficial but very powerful homosexual union. They look out for their own. When one gets into a position in a certain business, he will hire only homosexuals. They have literally taken over in some industries.

An off-Broadway actor my mother has dealt with in our Lost Coin coffee house is an *actress* in the theater. He dresses like a female and plays woman parts on stage. He, or she, comes to the coffee house beautifully dressed as a female with blond hair and blue eyes and a very womanly shape. As a homosexual he plays the female role with male lovers.

Quite a few Hollywood homosexuals are married — purposely married — to present an image of normalcy. Most of these marriages, however, end in divorce. One famous star, a homosexual, was married for appearance sake, only to be divorced a year later. Some marry in hopes of overcoming their problem only to find out they are still attracted to males. One Hollywood wife of a male star suspected her husband was having an affair with someone else. He was — with another male star. Most of the Hollywood types of homosexuals are masculine looking, bulging with muscles. They walk, talk, and make love like a man but are males in looks only.

The problem is not confined to the stars. In Hollywood and on Broadway homosexuals are powerful as directors, composers, producers, playwrights, even backers of many productions. Since there is an unofficial homosexual union (one homosexual making a practice of hiring another homosexual) it is easy to see how many shows can have a number of homosexuals in predominance. Often those who do the casting will choose a homosexual — have an affair with him — and then fire him if the relationship does not work out.

There are a number of organizations promoting "gay power." "Civil rights" groups for homosexuals have sprung up in various forms across the country. New York and Los Angeles homosexual organizations banded together in the summer of 1970 under the banner of the "Gay Liberation Front." They staged "Gay Liberation Week" activities in those cities. Sunday, June 28, thousands of homosexual men and women marched up Sixth Avenue, New York, from Greenwich Village to Central Park, carrying banners and wearing buttons with slogans such as "Gay is Good" and "Homosexuals Are Human."

The serious thrust of such efforts is a demand that homosexuals be granted the same basic rights as their heterosexual peers to hold jobs, to wear military uniforms, to be free from harassment, and to gather publicly. Underlying this effort is the hope of homosexuals to overcome two main public attitudes toward homosexuality: (1) it is a sin, and (2) it is an aberration from the norm, a sickness that requires psychiatric treatment.

Homosexual "rights" literature says, "We will rally and petition our government. If necessary, we will bring a thousand drag queens to suburbia. We must encourage the entertainment industry to depict us as we really are. . . . Help bring about the day when we can openly love whom we choose."

The Mattachine Society, one of the oldest, best organized, and most well-known homosexual organizations, claims there are some twenty million homosexuals in America, with one million in New York City alone. These figures are, however, unrealistic. Homosexuals like to claim large numbers to promote the idea that it is normal to be a homosexual and that "everybody's doing it." The Kinsey Report states that ten percent of American men have long periods of more or less exclusive homosexuality; only four percent (two percent of the women) are exclusively homosexual all their lives. These may be inflated figures also, but most experts do agree that there are about 2,600,000 men and 1,400,000 women who are exclusively homosexual in the United States alone.

From the above figures, and from the information that

is available about the inroads homosexuals have made into business, industry, and the entertainment world, it is apparent that the Christian counselor and the church must get involved in ministering to homosexuals. Until recently even the word homosexual was taboo in Christian circles. The mere mention of the word from the pulpit made people cringe. One prominent pastor in New York City, who dared to speak out concerning homosexuals, said afterward, "A half a dozen men walked out of the service during my message on the subject."

The church must come out of the Dark Ages and recognize the existence of the problem; that many homosexuals have infiltrated the pew, the choir loft, the organ and piano bench — and even the pulpit. This is not to suggest that they must be thrown out. First, they must be counseled with and pointed to deliverance from the evil. If that approach does not succeed, then the problem must be dealt with in another manner. Such conditions in the church must be reckoned with. But the greatest challenge is outside the church. The church and the Christian worker must make it known to the homosexual that there is help available, that they will help him with his problem and show him the love and compassion of Christ.

There are cured homosexuals in the church who have been helped through their conversion to Christ. But these are not many and they often live a lonely life, battling severe temptations, suffering in silence because they feel there is no one who will accept them or understand them if they do share their problem. Counselors are needed, therefore, in the area of follow-up, witnessing and in prevention. Many young people on the verge of becoming homosexuals could be turned away from a lifetime involvement in homosexuality if a trained, alert counselor were available to speak to them.

One of the reasons it is difficult to find male counselors who are willing to work among the gay people is that homosexuality is so repulsive to the normal man. It goes against everything he feels and is as a man.

One of our workers rebelled when a Teen Challenge team was going out on the streets to distribute literature specifically to homosexuals. "Do I have to go?" he asked. When we asked him why he didn't want to go, he said, "I hate them." What he was really saying was, "I am scared of them." The homosexual whom the counselor works with — or even talks with — may reflect something the counselor sees inside himself. Perhaps he may have had some homosexual involvement in his teenage years and is afraid that it might break out again.

But most of all, there is the problem of finding the counselor who has the patience, faith and the hope that Christ can cure the homosexual. This is a ministry that subjects the worker to abuses and exposes him to people whose personalities often have been totally warped by their way of life, and who often have temptations even after they are converted to Christ. There are minimal results, compared to the results of counseling other types of people. The road to recovery is terribly long. Yet the homosexuals represent a harvest field. Christ also died for them. The call goes out, "Who will go?"

In the book, *Parents on Trial,* the author states:

> It is not necessarily true that once a youth has become a homosexual, nothing can be done about it, but it is true that the rate of cure is very low. Everyone who has tried to help homosexuals — psychiatrists, psychologists, and pastoral counselors — are in agreement that theirs is a very difficult pattern to change. But there are cases in which homosexuals have made adjustments that have enabled them to marry and have children, and, most important, abandon their homosexual ways. The chief difficulty we encounter is the large number of homosexuals who do not want to change. They like being the way they are. One cannot read their literature without becoming acutely aware that they feel theirs is a superior way of life.[1]

Those who have encountered homosexuals who want attention and not a cure find it difficult to develop a ministry and a burden for them. They tend to ignore or openly refuse to help the homos. Or they preach against the sin of homosexuality, losing sight of the person behind the sin.

We have been greatly encouraged of late with regard to the possibility of a cure for homosexuals. There was a time when we felt it was virtually impossible — or that 98 percent did not want to be cured — but we are finding more and more who do seek help and who are being

[1] David Wilkerson with Clare Cox, *Parents on Trial* (New York, Hawthorne, 1967) pp. 124, 125.

freed from the habit. Admittedly, the numbers are small, but the point is: *homosexuality can be cured.*

The church must believe and preach that there can be hope for homosexuals. As it does so, I believe more homosexuals will come forth seeking help. The reason they haven't, is because Christians have allowed the failures of the past to hold them back from proclaiming the power of Christ to cure. If only one in a millon is cured, it means one thing: a cure is possible. The odds are, of course, not that severe.

Many liberal churchmen and theologians are doing much to "help" the homosexual — they are condoning the practice. This helps those who are looking for justification and acceptance by the church and society. One clergyman said regarding two homosexual friends of his, "Both of them are very happy and very much in love. They asked me to bless their marriage, and I am going to do it" (*Time,* Oct. 31, 1969).

Homosexuals do need compassion and understanding. They need acceptance, but not the kind of acceptance that says, "You have a right to be the way you are; the church will condone your practice." The homosexual needs acceptance in terms of the counselor's willingness to help cure him. There is a place for the Christian in counseling homosexuals. The question is, will we find a place in our hearts to love the person who practices homosexuality? Until the counselor is ready and able to make this commitment, the homosexual will continue to be outside of Christ and in bondage to his vice.

The Roots of Homosexuality

Homosexuals are made not born. All males are created equal. Most experts now agree that homosexuality is *not* the result of a genetic or hormone predisposition. Male and female homosexuals do not constitute a "third sex"; biologically they are full men and women.

What are the factors that contribute to the making of the homosexual?

1. *The home.* Today the scientific consensus holds that homosexuality is largely conditioned by the environment in childhood, and most particularly by parental influence in the home. Sexual repression in the home is one of these

factors. Children who are constantly being warned about the dangers of sex activity grow up with a gray if not dirty feeling about it. Natural sexual feelings in their teens are interpreted as unnatural and inspire feelings of guilt. Children may be taught to fear members of the opposite sex. Parents who have their own hangups about sex often reflect these, consciously or unconsciously, to their children.

Parents who raise their children in a sexually healthy home need not worry about raising a homosexual child; he will most likely grow up normally. In the sexually healthy home there should be a steady flow of impressions that will enable a child to conclude gradually and naturally that the heterosexual way of life is not only normal and right for him, but also productive and fun. Sexually well-adjusted parents know quite instinctively how to encourage masculinity in boys and femininity in girls; few adults require expert advice to determine what psychiatrists call "age-appropriate" behavior in their own children.

Sex is not the only factor that contributes to homosexuality. Just as important is the ability of mother and dad to play their proper roles in the home. Studies show that homosexuals suffer from a lack of a solid identification with the parent of the same sex, and from deeply divided feelings for the parent of the opposite sex.

Mothers can contribute to homosexuality if they (1) are domineering; (2) are overly protective; (3) show preference; (4) play the son against the father; (5) have a poor sexual relationship with the husband which results in showering affection on the son; (6) are hostile; (7) reject the child; (8) have an unconscious desire to make a girl out of the boy, or vice-versa; (9) tell the child he was unwanted, or a "mistake"; (10) are puritanical; (11) demand to be made the center of their son's attention; (12) make him mother-dependent; (13) act seductively toward the child.

Fathers can contribute to the homosexuality of their child if they (1) are weak persons; (2) are detached from their sons; (3) humiliate or belittle sons; (4) are cruel in punishment; (5) prefer one son over another, perhaps the son who is more like the father, or more masculine; (6) reject their son for other males. Psychiatrists agree that they "never saw a homosexual who had a good relationship with his father."

2. *Sociological factors also contribute to the making of a homosexual.* If some of the factors above exist in a home, it does not mean that the child will automatically be a homosexual. Usually homosexuality is the result of a combination of factors in the home and in society as a whole. It can result from the home alone, but studies show that experiences outside the home and in society at large also help make the homosexual.

Social factors which lead to homosexuality include: (1) the feminization of the male, masculinization of the female; (2) the high premium of male competition, along with female competition, (also competing with the male); (3) the diminishing importance of the parental role in the home; (4) the greater insistence on sexual "performance" or Playboy exploits; (5) the permissive attitude of the entertainment industry toward homosexuality; (6) the acceptance of homosexuality in society as a whole; (7) the demoralization of marriage; (8) the portrayal of sex as a game; (9) the American ideal which seems to equate virility with physical strength and prowess, and which leaves the less physically well-built male to be looked upon as a sissy.

3. *Experiences related to childhood may contribute to homosexuality.* Experiences can often create homosexuality in childhood, or they can help to develop a pattern that results in the outbreak of the problem later in life. Some young people may participate in occasional homosexual activities in childhood, yet make a satisfactory heterosexual adjustment later in life. It is usually only the combination of a poor relationship with parents, plus a bad experience outside the home, that results in the establishment of the homosexual pattern of behavior.

Time magazine says that it is agreed by most experts that children will not become homosexuals unless they undergo many disturbing experiences during the course of several years. Also, while only one-third of the confirmed adult homos can be helped to change, larger numbers of "pre-homosexual" children can be successfully treated.

Types of Homosexuals

As with alcoholism, most homosexuality is hidden. That is, it is hidden to the average American. However, "it takes one to know one." It doesn't take long for two homosexuals to "make connection."

A favorite meeting place is the gay bar. It is fast becoming a social insitution in America. Men go there, not primarily to drink, but rather to socialize with other homosexuals. The evening usually ends in pairing off and departing to one or the other's apartment. Those who do not make connections must resort to walking the streets, going to certain gay parks, or making contact in restrooms or baths. The latter is almost as popular as the gay bar. It is sometimes referred to by the clientele as an "orgy room."

Most homosexuals go from one relationship to another. To find new partners, some homosexuals "cruise." They engage in gestures that immediately identify them to each other. Like the male girl-watchers, the male boy-watchers do most of their cruising with the eyes by making prolonged surveillance of the other man's body. It is also done by lingering in each other's presence, and over the shoulder glances. In bathrooms it may be done by a foot-tapping signal.

While taking a minister on a tour of Times Square one night, I decided to show him how such a possible contact could be made. We sat in a restaurant in the row facing the street and sidewalk. As crowds strolled by we started looking carefully at different individuals. One middle-aged man caught our eyes. He passed on, then came back and looked at us again. We returned the gaze. Then he disappeared. About three minutes later we turned and saw him taking a seat right next to us in the restaurant. We got up and walked out — and he followed. Soon, however, we lost him in the crowd. However, it was apparent he thought we were "cruising."

One client, a homosexual, came and said, "I quit my job." When asked why, he confessed that another worker on the job was giving him the eye. He confessed, "I tried to avoid him, but my old habits and homosexual gestures, I guess, are still a part of me and I think he knows I'm gay. I just had to get away from that place before I fell." Homosexuals seem to have that natural instinct for recognizing each other.

Although there are some homosexual marriages that last some time, most homosexuals go from one partner to another. Long term relationships between two males are notably few. This is one of the miseries of such a life. When the homosexual gets older, he begins to have less appeal and often he has to buy sex.

One thing is for sure regarding the life of the homosexual, it is far from gay. Most of them present a picture of an average life style of any male, but behind the scene is a life of transitory relationships, lovers' quarrels, jealousy, and romantic power struggles. There is also the fear of exposure — even blackmail — and for the more desperate there is danger of arrest, of making advances toward a non-homosexual and perhaps a resulting beating. Even those relationships in which the partners agree that they are married (it is of course not a legal marriage) rarely last more than several years. The Kinsey Report of 1948 found that "long term relationships between two males are notably few."

To help the counselor better understand the different types of homosexuals, these are their main characteristics as given in *Time:*

1. *The blatant homosexual.* These include the catty hairdresser or the lisping, limp-wristed interior decorator, the hip-swinging waiter, and so on. His lesbian counterpart is the "butch," the girl who is aggressively masculine to the point of trying to look like a man. Blatant homosexuals also include "leather boys," who advertise their sadomasochism by wearing leather jackets and chains, and certain transvestites. Blatants often draw sneers from other homosexuals; many of them are only going through a phase. Having recently "come out" — admitting their condition and joining the homosexual world — they feel insecure in their new roles and try to recreate their personalities from scratch. They try to act the way they think gay people are supposed to behave.

2. *The secret lifer.* Ninety percent of the nation's committed homosexuals are hidden from all but their friends, lovers, and occasionally, psychiatrists. They prefer subdued clothes and close-cropped hair. They may dress more conservatively than flamboyant straights. Many wear wedding rings and have wives, children and employers who never know. They range across all classes, races and occupations. To lead their double lives, these full or part-time homosexuals must pass as straight; most are extremely skilled at camouflage. They can cynically tell, or at least smile at, jokes about "queers."

3. *The desperate.* Members of this group are likely to haunt public toilets or Turkish baths. [One young man I dealt with,

who was faithfully endeavoring to live a Christian life, would suddenly become tempted while coming home from work. He would run into a subway toilet and engage in a homosexual act. It was as though an evil spirit came upon him.]

The desperate homosexual may be pathologically driven to sex, but emotionally unable to face the strains of sustaining a serious human relationship. Or, he may be a married man who hopes to conceal his need by making contact as anonymously as possible.

4. *The adjusted.* For the most part, these homosexuals live conventional lives. They have a circle of friends whom they meet at gay bars or at private parties. Often they try to settle down with one lover.

5. *The bisexual.* Many married homosexuals fake enjoyment of intercourse with their wives. Some researchers, however, have found a number of men and women who have a definite preference for their own sex, but engage in occasional activity with the opposite sex and enjoy it.

6. *The situational-experimental.* He is a man who engages in homosexual acts without any deep emotional motivation. Many drug addicts in prison will engage in homosexual activity while there, but return to normal sexual activity when on the outside. The same often happens in the armed forces.[2]

Developing a Counseling Ministry to Homosexuals

Few Christian workers are called to work exclusively with homosexuals. Several converted homosexuals work full- and part-time for Teen Challenge with homosexuals. Our workers distribute literature to homosexuals in Greenwich Village. Roger Dean, a converted homosexual, has written a tract for homosexuals, called "Gay," which we distribute.

The Mattachine Society sometimes sets up its literature table in front of our workers. When we give literature to homosexuals, some of them curse, or throw the literature in our faces; some walk on slowly after taking a tract and then tear it into little pieces. Homosexuals don't like to hear what the Bible says about their practices, nor do they want to hear that there is a cure. Admitting there is a cure means they should do something to help themselves. They would rather believe God made them the way they are, or that they have an incurable sickness, or that homosexuality is as natural as heterosexuality.

[2] *Time*, "The Homosexual: Newly Visible, Newly Understood," October 31, 1969. Reprinted by permission from *Time*, The Weekly Newsmagazine; copyright Time Inc., 1969.

Christian counselors are needed to work with homosexuals. It is true, most homosexuals need professional help, and the average counselor may not feel equipped, but he can at least present the witness of the Gospel and give hope through Christ.

Christian workers should learn as much as possible about the problem. The counselor who is alert to pick out the signs can find the hidden homosexual. Realizing that homosexuality may be hidden behind another problem can be most helpful in knowing how to proceed with certain cases. If I'm interviewing someone whom I suspect of homosexuality, I ask politely, "Have you ever been engaged in homosexuality?" If the answer is yes, I ask next: "Are you now a practicing homosexual?" Knowing the answer to this at the beginning of the counseling session saves a lot of time.

As alcoholics and others often do, homosexuals may come to the counselor with a problem that is only a smoke screen to conceal a deeper problem. Usually the problem they present is the result and manifestation of homosexuality. If the counselor does not know the primary problem, he will be trying to treat the symptoms and not the cause. It may be possible to help a homosexual without knowing he is one, but such help would be in spite of the counselor and not because of his knowhow.

How to Counsel Homosexuals

The following suggestions are for the counselor who is knowingly treating a homosexual. If the counselor suspects the person with whom he is dealing is a homosexual, he should either ask him directly or work toward the goal of uncovering the problem. Once admission of homosexuality has been made, the counselor can proceed according to the following outline.

1. *Find out if the homosexual views his activity as a problem.* There must be motivation. Why did he come to you? Does he consider his homosexuality a harmful, self-destructive habit that must be removed? Does he want to become "straight"? These questions should be first in the mind of the counselor. He should look for evidence of whether the homosexual really wants to change. The homosexual may be saying, "Make my life more comfort-

able and take away the pain, but don't change me." He may want the counselor to help him get rid of his guilt, but not his pleasure.

2. *Expect strong initial resistance.* The homosexual is a difficult patient because he is ruled by the bundle of fears that made him a homosexual in the first place. He has an unconscious fear of discovering heterosexual wishes and feelings, and an even greater fear of acting on such feelings. He is afraid of discovering the inevitable emotional bankruptcy of homosexuality. He fears his inability to shift to heterosexuality.

Added to these fears is his resistance to the message of the Gospel. Some homosexuals are deeply bitter toward God for the way they think He made them, or for allowing the conditions to exist during their childhood which set the stage for homosexuality.

If the counselor understands that resistance in the early stages of counseling is normal for this type of person, it will help him. One young man I dealt with would get angry, say abusive things, even vulgar things, but he would always come back, and each time his resistance was lower.

3. *Find out what type of homosexual he is and the extent of his involvement in homosexuality.* I have dealt with those who were more homosexual in their fantasies than in reality. Often young people are in the early stages of homosexual involvement and can be saved from it. Their fear of becoming a confirmed, life-time homosexual is usually their biggest problem. They must be shown that just because they engaged in mental homosexuality, it does not mean they are a confirmed homosexual.

A young man in his thirties came to see me and the first thing he said was, "I am a homosexual." During our first conversation he stated that he had never engaged in homosexual activity with another male, but he had dreamed about such a relationship and had lusted in his mind after other men. From childhood he had engaged in homosexual fantasies, but fortunately he had never actually practiced it. He was helped by the reassurance I gave him that he was not an overt homosexual, but rather had latent tendencies in that direction.

The counselor will meet many who have latent tendencies toward homosexuality and he should encourage them to talk about it. Pastors should encourage this by having frank discussions with young people, and by informing them about sex and sex deviations. If I were a pastor, one of the first things I would do is either conduct a sex education course myself, or bring in some person competent in the field to do it. The prevention of homosexuality is one of the most neglected areas of Christian counseling and teaching.

In short, the counselor should look for homosexuality in all of his dealings with others. He may discover either a latent or an overt problem.

4. *Beware of false confessions and contrived contrition.* One young man we dealt with at Teen Challenge wept and cried every time we talked with him. He said he was sorry. Whenever he could, he put his head on my shoulder, or on someone else's shoulder who was counseling him. He was mentally and emotionally disturbed, but he is an example of some who will come to the counselor with high-sounding confessions and emotional outbursts of sorrow. The counselor should not allow himself to become overly impressed by mere confessions or even deep contrition. Both of these are normal reactions for the homosexual during counseling. Such confessions must be weighed against further actions and steps that the homosexual takes to help himself.

Some homosexuals want relief from the guilt of their deviation; they get a certain amount of release by their outbursts of confession. Often they go through a regular cycle of confession, reversion, confession and reversion all over again. We have had to stop some homosexuals from seeing us or calling us, because we sensed they only wanted to use us to unload some guilt; they did not want to change.

There is also the religious homosexual who says, "I love God. I feel God is with me." They have convinced themselves that God accepts them the way they are and that He understands them. They have no desire to change.

5. *Teach what the Bible says about homosexuality.* The homosexual will not be cured until he looks at the underlying root of his problem. There are surface and psychological causes of homosexuality, but understanding them is not sufficient to lead to a cure.

The surface cause is that homosexuals have a fixation

for members of their own sex that prevents them from having satisfactory relations with members of the opposite sex. When we asked a homosexual why he was one, he said, "I just happen to like men. As long as I can remember, I have been attracted to other men. I can't help it — my flesh just cries out for another man's flesh."

Psychologically, homosexuality is an acquired abnormality. It can be caused by the pampering and petting of overly affectionate parents, by an unnaturally close relationship between a boy and his mother, by fear of normal sex, by childhood training that sex is dirty, sinful, vile, and by the bad example of promiscuous parents.

Homosexuals know the theories and explanations of their behavior. They seek sympathizing psychiatrists who will try to help them adjust to a hostile society, or to rationalize and justify their behavior. Psychology can blame phobias, compulsions, obsessions, fixations, parental failures and misguided childhood behavior patterns for causing homosexuality. Consequently, the homosexual can blame God, his parents, society and bad breaks for his condition, but rarely does he accept any responsibility for it himself.

This is why it is so important for the counselor to lay a biblical foundation for the root cause of homosexuality. The counselor must help the homosexual look at the basic cause, which is *creature-Creator distortion* (Rom. 1:25). We base this on a simple outline of Romans 1:18-32. The counselor should take the homosexual through this outline as he seeks to lead him to Christ. This will set the framework for a cure.

(a) Man's basic rejection of God's deity (21a, 23). Man refused to honor God and refused to give Him thanks. Instead, man humanized God.

(b) Man's rejection of God's revealed truth (19, 20, 21b, 22). What can be known about God is plain to men, that is, His eternal power and deity. But men suppressed the truth by their wickedness. As a result, man's wisdom has ended in futility and darkness. "Professing themselves to be wise, they became fools."

In the case of the homosexual, the truth of this is particularly evident. The homosexual practices his sin because he chooses and professes his own wisdom, contrary to God's. He has substituted futile thinking for truth and reality. Homosexuals generally tend to be full of answers, based on humanistic observations sprinkled with some psychology and even a little religion.

(c) Man's glorification of the creature instead of the Creator (v. 25). The Scripture attributes "dishonoring their bodies among themselves" and women's exchanging "natural relations for unnatural" and men's giving up "natural relations with women . . . committing shameless acts with men" (RSV) specifically to this glorifying of the creature. Overt homosexuality can be traced to serving the flesh, rather than God. When a person no longer honors and serves God, he is susceptible to becoming a slave of the flesh. Before one can become a life-time homosexual, he must ignore the voice of conscience, his knowledge of right and wrong, and follow a premeditated course of disobedience and stubbornness. A homosexual is a victim of a mind and imagination given over to the worship of the flesh. The homosexual feeds on filthy literature, on dirty pictures and lewd novels. His dreams, thoughts and imagination have been taken over by the demons of lust.

A converted homosexual once said, "My whole life I sought for love. I was always looking for that one special lover. I wanted to nestle into another man. I wanted to get into his personality, to take of his strength, his virility, and make it a part of myself. Then I realized this was a bizarre distortion of the love I was actually seeking in God. The love of God and the love of man are two extremes on the pendulum of love. I rejected true love and accepted the perverted kind. It was hell's parable of heaven's reality. . . . Homosexuality is the complete distortion of everything God promises.

"Only after I accepted Christ, and received the teaching of the Word, did I realize I had distorted the concept of love. I was loving the creature more than the Creator. I now worship the Creator and I have finally found the true meaning of love, and the means whereby I can ward off the lust of the flesh."

6. *Be prepared for a long counseling relationship.* Next to the mentally ill, the homosexual demands the longest period of time for healing. The fact that a homosexual will submit to lengthy counseling and therapy is in itself a great accomplishment. Only those who have found hope

in Christ will stick with treatment, especially if the counselor is trained enough to see whether actual change is taking place.

The counselor should make himself available as much as possible, both by personal visits and by telephone contact. While trying to help one young man, I told him, "Here's my phone number; when you are going through a severe temptation, call me and we'll talk and pray." One of the biggest hurdles for the homosexual is to find a relationship of warmth, trust, and confidence with another person to whom he can turn in the moment of his most urgent need. True, he must turn to God, but he also needs a human instrument to assist him in his contact with God.

The counselor must be prepared to help the converted homosexual go through his "burning out" process. Roger Dean said the first four weeks after his conversion his life was blessed and wonderful, but then he faced great temptations. "I thought Christ dismissed all my problems," he said. "He did take away the old habits, the hustling, and all the old practices, but he did not take away the temptation. I still got shook up when I saw a man walk by."

He went through what he calls the "burning out process" when Christ had to destroy him. During this time, he said he wanted sexual relations with someone, with anyone. His lust was being burned out. "I told God I'd rather die than go back," he said. Meanwhile, his Christian friends and counselors faithfully stood by him. He did not want to be alone to battle the temptations.

Perhaps Roger's motivation was rare, but it was evidence of God's power to change the homosexual totally. The counselor should always let the hooked homosexual know that others have made it and conquered the habit. Most homosexuals will ask, "Do you know one homosexual who has made it?" He should be told that many have, and that it is possible for him to receive the same cure.

There are some homosexuals who fear being cured. Homosexuality is their security. They are afraid of what would happen if they were to become normal. Their problem also gives them an excuse for other things they do, which may or may not have anything to do with homosexuality.

Some justify drinking by the fact that they are homosexuals. Another homosexual client would constantly complain that he was not being accepted by other people because he was a homosexual. However, in his case only an experienced counselor would be aware of his problem. He used this as an excuse to cop out from counseling. He said, "Since nobody else will accept me, I'll just go back to my old friends — I know they will accept me."

The counselor must do as Jesus did. He appealed to a man's desire for health, healing and wholeness. "Wilt thou be made whole?" he asked one man. The question was not, "Do you want to get rid of your sickness?" but, "Do you want health?"

7. *Learn how to handle the homosexual's periods of regression.* Most converted homosexuals do not have an easy time "burning out" their homosexual lusts and appetites. Deliverance from homosexuality is much different from deliverance from drugs or alcohol, because homosexuality is a problem connected with the sex drive. One minister who had recovered from homosexuality and had married and had children, suddenly was faced with the old temptation again after many years of freedom. Whether this had anything to do with a coldness in his spiritual life, I do not know, but his case points out the difficulty of long-term recovery.

The counselor must be understanding when regression takes place. It must not be interpreted as the counselor's fault. Angry outbursts, lectures, threats of breaking off the counseling, humiliating and belittling the client will do no good. His faith will need to be bolstered. A direct, biblical thrust needs to be made to build his hope. Then an effort can be made to see why he reverted. Christ is not only the cure for the homosexual's sin problem, He is the cure for his search problem. The homosexual has sought in a relationship with another man what can only be satisfied when he is "in Christ." One homosexual told me, "I sought for a lover. I was on a constant search for true love." This need for a vital relationship with a person is met in a saving relationship with God's Son.

Eddie sat in my office; a steady flow of tears ran down his face. "I don't want to live anymore," he said. "I can't go on like this. What's there to live for?" The slashes on his wrist confirmed that he had tried to take his life the night before.

Eddie had fallen back into his homosexual habit once again. It was a discouraging blow to him. When I asked him what had happened, he said: "I was riding home from work on the train when my eyes met this other fellow. Before I knew it, I was following him to his apartment." This had been his sixth relapse in the year since he had accepted Christ. "I tried," he said, "the Lord knows I tried. I've done everything you've told me to do."

Just how much he had tried to avoid temptation was difficult to determine. Eddie's problem was that although he wanted to be free of his habit and serve Christ, he had not yet reached the point of total despair and hate for the kind of person his homosexuality turned him into. But the more he enjoyed freedom from the habit over a long period of time, the greater effect each new fall had upon him. Finally, after yielding to this last temptation, he was ready for the first time to give up completely his own ability to stay clean and yield totally to God for strength.

What should a counselor do in such a situation? I wondered if I should condemn him or comfort him. I first thought of condemning him. Three or four times Eddie said, "I'll leave if you want me to." Then I said, "Eddie, if you had really wanted to end your life, I'm quite sure you would have done it. I don't think you have given up hope. I think you slashed your wrist because you felt you needed to suffer for what you did."

In spite of Eddie's seeming hopelessness, I was quite sure because he had come to see me that he had not given up hope. Once I was convinced of this, I began to try to feed his faith. Through prayer and the assurance to him of God's forgiveness, his sobbing turned to tears of comfort and assurance that the Lord had forgiven him.

This case shows what a counselor may have to go through in dealing with a homosexual. The temptation will be to give up or to threaten him. This should be avoided until it appears that the last thread of his desire is gone.

7

SOBER OR FREE?

One of the things I fear, is that in the midst of the attention drug addiction is receiving, we are losing sight of the terrible plight of the alcoholic. Is society hiding its booze addiction behind the youth drug problem? Is our concern for the dope addict a genuine concern, or is it an evasion of the alcohol problem? For many, it is an evasion. No parent can honestly lecture his child about the dangers of drugs while holding a whiskey glass in his hand.

One of the arguments I find it difficult to contend with when I'm talking to young people about the dangers of drugs is: "If our parents drink, why can't we smoke pot? It's no worse, and even less harmful." Whether marijuana is less harmful than alcohol has never been proved, but the young people do have a point when they say, "You have your thing; why can't we have ours?" Of course, two wrongs don't make a right. The use of one poison does not justify the use of another. However, if marijuana is wrong, then so is alcohol.

Perhaps society's concern for drug addiction results from the number of teenagers involved; the cost of supporting the habit; the quick physical tolerance the body builds up toward it; and the ever-present danger of an overdose.

Alcohol, on the other hand, is socially acceptable; part of the American way of life; taken in moderation by millions of people. Alcohol deteriorates the body and mind more slowly than hard narcotics do. Alcohol addiction simply does not stir the same emotions drug addiction does.

From our experience in dealing with both types of addicts and addictions, we believe there is a greater potential for success with the hard-core drug addict than with the hard-core alcoholic. Both in terms of rehabilitation and in terms of recovery, the drug addict seems to fare better. Emotional conflicts within the two often are the same, but the physical and psychological craving for alcohol is more difficult to overcome in the long run.

Therefore, there is a great challenge for the church and the Christian counselor to reach the alcoholic. Counselors will come in contact with more alcoholics than drug users. Statistics bear this out. For every one hundred adults in the United States, 4.2 are alcoholics. In Nevada, 6.6 out of every hundred are hooked, in California, 6.4. The number of alcoholics doubled between 1940 and 1966, from 2,600,-000 to 5,000,000. Alcoholism is five times more prevalent than cancer. Every year in the United States 250,000 people become alcoholics, or 1,200 a day. The national family relief cost of alcoholism is $2,600,000. Alcoholism takes approximately 12 years off the alcoholic's life.

Alcoholics — Who Are They?

For many, the typical alcoholic is a skid-row bum. Often, this is the type pastors and Christian workers are most in touch with. This is the kind we have dealt with most often in our Teen Challenge program. Many of them have become hardened to the gospel. They think of the church only in terms of soup and sandwiches. The gospel service is the penalty they feel they must pay for their meal. If they had money for food, they would rather pay for it than go through the gospel service. They also learn the language of Christians; they learn what to say to "con" well-meaning Christian workers and to panhandle from them.

We have had little success with the rescue mission conditioned alcoholic. Perhaps this is partly because the kind of alcoholic who ends up on skid row is in the worst condition and thus frequents mission halls out of desperation.

Some of these alcoholics have been helped. We have seen some marvelous transformations at Teen Challenge. But I wonder if in one way the rescue missions have· not helped to perpetuate the problem. Have the gospel missions inadvertently helped to keep the alcoholic in alcoholism? Have we — I include Teen Challenge in this, for in a sense we too are a mission — unknowingly allowed the mission to be used as a flophouse? Have we let it be used as a place for young preachers, or would-be preachers to practice or to satisfy their preachers' itch? Have we used the skid row alcoholic as a "gospel guinea pig"? These are serious, probing questions. They have to be raised and answered. Those of us who work with alcoholics must especially answer them, as we try to develop effective programs to help and cure alcoholics.

But the skid row alcoholic is not the typical alcoholic. We must turn our attention to the "hidden" alcoholics. Outwardly, they seem to function normally in society. A survey in one city, taken by an organization which treats alcoholics, found that among 30,000 who applied for a "cure," there were 600 medical doctors, 300 priests and clergymen, 170 dentists, 650 lawyers, 18 judges, and more than 1,000 tradesmen and heads of industries.

Following is my own analysis, including the research of others, of the different types of hidden or unnoticed alcoholics. Most of them do not see themselves as needing help. Later, I will discuss the question of how to help the drinking person see that he does have a problem.

Types of Alcoholics

1. *The working or social alcoholic.* The largest number of alcoholics are in this category. Such an individual works, does his best to provide for his family, and to some degree carries on the functions of father and husband. He may lose time off from work, but he manages to hang on to his job. Others at work may be aware of his drinking problem and protect him from losing his job. In so doing, they may also unknowingly be keeping him from seeking help, because of the sense of security his job gives him.

His wife may also sympathize with his drinking and protect him from the children, other relatives, and friends. She may enjoy mothering him or caring for him as a patient. I have seen cases, both with addicts and alcoholics, in which after the husband was rehabilitated, his wife no longer showed an interest in him because she no longer had a sick patient to care for. The fact that there was now a man in the house who could look after himself and the rest of the family meant that she had to step down from the throne, so to speak.

2. *The hooked alcoholic.* This is the alcoholic who is psychologically and physically addicted. "It is possible that some irreversible change in biochemistry gives the alcoholic a sensitivity or 'allergy' to alcohol, so that one drink sets off a chain reaction leading inevitably to a drunk. . . . The phenomenon of craving which helps perpetuate a binge may be caused by one or more of several x factors of a physiological nature — depletion of chlorides in the blood, faulty elimination of certain waste products produced in the metabolism of alcohol, lack of vitamins in the brain, or some upsetting of the enzyme balance."[1]

The hooked alcoholic is the one who suffers withdrawal pains when he tries to stop drinking. He may be working; he may be the social alcoholic; he may be the skid row alcoholic. When and at what point someone turns into a hooked alcoholic, no one knows. There just seems to be a point at which those who drink steadily find themselves physically and psychologically hooked.

The hooked alcoholic reaches this condition by several progressive stages:

(a) *Social drinking.* Probably 98 percent of all alcoholics start on the road to their addiction by social drinking. The social drinker may be compared with the drug user. Social drinking is the first link in the chain of alcoholism, but just as all drug users do not become drug addicts, so all social drinkers do not become alcoholics. But as with drug use, no social drinker is immune to becoming an alcoholic. Every social drinker is a potential alcoholic.

(b) *Steady drinking.* Social drinking leads to more social drinking, and the next step is steady drinking. The drinking may be alone or with others.

(c) *Problem drinking.* The problem drinker is the steady drinker who finds that he now has a physical crav-

[1] Howard Clinebell, Jr., *Understanding and Counseling the Alcoholic* (Nashville, Abingdon, 1968) pp. 68, 69.

ing. He may drink out of habit, or he may drink more when pressures and problems pile up on him. His drinking has become a problem either because he has started to use alcohol steadily, or because he finds it has become the answer to other problems. Or it could be a combination of both reasons.

(d) *Addiction*. The problem drinker is now hooked or addicted. The flame has gone out of control. He has a physical craving that can only be quenched by alcohol. The question from this point on is how he can control or manage his addiction. Can he work and wait until the weekend? Can he get through the day? He may become a nipper or a binger. One out of ten or fifteen end up on skid row.

3. *The nipper.* The hooked drinker may develop the habit of sneaking off regularly to take a nip: a nip in the morning, a nip at noon, a nip at night, and maybe a few nips in between. He usually is never drunk; he is the most hidden of the hidden alcoholics. Many housewives and businessmen are in this group. The housewife can easily nip during the day at home, and the businessman or office worker can pull a bottle out of the drawer and sneak a quick one.

The nipper likes to maintain a certain level of inebria all day, rather than drink heavily at one time. This is the reason the nipper usually is never drunk, or doesn't have the appearance of being drunk. Only someone who knows this person well can detect the mild drunkenness or inebria.

The nipper is the most difficult to reach because of the hidden factor, and because he is able to maintain normality. The working or social nipper goes to great lengths to get his nip and to hide the fact. He must lie, deceive, and cover up. No matter who he is, and how honest he may be in certain affairs of his life, when it comes to satisfying his craving for alcohol, he will go to any extreme to have that one swig.

4. *The binger.* Some alcoholics drink heavily at times, then level off, or they use none at all for several days. There are men who disappear for three or four days — out on a drinking binge — then return home and stay off the bottle for weeks or months. Why they go on the binge and how they are able to stay clean for such periods of time is not

known. Often the binger suffers from deep-rooted guilt feelings that rise up periodically and thus trigger the drinking. Or, he may be a person subject to severe depression and moods, which also serve as a trigger.

5. *The skid row alcoholic.* It is estimated that only about ten percent, at the most, of the alcoholics end up on skid row. Some working alcoholics, nippers and bingers may spend short periods on some skid row, but those who end up there permanently, fortunately represent only a small number of the total alcoholic population. Those who do become a part of the row do so not because they want to be with other alcoholics, or because it is a good place to go to drink; they go there out of necessity. They are homeless and jobless. The flophouses become home. Some drift into skid row, not because of alcohol, but to find a cheap place to live. But after being exposed to conditions in skid row, they develop a drinking problem.

Skid row alcoholics not only have an addiction to alcohol, but to the atmosphere found on skid row. In skid row the alcoholic finds friends and fellowship, held together only by alcohol. Some of them find it difficult to leave the friends and fellowship behind. Conditions on skid row, of course, are deplorable. Most skid row alcoholics who come into our Teen Challenge Center suffer from some physical infirmity: malnutrition, liver infection, nervous and gastric disorders, stomach ulcers, and skin infections known as wine sores.

The Roots of Alcoholism

Where does alcoholism begin? Does it start in the person or in the bottle? Is the alcoholic sick because he drinks, or does he drink because he is sick? Is the problem physical, psychological, emotional, or spiritual?

There are those who teach and believe that it is the alcohol which causes alcoholism. Others believe it is caused by the alcohol along with inner conflicts that have nothing to do with the physical or chemical properties of alcohol. My own beliefs lie somewhere between these two opinions. Some people seem to get hooked just because they drink too much. Their bodies build up a physical craving, then a tolerance, and thus the craving for more and more alcohol. But what about those who drink and never become alcoholics? And what about those who take one drink and are hooked immediately? Does a lifetime of drinking in moderation prevent physical craving? Does a personality disorder or emotional conflict make a person ripe for addiction?

The cause of alcoholism seems to be both in the person and in the alcohol. There is no doubt that some people are addiction-prone. It is also a fact that alcohol itself creates additional psychological and spiritual problems that perpetuate its use. The problem for some is first in themselves; later, in the bottle; and later still, in the bottle and the person. With others, it may work the opposite way. There may be nothing wrong with the person. It is the bottle. They like to drink. The body builds up a craving. As a result of turning to the bottle, something goes wrong inside the person.

I think it is an oversimplification, however, to lay the blame on the alcohol alone. If this were so, then the solution would be to isolate the alcoholic for a period from all use of alcohol. Get the alcohol out of his veins. But the psychological craving would still be there. And the emotional disorder that either preceded or resulted from alcoholism would still be there.

"Repetition alone won't produce addiction. It only comes when there is a motive for repeating. Alcohol is not habit-forming in the sense that a drug like morphine is. Rather than calling alcohol habit-forming, it is more accurate to say that it is a substance that lends itself to those who form compulsive habits easily."[2]

It is a fact, however, that alcohol is addictive. It is a poisonous substance that can and does create habituation, craving, and addiction. The question then is simply this: Does the poison alone do this, or are there other factors that have nothing to do with the alcohol which either produce or add to the addiction? Probably, it works both ways.

What are some of the factors that can cause alcoholism, or cause social drinkers to become alcoholics? Persons who have inward disorders or conflicts do not turn to alcohol necessarily because of those conflicts. They first drink so-

[2] Howard Clinebell, *Ibid.*, p. 44 .

cially; then, because of the inner conflicts, they are triggered into alcoholism. Two people may have the same type of personality disorder and the one is an alcoholic and the other is not. Just because a person suffers from some emotional weakness does not mean he or she is going to become an alcoholic. It is true, however, that persons with distress, anxiety, guilt complexes, and so on, are more likely to become alcoholics than others are.

In examining the roots of alcoholism, or the roots of emotional distress that can make a person susceptible to alcoholism, one must first look into the family background and the home. What kind of parents sow the seeds of alcoholism in their children?

1. *The "iron fist" parent.* This is the parent who rules the home like a dictator. Father is the man with the iron fist. He is to be obeyed rather than loved. He is the first and final authority. Children of the iron-fisted father grow up hating him. They live in fear and react to discipline out of fear. The children can never identify with their father. They look for the day when they can leave home and be free. The child of the iron-fisted parent is a puppet. He learns that to be loved, he must obey. He has to learn love through obedience. He is not loved because he is the child; he is only loved if he is the good and obedient child.

The result is that the child feels emotionally rejected and has great feelings of inferiority. Such instability can make it impossible for this child in later life to function as a man, a husband, or a father. One client told me, "I hated my father with a passion. I couldn't wait 'till he was dead. One day somebody walked up to me on the street and told me that my father had died. I remember being so happy and laughing. But then I began to feel so guilty for hating my father. First I drank because I hated him. And after he died I drank because of the guilt over hating him."

2. *The "success ladder" parent.* One father said, "I'm going to make sure my children have all the things in life I was deprived of." For this father, the child became the reflection of his own ego. The goals this father could not achieve he wanted fulfilled in his child. The hippie generation is the product of the success ladder parent. The child grows up hearing over and over again, "Get the right job, go to the right school, get the right position,"

and so on. Why? Because it makes mom and dad look good.

The "got-to-succeed" child is smothered by those parental ambitions. He cannot find himself, or choose his own goals. He is a creature of parental ambition. He also learns that love has a price: success. The more he succeeds, the more he is loved. The less he succeeds, the less he is loved, and the less he gets in the way of material pay-off. When the child cannot climb the success ladder, when he cannot live up to the lofty goals mom and dad have set for him, he either rebels or withdraws into guilt feelings. Several alcoholic clients in our dealings have been only children. In such cases they seem to have had intense pressures put upon them to excel according to a mother's or father's desire. In one case when the client could not and did not wish to fulfill his parents' ambitions, he rebelled by finding acceptance among a peer group in which the popular thing to do was to get drunk. At home he could not be a success, but among his friends he was.

3. *The legalistic parent.* These are the strict disciplinarians; they take a legalistic approach to life. If son or daughter lives according to all the rules, they are termed good and they are loved. The parents are usually religious, or have come from a moralistic background. Children of such strict parents can't live up to the rules and thus feel insecure. They either give up or become obsessed with the desire to be perfectionists.

The above outline does not mean that all alcoholics are the result of their parents' mistakes. Surveys show that some alcoholics had a poor relationship with their parents, but one must not assume that because a man becomes an alcoholic, his parents are to blame. Often there are purely sociological reasons for the use of alcohol. The availability of it, one's circle of friends, social activities, and other factors can enter into the use of alcohol in the first place. Also, stresses often develop later in life and create inner conflicts that can make a person prone to alcoholism.

Further proof that sociological factors can cause a person to become an alcoholic is found in the fact that the same personality traits and conflicts which show up in alcoholics also appear among non-alcoholics. Why didn't the latter become alcoholics? Perhaps because of their religious or cultural upbringing. Sociological factors prevented the outbreak of alcoholism. Social conditions can cause its outbreak, whether the symptoms that sometimes cause it are present or not.

I have often said to parents and church people in rural communities, "Given another set of circumstances, if your children were raised in an urban environment, or in a situation where drugs or alcohol were more prevalent and available, they too might have become addicts." Some young people find themselves working and living in social and cultural circumstances where there is much drinking, and their chances of addiction are, of course, much higher than if they had not been exposed to such pressures. During the years of prohibition, the *per capita* rate of alcohol consumption dropped by 25 percent compared to previous years. The result was that many alcoholics were checked during that period. However, the present rate of increase in alcoholism seems to coincide with the increased consumption of alcohol. Is there more alcoholism now because people are getting worse, or are people getting worse because the use of alcohol is growing? Regardless, one fact stands out: we have become an alcohol consuming society, and we are paying for it in the ruin of lives.

How to Counsel the Alcoholic

1. *Understand the difference between alcohol and the alcoholic.* In other words, separate the sin from the sinner. We must condemn the use of alcohol and detest what it does to the individual, but love the person who is an alcoholic.

The alcoholic will not come to the counselor who cannot see the difference between the evil of alcohol and the person who is the victim of its use. Many evangelists and pastors are so obsessed with removing alcohol and other evils in society that they never have time to help those who are the *products* of the social evils. When they work or counsel with alcoholics, they are more concerned with preaching, lecturing and moralizing on the dangers of alcohol than they are in getting through to the person with the problem. Such Christian workers get a reputation for being crusaders rather than helpers; the alcoholic will not come to them or respond to them.

2. *Uncover the problem.* Most alcoholics belong to the "hidden" category. They are not easy to uncover. One has to become a detective. The counselor must try to remove the barriers that prevent the alcoholic from coming forth. This can be done by building up a relationship of trust. The counselor's trust relationship will knock down the barriers and bring out the knowledge of the addiction. When the counselor suspects alcoholism might be behind a certain problem, the revelation of it, or the mention of it, to the person being counseled can create a strain, even a disruption of the counseling process. Only if the person trusts the counselor will he open up and face his alcohol problem.

How can the hidden alcoholic be uncovered?

(a) *Advertise.* Advertise your concern, compassion and willingness to help by pulpit sermons, by Christian witness, and by normal everyday conversation. Build up a reputation for helping people in general. Pastors can further show their interest by promoting seminars, educational programs and rallies on the prevention and cure of alcoholism. All of these activities let the hidden alcoholic know that you are interested and want to help. He can come out of hiding.

(b) *Recognize the prevailing symptoms surrounding alcoholism.* By knowing some of these signs the counselor in the normal course of church visitation, or on business activities might be able to uncover alcoholism. Often behind marital problems, financial or job problems there may also be an alcohol problem. By watching for some of the prevailing signs that precede alcoholism, the counselor can help the person while his drinking is in the early stages.

(c) *Watch for alcoholism hidden behind other problems that a client or contact may bring to a counselor's attention.* Part of the alcoholic's dilemma is to recognize and admit that alcohol is his real problem. The problem drinker will hold out as long as possible before making this admission. He may not see that his drinking has anything to do with his problem. Therefore, he will not mention it because he does not think it is relevant to his problem. However, the problem he wants help with may be the cause of the alcoholism, and it may be making it a more serious problem.

3. *Make yourself accessible to people in general.* Coun-

seling alcoholics is like counseling anyone else. Some of the same general principles outlined in previous chapters must be used with alcoholics. The counselor must bridge the problem gap. This can only be done if he attracts people to himself. People must feel he is approachable, accessible, thoroughly sincere, and sense that he really cares about them. Some ministers and Christian workers get the reputation of being professional and aloof. "He's just not the kind of pastor you feel comfortable about telling your problems to. He just doesn't seem to understand," a person told me when I advised him to see his minister.

The Christian counselor who seeks to help the alcoholic must develop rapport with people, have a pleasing personality, allow other people to be themselves, and not be preachy and authoritarian in his manner.

There are many simple things the counselor can do to become an accessible person. You have to let your concern be known. Take time for brief conversations with families in church. Ask short questions that do not make you appear to be nosy but show that you are interested. When you get a report about someone's difficulty with a certain situation, make a brief inquiry about it so that the door will be open for you to minister in that situation. Ministers, church workers and counselors should never assume that people will know they are available to help; their availability must be advertised. People who desperately need help often cannot break the barrier to ask for help or to unburden themselves to others. Pastors must constantly make it clear that counseling is a part of their ministry — not a burden but a desirable part of the Lord's work. Some people assume a pastor is too busy, or that their problem is insignificant, or that the minister is not interested or doesn't understand.

A young woman stopped me one day in the hall of Teen Challenge Center and asked if she could speak to me. "I'm quite busy right now; I'll have to see you later," I said. But later it occurred to me that she was my business. I had at the time been doing some paper work. I realized that I had been called to work with people, not paper.

4. *Be alert and sensitive when dealing with the alcoholic.* The counselor must have eyes and ears alert to hear what

the alcoholic is saying. Listening, more than talking, helps to build rapport and to bridge the problem gap.

Mannerisms also are important. It is easy for a counselor to mumble, "Yes, I see," and yet have his mind on something else, so that his client knows he is not really listening. I have the habit of sometimes scribbling letters, or leafing through papers when someone is explaining a problem to me. It's a nervous habit. It distracts the other person. He needs the counselor's undivided attention.

The counselor should also look the other person in the eye. Most people, however, will find it difficult to look the counselor back in the eye. However, by doing this the counselor can get the other person's attention and show him that he is listening. The counselor's mood, position and facial expression all have something to do with showing he is listening and being alert and sensitive.

Listening helps the counselor to get into the alcoholic's mind and into his world. It helps him sense his feelings and conflicts. The only way the counselor can get the picture is by the words that come from the alcoholic's lips. They are all the counselor may have to go on, if he does not know the individual personally.

From the counselor's alertness and sensitivity the alcoholic will feel his empathy. The process of building up a relationship of confidence and trust is essential as the counseling process goes on and reaches the stage when the counselor gives instruction and guidance in recovery and rehabilitation.

5. *Let the alcoholic unburden himself.* The alcoholic may only want sympathy or someone's shoulder to cry on. However, the start of all rehabilitation begins with the release of pent-up feelings, inner tensions, and the talking out of personal problems. This spilling out of sour feelings is in itself therapeutic. Some of these feelings are buried deep within the alcoholic. It may take time for them to come out. With every drink, these feelings have gone deeper and deeper into the caverns of his mind. They cannot come out easily. They must come out and the counselor must not only be a good listener, but also skilled in drawing out these feelings.

The unburdening process is essential for recovery, but it is like breaking open a boil on the neck. At first the poison is slow in coming, then it may flow profusely. When this happens, the counselor should not be shocked, disturbed, or uncomfortable; rather, he should be encouraged by this sign of progress. He should use brief questions and comments to keep the unburdening process going until he is sure the alcoholic has been emotionally cleaned out.

Beware of drawing quick verbal conclusions from these poured-out feelings. That can stop the flow of words. Be careful not to apply a bandage too soon. The client must let all the infection out before you can apply healing counsel. Much of the information the counselor needs to understand the alcoholic and to formulate instruction comes from this unburdening process. The alcoholic must feel free to express his feelings of anger, hostility and hate. That is one reason the alcoholic has been drinking, to suppress his feelings. To tell him that his feelings are wrong will not do him any good either. He must get those feelings out in the open so that together with his counselor he can explain the reasons for them.

6. *Find out the degree of motivation.* As with the drug addict, the first step in counseling the alcoholic is to determine if he wants help and if so, how serious he is about getting it. The counselor may be ready but not the alcoholic.

It is good to evaluate what is behind his desire to be helped. How much pressure are his wife, parents, or others putting on him? Is he just in the mood for love or attention? Does he just want to be consoled? Is he looking for sympathy? Has someone or some circumstances forced him to seek help?

One of the city sanitation workers who picked up garbage at Teen Challenge was brought to us one day by his fellow workers. They asked us if we could help him. He said he wanted help. He checked into our program, but soon left. We found out later that his job was in jeopardy and he was pressured into seeking help. He was not sufficiently motivated for us to do anything for him.

Sometimes external factors can motivate someone to seek help, but only if there is first a desire on the alcoholic's part. The first and most important motivation must be internal; other external forces can reinforce and support his motivation.

The counselor must also find out what kind of help the alcoholic wants and how much. Is he looking for temporary relief, or a total cure? Does he believe he can be helped? He may have doubts about his ability to be cured, but does he have a degree of motivation — at least to start? Does he believe you are the right person to help him? Why did he come to you?

When interviewing prospects for Teen Challenge Center, we ask who referred them to us and why they came. We want to find out how much confidence, if any, they have in us and in the type of cure we offer.

I find alcoholics are never ready, or motivated, as they should be. If the alcoholic is motivated enough to start the motivation can be increased later through a conversion to Christ. The question is, is his desire to stop drinking stronger than his urge to continue drinking?

During the counseling process the alcoholic's motivation runs in streaks. One day he may be highly motivated, the next day he may have no motivation. He is pulled by opposing forces. The desire to quit and the urge to drink are two forces which both run through his mind.

He may want to stop because of the consequences of his alcoholism, but he may want to continue because alcohol has become the solution to pain and distress. Even after quitting for awhile, he may forget the miseries of drinking when the temptation to drink becomes strong again.

In the twelve steps to recovery of Alcoholics Anonymous, motivation is essential to starting on the route to recovery. Step one is: "We admitted we were powerless over alcohol, that our lives had become unmanageable." The Christian counselor must determine whether the alcoholic he is dealing with has admitted this.

7. *Through prayer, lead the alcoholic to the "new creature" experience of the Gospel.* The counselor must believe that if "any man (alcoholic) be in Christ, he is a new creature: old things (drinking, personal problems) are passed away; behold, all things are become new" (II Cor. 5:17). The right moment must be found to present this message and to introduce the alcoholic to this experience. It must not come too soon or too late. Is it ever too soon to attempt to lead a person to Christ? In the case of alcoholics,

yes. He must be ready for you, the counselor; he must also be ready to give himself to Christ. You must first lay a scriptural foundation. You must discern his spiritual understanding and hunger. If he wants help, does he want Christ's help?

He may have a gospel hangup or he may be hardened to the Gospel. If he is a mission drop-out, he may have become calloused to the Word of God. He may still be bitter about having had to swallow the bait (gospel services) that many missions offer before they will admit the alcoholic for meals and a bed. He may have had a previous emotional religious experience, but either had no desire to follow through, or he was never taught how to follow through. Thus he has lost confidence in religion or conversion. He may have a negative outlook on the Gospel — a set of do's and don'ts. He may never have realized that a person can "taste and see that the Lord is good." Find out what is behind his resistance to the Gospel. Is it based on past experience, misunderstanding, or rebellion against God?

Regardless of his past knowledge of the Gospel, the alcoholic must be presented the truth that can set him free. I like the way a group called Alcoholics Victorious approaches conversion. In its creed, step number one is: "I realize that I cannot overcome the drink habit myself. I believe the power of Jesus Christ is available to help me. I believe that through my acceptance of him as my personal Savior I am a new man." Step four is: "I can be victorious because I know that God's strength is sufficient to supply all my needs."

The counselor who takes this strong evangelistic approach has the greatest potential for a cure and the most comprehensive type of solution to present to the alcoholic. Christ can change the alcoholic. He can be made into a completely new person. Such a transformation gets to the root of all of the alcoholic's outward problems — his alienation from God — as well as the manifestation of that alienation, his emotional and mental conflicts. Christ removes the need for the bottle by changing the person.

Howard was thirty-six when we first met. He had been a chronic alcoholic for eighteen years. "I had made up my mind even before I was an alcoholic that I was going to be one. I used to dream about it. I'd see pictures advertising whiskey or beer, and would get a thrill out of it," he told me. His mother and father separated, and when she died he was left with an inheritance. At the age of fourteen he began drinking and by eighteen he was hooked. Within three years he had swallowed up his entire inheritance. "I've been in at least twelve different state hospitals in twelve different states. I'd stay for a few months to get dried out so I could go out and enjoy drinking better." He said he had too much pride to go to missions so he had little contact with the Gospel. However, he wandered into a storefront church one night in Brooklyn where some Christian people presented him with the message of salvation, and then took him to Teen Challenge. He went through his withdrawal, worked hard as a resident of the program, and openly and outwardly responded to spiritual things, but he said, "I only read my Bible and got on my knees and went to church because I was told I should. I learned to respect the people who were trying to help me." But there was never complete surrender to Christ. He began to question and analyze the Gospel. As many times as he was counseled, he refused to yield his life to Christ. As a result he was back on the streets and back on the bottle. And now he had found a new scapegoat to blame for his addiction — the Christian. He projected his failure onto those who had counseled him. When he was drunk he would stand outside Teen Challenge and vent his anger. Through later contact and later counseling, when sober, he displayed the attitude that the Christian owed a debt to him. He sought material assistance and wanted his Christian counselors to be his errand boy to help him every time his drinking got the best of him.

Contact with him was lost for a period of time. Then one night in a hospital a staff worker met him. He was in severe withdrawal pains. "What are you doing, Howard?" the staff worker asked.

"Getting some formaldehyde. I am very, very sick," he replied.

"Why don't you come back to Teen Challenge?" the counselor asked.

"They won't have me," Howard stated.

"But Jesus wants to heal you. Come on, we are going

back to the Center. That's where the Lord wants you," the worker insisted. In spite of the fact that there was no room for him and of our reservations about his sincerity, he was permitted entrance.

"I was so sick when I came into the Center that time that I was drinking Vitalis. Besides that, I had a hole in the back of my head — don't know where I got it — somebody must have hit me with a bottle. When I was withdrawing I kept seeing color television. The programs were all hallucinations. A horse leaped out of the TV and started talking to me. I was so sick. I couldn't take the pain anymore so I tried to walk out the door. But my hands were shaking so much from the DT's (delirium tremens) that I couldn't grab the door handle. Then I fell down on the floor in front of the door. A brother came over and started praying. I told him I was going to die. Then they took me to my bed. I was so sick I couldn't move. I remember it was December 27th and something told me, 'Howard, if you make it through this year, you'll make it all the way.' Thank God, I did make it through the next few days and the new year came. But still I was not converted. It wasn't until a few weeks later when I was filled with the Holy Spirit that I finally believed I was really cured and that Christ had totally delivered me. Before the night when the power of God came upon me, I still didn't enjoy reading the Bible or praying or even going to Church. It was a chore to me. But after that experience with Christ — and that in-filling of the Holy Spirit, it was like eating steak. I wanted to eat and eat and eat." Happily he is still eating spiritual food.

After the "new creature" experience takes place, is the former alcoholic *sober* or *free?* Is he a sober alcoholic, or is he a free and whole person? It disturbs me that some sober alcoholics have this philosophy: "I am an alcoholic. I shall always be an alcoholic. I live one day at a time and promise myself only to stay sober for one more day. Tomorrow I may go on the worst binge I have ever had." Such a philosophy certainly falls short of the cure Christ offers. It is faith in oneself to get through a day, rather than the faith in Christ which can cause the alcoholic to say, "I can do all things through Christ who strengthens me."

In almost every church where I go to speak, a former alcoholic will come up to me and give his testimony of freedom from drinking. Each one, through a dramatic conversion to Christ (most often as a result of one visit to church and the altar), has found a complete deliverance from alcohol. When they get up in the morning, they do not fear that perhaps this will be the day when they will go on a binge. They wake up with Christ on their mind, not the bottle. This does not mean they never have temptations. They do. But when temptation comes, they can look to Christ to deliver from the temptation.

Most of these men also testify to the fact that the craving for alcohol is gone. They may have temptations, but not because of a craving that has never left them. The devil comes back to examine "the house" to see if Christ is still the occupant. Christ came in and transplanted the old heart, with its craving for drink, and put in a new one with its craving for God.

The "new creature" alcoholic emphasizes the cure, not the problem. A sober alcoholic considers himself still to be an alcoholic. The only difference between him and other alcoholics is that he is not drinking. The only thing between the sober alcoholic and alcoholism is a bottle of alcohol. Between the free alcoholic and alcoholism, however, is Christ. The one seeks to stay away from the bottle, the other seeks to stay with and in Christ. It is much easier to "walk in the Spirit" and not fulfill the desires of the flesh (alcoholism). The sober alcoholic says, "Once an alcoholic, always an alcoholic." The free alcoholic says, "If any man be in Christ, he is a new creation."

Does this mean the free alcoholic can drink again? Of course not. To touch a drop would trigger his alcoholism This is not because his alcoholism was always there and not manifested. Instead, it is because the devil would bring back seven evil spirits worse than before. For one who has experienced the new birth to return to alcohol means that the old symptoms that brought on alcoholism in the first place had returned. The craving for alcohol would be the result of his having failed to pray, to have fellowship with Christ and Christians, to read the Bible and perform other Christian duties. The relapse would not be because of the power of alcohol, but because of his loss of

Christ's power. No freed alcoholic who has walked in the Spirit and continued in the faith has ever suddenly reverted to the use of alcohol. The problem is not with the alcohol, but with the person who fails to keep the faith.

8. *Help the freed alcoholic to bridge the family gap.* The tragedy of alcoholism is that for every alcoholic there are an average of three to five others who suffer because of it. The alcoholic's family must be involved in his recovery. This is not always easy. The damage and division brought on by the past years of drinking do not heal easily. The new convert may expect too much from his wife, parents, or children, too soon. He will want them to accept him with open arms. The wife may want to, but she may be afraid to believe in him. Usually, the family will want to "wait and see." The counselor should advise the converted alcoholic to prove himself and give his loved ones time to accept him. Once they are convinced of his sincerity and his deliverance from the habit, they can begin to bridge the gap. Both the convert and his family must forgive past sins. Old wounds and tensions should not be reopened.

If the wife or family will not accept the converted alcoholic, the counselor should invite them in for private counseling and, if they are willing, talk about their feelings and problems. When the counselor feels the time is right, he should bring the parties together to discuss their differences. Both sides must give and take. The converted alcoholic's family should not be brought into the counseling process too soon. By having a private session with the family first, the counselor can better decide the best time to have a joint session with the new convert.

Pressure is often put on the converted alcoholic to return home and take care of his wife and children. In most cases, he can do this, but the wife should be instructed to give her husband as much time as possible — if he is in a treatment program — before asking him to come home. Sometimes the wife may want her husband back purely for financial reasons. Usually, the wife of an alcoholic is being supported from other sources. The counselor should encourage her to continue receiving such aid until her husband is strong enough to return and assume all responsibilities of support.

Another problem the new convert may face on his return home is opposition to his conversion. The wife of one of our converts told him, "I'll accept you as an addict, but not as a Christian." Often a converted alcoholic will get the same reaction when he returns home to live with his wife, children, parents, or brothers and sisters. They will say, "That was all right for you; you really needed the help. We don't have your problem, so we don't need that religious stuff." This can be discouraging, even shattering, to a new convert who is proud of his new life and wants to give Christ the glory. The convert will need counsel about his attitude toward this reaction from his family. He must understand that they may accept him, but be reluctant to accept his Savior. He should be encouraged to live his testimony, carefully sow the seed of the Word, and pray about the matter. In time he may see some marvelous conversions take place in his home. We have seen whole families converted. The counselor should inform the family that the only adequate way they can help the converted alcoholic's rehabilitation is to share his spiritual experience. The same Christ who made the alcoholic a new creature can make his family new also.

The counselor should recommend the following steps for a family seeking to help an alcoholic loved one respond to treatment: (a) don't force or threaten him to seek help; (b) make suggestions that he seek help; be firm but not pushy; (c) don't baby him; (d) if he is living away from home, keep in touch with him; (e) don't support his habit; (f) keep from getting bitter or hateful toward him; (g) ask others who are knowledgeable to speak to him; (h) through faith and prayer, never give up; (i) don't blame yourself.

Even if a converted alcoholic should revert to alcohol, quit the counseling sessions, or drop out of the rehabilitation program, the counselor can and should maintain contact with his family. They may start coming to church to bolster their own faith, as they endeavor to live with the problem of seeing their loved one continue in alcoholism. I think of one man who returned to alcohol, but later he was motivated to seek help again because the members of his family became Christians and showed a new love and understanding for him. All the hostility and reasons for his continuing to drink were removed by the conversion of his family.

Occasionally, when the converted spouse returns home, he meets an adverse reaction from the wife who formerly controlled him or treated him as a patient. She loses her domination of the home because her husband can now assume leadership. This situation is not common, but the counselor should be aware that it can happen. Such cases will take lengthy, careful counseling to work themselves out. It is like starting marriage all over again. The marriage must be built on a different premise and relationship. It can no longer be tied together by the alcoholism and weakness of the husband.

9. *Help the rehabilitated alcoholic face his responsibilities.* Some converts want to go back to work, or even into full-time Christian service, too soon; others, not soon enough. The counselor must know when the time is right. When the convert is able, he must — whether he wants to or not. He must be challenged and instructed to do so.

The family should let him "stand on his own two feet." Many are afraid to let him assume any responsibility, because they are afraid the pressure will cause him to fall. However, the family should be told that responsibility is essential for the convert's regaining his self-respect.

The counselor must firmly aid the convert to face reality. He may make excuses, find fault with those he works with, complain that he can't find a job he likes — all of which are characteristic of past patterns of behavior. The counselor should "lay down the law" and urge him to accept the program of recovery that has been worked out for him. At this point in his rehabilitation he should have reached a certain level of victory to be able to take such firmness and "tough love."

10. *Begin to phase out the relationship with the recovered alcoholic.* The attachment and relationship so necessary for successful counseling in the early stages of contact with the alcoholic can be detrimental during his recovery stage. The counselor must release him, emotionally and spiritually. During follow-up contact should be maintained, but the counselor should not impose himself on his client, nor should he allow him to call or visit with every little problem. Encourage him to make his own decisions. Don't

do for him the things he should be doing for himself. The responsibility for recovery must be the alcoholic's, not the counselor's.

The converted alcoholic must learn that he can stand "on his own two feet." But he won't make it if the counselor gives him the impression that the alcoholic needs him, or that he is making it because of him. If the alcoholic gets the impression that the counselor needs his recovery to feed his own ego — and aid the counselor's personal success — the alcoholic will feel exploited. In many cases, a pastor, layman or Christian worker will strive to get an alcoholic reformed just so they can prove something to themselves, colleagues, or others. The result is a "my convert" relationship, in which the counselor babies the alcoholic, smothers him, and finds it difficult to release him. If the rehabilitation fails, the counselor sees it as a personal failure; if there is success, it is viewed as personal success. This kind of attitude puts great pressure on the alcoholic, who senses that he is just like a guinea pig in an experiment, or that his testimony is needed by the church or by some organization to prove it is doing a good work. This is the worst kind of exploitation.

11. *Help him develop a strong spiritual life.* The recovered alcoholic needs a "brimful" experience of and relationship with Christ. He must be, as young people at Teen Challenge like to say, "on fire for God," and "up tight with Jesus." The ex-alcoholic must depend totally on the Lord for his freedom from alcohol, and to maintain his new life.

Three things are necessary for the development of a strong spiritual life:

(a) *Daily prayer.* Just as he took a nip of alcohol in the morning, a nip in the afternoon, and a nip at night, so he needs to learn to whisper a prayer in the morning and throughout the day. Alcoholics who have been a part of a resident rehabilitation program must learn to discipline themselves to pray when they are on their own. They may experience a let-down because they are no longer in a spiritual atmosphere where they were encouraged to pray. When they are working and facing responsibilities at home, they must set their own schedule for prayer.

(b) *Christian fellowship.* The rehabilitated alcoholic

needs the fellowship of other Christians. Finding him the right church is important. The right church is one where he can sense the presence of the Lord and where the people are friendly and helpful. Remember, the alcoholic previously spent much time in bars and taverns where he found fellowship, friends and an atmosphere that meant a lot to him. The church must be everything, and more, that the local bar was. The recovered alcoholic also needs the friendship and fellowship of other Christians in his home. Because he does not drink anymore, and because all of his old friends were drinking people, he needs new friends. Pastors should introduce couples to the recovered alcoholic and his wife, people the pastor feels would understand him and be compatible with him.

(c) *Christian service.* Alcoholics are notorious receivers; they never give out. After conversion, almost always they naturally want to give. They need to know when and how. Help them to find a place of service that is within their abilities. Take them to evangelistic services, on witnessing ventures, to retirement homes, jail services, and so on. Let them give their testimonies; that will help to strengthen them. A word of caution: too much activity, too soon, can do more harm than good. The converted alcoholic must be ready for Christian service. Don't try to make him an example until he is ready. He may want to take on more responsibility than he can handle. Involve him in Christian service gradually, and keep a watchful eye on him to see that he is maintaining his prayer life.

8

REBELS, RUNAWAYS AND REVOLUTIONARIES

THE END OF THE REBEL

Man Dies in Train Leap

A 21-year-old man was killed late Wednesday night when he fell or jumped from a Baltimore-bound Penn Central train a mile north of here.

The dead youth was identified as Richard Lee Beers, who is believed to have lived most recently in Greenwich Village, New York City.

Maryland State Police at North East said they found LSD, "speed," and other drugs on Beers' body and also on his traveling companion, Sandra Santana, 17, also of New York City.

A police spokesman said yesterday the girl told them Beers had taken LSD before the incident. He said that she claimed she saw Beers jump from the train, which police said was traveling through a wooded area. at 60 miles per hour, and reported it to a conductor. Police were notified by Penn Central personnel in Baltimore.

Beers was pronounced dead on arrival at Union Hospital, Elkton.

Miss Santana, described by police yesterday as being "incoherent," is being held as a material witness.

Beers' father, Lee, a factory work in Philadelphia, said his son left home three years ago, shortly after the death of his mother. The elder Beers said his son, an only child, "just wanted to be on his own."

The elder Beers said his son was a talented guitar player who, the father said, "expected to make it big right away."

According to the father, the youth played with the Wissahickon Folk Singers, a group which made one record and appeared on the Ted Mack Amateur Hour. However, he said the group never achieved success.

Beers said his son, who attended Wissahickon High School near Ambler, Pa., "didn't care for school or work, but was good with his hands and his guitar." According to the father, Beers had no police record.

Beers said his son "became a rambler" after leaving home, unwilling, he said, to hold a job. The father said the youth had no apparent means of support except through money earned playing his guitar. The father said he had not heard from his son in more than a year, but thought he last lived in Greenwich Village.

The elder Beers said he suspected, but did not know, that his son was apparently using drugs. He said his son, who once was husky, became drawn and ill-looking in recent years. "He wasn't the same boy the last few times."

—*from a newspaper report*

Mr. Lee Beers, the boy's father, has put Richard's story into poetic form:

THE END OF THE REBEL

I have a story that I must tell
To all the youth who wish to rebel.
Remember the one, too young to die,
If you think it's fun to get high.

My son is dead: I wonder why
He had to be so young to die.
Why rebel, leave home and me?
Why the drugs, the L.S.D.?

Was it because I condemned his hair?
Did he believe I did not care?
Maybe the love in my heart, so true,
Somehow failed to shine through?

He left home just eighteen.
Went on his own; joined the Hippie scene.
Lived the life that the Hippies led.
Now, at twenty-one, the rebel's dead.

The rebel was very much alive
Aboard train number one fifty-five,
Till he and his girl took L.S.D.
For him, both trips ended fatally.

Somehow he managed to take a dive
Off of train number one fifty-five:

Was he pushed; did he jump, or fall?
Only our good Lord knows all.

Maybe the Lord forgave and set him free
From the life he'd lived and its misery.
And for all youth to note, and see,
Just what the end of a rebel might be.

Please heed this warning that the good Lord sent,
Don't go the way this rebel went.
Or do the things that he did wrong.
Stay at home, where you belong.

Believe me, your parents really care,
The love you seek is really there.
Maybe not always a shining glow,
But it's there, believe me, I know.

—Lee Beers

Tony was an upper-middle-class teenager. His parents provided him with a good home. He attended one of the better schools in his city. He always had pocket money. At the age of fourteen he had his own television set and a telephone in his bedroom. At sixteen he was given an automobile. Tony dressed very well, again thanks to mom and dad.

But the more his parents gave him, the less Tony appreciated it and the more he rebelled. Why? Ask Tony and he will simply say, "I don't really know." Perhaps a social worker would say that his family stuffed his pockets but starved his emotions. "There never was really any open conflict when I was younger, but neither was there real togetherness," Tony says.

His rebellion was mostly hidden, or controlled. There were occasional outbursts of anger toward his parents, but the open differences were minimal. Occasionally he would purposely disobey them. Perhaps unconsciously he was getting even with them. Until he was eighteen Tony lived at home and carried on an outwardly normal relationship with his family.

Then Tony went to the university. There he picked up other ideals and philosophies. To the rebellion against his parents was added a dash of social rebellion and a dose of "anti-establishment" resistance. Over the period of a year Tony became a runaway who didn't actually run away; he was a runaway at home. He lived under the same roof as his parents and he slept in the same bed he always had, but that was about the extent of his home life. He ate a few meals at home and spent less and less time with his parents and the rest of his family.

When he was at home Tony spent most of his time alone in his room. His room had become a psychedelic pad with posters, hippie art, rock music, incense, and other paraphernalia of the hippie sub-culture in which he was becoming immersed. Emotionally, socially and spiritually, he was a runaway. He had, in spirit, left home and joined the runaway generation. Like many teen-agers of today, Tony joined the "get as far away from home as possible" generation.

The actual making of a runaway in his case came about in a simple and seemingly harmless fashion. He didn't sneak away from the house. He convinced his parents that it would be best for him to live with a few friends in his own apartment. This, he reasoned, would help him "learn to be a man" and to "face life." It sounded so good; it was a smooth job of cutting off the home ties and taking the ultimate step in expressing rebellion against his parents. "The best part about it," he told his friends, "is that mom and dad bought it and I didn't have to hassle with them."

Now Tony was a full-fledged runaway. He attached himself to his new way of life; his feelings, attitudes and philosophies were radicalized. He started to smoke marijuana and occasionally dropped acid (LSD) to "expand his mind." "It was groovy," Tony commented.

He joined his friends' peace movement, at first only in theory, then later he became an activist because "I had nothing else to do." He carried protest signs, "yelled a few obscenities at the pigs," and threw a few bricks. At first, Tony says, it was "more like a game than anything else." Then, "I began to get serious about it. We started to find issues. Soon I was committed to overthrowing 'the system.' The more I was in the movement, the more reasons I found — or was taught — why the system needed to be overthrown."

Tony had found a new target for his rebellion. Next, he joined a "revolutionary camp." There he learned the tricks of the revolutionary trade: how to protest, to resist, to sit-in, stand-in, lie-in; and if none of that worked, how to bring about an open revolution. It grew on him. It became his cause. He believed in it. He was now a revolutionary.

The turning point in Tony's life came when he first realized what had happened to him since he had left home and joined the "movement." It took place while he was taking part in what had been billed as a peaceful anti-war demonstration.

"There wasn't supposed to be any violence," he explained. "But as I listened to our leaders talking about the injustice of war, of capitalism, parenthood, society, and so on, I suddenly realized they were carrying guns in their pockets and were ready to make violence themselves. And here they were, spilling off about peace. I looked at the peace symbol under my neck. I thought about the guns in their pockets. And for the first time it didn't make sense. It didn't add up. So I made up my mind then and there that I was getting out. This was not for me. This wasn't my bag."

Tony then went back to being a nonprotesting rebel and runaway. He dressed mod, or what others would call hippie. He wore beads, grew a beard, and "dug the Beatles, Dylan, the Jefferson Airplane and all the other rock stars." More and more he smoked marijuana and "tripped out" on LSD and "speed." Then, at a party, someone introduced him to "smack" (heroin). After about six months, he had a $25-a-day habit.

"You know," he reminisces, "when you go to one of those things you never know who is there. And with drugs floating around, you never know what kind of drugs are being pushed. I guess there were some guys there trying to turn some of us 'speed freaks' on to the hard stuff, because they knew there was more money in that for them. I was so stoned I didn't know what I was doing. I took 'horse' and liked it. It was a different high than I had ever experienced before.

"Another reason why I think I took the hard stuff — because no one gets hooked by intention — is that I was so low emotionally. My lows were getting lower and my highs were not getting me high enough. I guess when I went to that party I was at my all-time low. And 'smack' got me — wow, way, way up there, or maybe it was down there, I really don't know. Anyway, I said to myself, 'This is what you've been looking for. From then on I knew exactly what I was doing. I went looking for heroin and I loved it."

After three years on hard drugs, Tony turned to Christ and got "unhooked." Today Tony is a Christian. He doesn't carry a peace placard. "Now," he says, "I carry the Prince of Peace in my heart." Two steps brought about a spiritual revolution in him. The first he calls common sense; the second, Jesus Christ.

Tony's story illustrates three different kinds of young people: the rebels, the runaways, and the revolutionaries. Tony was all three. First, he was a rebel. That set the stage for turning him into a runaway. Finally, after he ran away, the stage was set for him to become a revolutionary. On top of that, he became a drug addict. Although labels can be misleading, for the sake of trying to identify the emotional, psychological, philosophical and spiritual make-up of today's youth, we will use the terms rebel, runaway, and revolutionary. They are not young people who come looking for help from Christian counselors, as the drug addicts do. The latter come because they know they need help. But runaways are not aware of their need. Tony sought help as a drug addict, not as a runaway. Were it not for his drug problem, he might never have sought help.

As outlined in the chapter on the addicted generation, the counselor must determine to what extent drugs are a problem with the rebels, runaways, and revolutionaries. If there is drug addiction, treatment must begin at this point. In the process, rebellious and revolutionary attitudes can be dealt with. Many rebels, runaways, and revolutionaries, however, are drug users but not addicts.

This does not mean rebels, runaways, and revolutionaries can only be reached if they are addicted. It only means they do not readily seek help. They are not restricted to the streets, hippie havens, college campuses, and the high schools; they are also in the home, at work, and even in the church. Christian youth are affected by the thinking of today's anti-establishment advocates. The number of so-called Christian radicals and Christian hippies is growing. Some are openly radical, others carry their attitudes within them.

There is a need to prevent young people from following today's radical ideologies. This can be done by watching for the signs of rebellion, uncovering the runaways at home, and checking trends of thinking that eventually keep young people completely away from God. Just as there are youth on the verge of becoming addicts, alcoholics or homosexuals, so there are many being influenced by forces outside the home and church to become rebels, runaways and revolutionaries. Following some of the suggestions outlined in chapters 2 and 3 will help to prevent their becoming such.

However, the greatest challenge lies outside the church. Among the confirmed rebels, runaways and revolutionaries evangelists and Christian counselors should find a harvest of souls. This can be done through coffee house ministries, through high school clubs and organizations, through campus ministries, by summer beach evangelism work, and through the more conventional out-reaches such as rallies, seminars, and other church-oriented programs. The counselor will not meet these young people on a client-to-counselor basis, but rather on a very loose social contact relationship.

Dealing with an addict is usually on the basis of his need. However, this is not the case with the nonaddict rebel, runaway or revolutionary. He senses no need. He feels he *has* what the world needs. The presentation of the Gospel to him means the confrontation of two causes. He may feel Christianity is outdated, and that his is a new "gospel" to save this generation. He may have a missionary approach in turning others to new ideas. He is addicted to idealism. As one revolutionary said, "We are not just a protest movement, we are literally a separate nation inside America." It is to this nation within a nation that the Christian must go, first as an evangelist and second as a counselor.

THE REBELS

Everyone rebels at some point in his life. Most people know how to work out their rebellion in an orderly and constructive manner. Others, either because they cannot cope with the situation, or because they are faced with obstacles too great to overcome, become bitter and infected with a rebellious nature.

The most common form of rebellion is that which pits the child against his parents. All men are endowed with a basically rebellious nature because of their inheritance from Adam. If parents do not check such rebellion, then it develops until it becomes more and more a part of the child's method of reacting to the world around him.

Childhood rebellion is also fostered by other factors. For example, a child may see his father continually come home drunk. He may see him slap his mother. The child may be beaten. One of the young people at Teen Challenge was tied to a table leg when he was a child, and left in the house alone for hours. Such traumatic childhood experiences add fuel to the flames of rebellion. Unchecked rebellion in childhood and in early teen years sets the stage for a lifetime of rebellion.

Rebellion, however, must have a target. The rebels throw their darts of anger, hostility and rebellion at their parents, at authority in general, and at the church. Parents are the first target. Parents sometimes are to blame for this. They can bring on rebellion if they do not discipline their children; if they are overly permissive; if they do not provide religious training in the home; or if they fail to expose their children to spiritual values that serve as a buffer to rebellion. Unconsciously children resent the fact that parents do not serve as a kind, understanding and loving buffer to their aggression.

Some children are rebellious for selfish, ambitious and "got to have my own way" reasons. Others are rebellious because they are deprived of the good things of life. They feel they have been cheated out of such things as physical beauty, material blessings and a good home environment. One mother told me, "When my son lost his father he became very bitter and rebellious. When his father was living we never had any trouble with him." In another home the teenage daughter was getting low grades in school, staying out late at night, and developing an ever-deepening rebellious attitude toward life. When her alcoholic father was converted to Christ and returned home, immediately her grades went up, she no longer stayed out late at night, and her rebellion completely disappeared.

In the home the parents are the authority figure. If they do not assume their proper authority role with love and understanding, then the child may have a distorted view of other authorities. Parents can either stand in the way of selfish desires, or starve their children of deserving ones. Outside the home there are other adult figures who are doing the same: the teacher, the school principal, the policeman, for example. If the child cannot relate properly to authority in the home, it is not likely he will be able to do so outside the home. The rebellion to authority may result from an adult's standing in the way of letting a child have his own way. Or, the adult may be repressive and not allow the youngster to have the breathing room he so desperately needs and searches for in his relationship with the world at large. The older the child gets, the larger becomes the world he faces, and the more authority he has to relate to. With the help of an understanding and instructive adult, rebellion can be completely removed.

The church often is another target of rebellion for two reasons. One has to do with the success of the church, the other has to do with its failure. If the church is successfully delivering "the whole counsel of God," some young people are going to look at it as their enemy. They will feel that God is infringing on their right to have a good time. To them, Jesus Christ is a kill-joy. If they become Christians, they think Christ will make them lose all their friends, turn them into "squares," and destroy other ambitions they have. Those who will not accept Christ's claim of ownership over their lives are going to rebel. They may aim their darts of rebellion at something in the church, but they are really rebelling against God. A church that is true to the Gospel is going to encounter such resistance. But if and when this young person decides he wants to accept Christ, this is the only kind of church in which his rebellion can be turned into regeneration and renewal.

Rebellion can also result from the failure of the church. Many young people have sought for a meaningful religious experience. They were at one time sincere in their desire to know if God is real and if Christ can be a personal Savior. But they were told that the Bible is full of myths, that Christ is only a great teacher, and that the Holy Spirit is not a person but an influence. To them, the church was like a social club, a place to go for one hour on Sunday. So they gave it up as a lost cause. They rebelled against it because it was a cold and dead institution. At the very time when they needed some answers to life's problems, they found none.

If rebellion is the result of the rejection of truth, it is something that can be understood and accepted as natural. But when rebellion is the result of spiritual apostasy — the withholding and denial of the truth — then it is a tragic, unforgivable blunder on the part of the withholders and deniers of that truth.

Every generation has had its own ways of expressing rebellion, and getting parents and adults "up tight." Youth in the past often rebelled by dancing the Charleston, wearing flappers, dressing in the mod style of their time, smoking cigarettes, getting drunk, or riding out to the local lovers' lane. At present the most common method of widening the generation gap is to wear long hair, dress in hippie garb, become rock music addicts, and of course the most serious form of rebellion — drug taking. Even giving the peace sign seems to irritate some of the over-thirty group, and young people find it a convenient way of expressing rebellion. Young people who do such deeds may only be expressing a preference in life style and taste, but they may also be expressing rebellion. Other common methods of venting rebellion by teens against parents may be by getting poor grades, wearing sloppy clothes, or dating someone the young person knows mom and dad do not like. One girl we dealt with rebelled by going to church. She knew her mother didn't want her attending a certain church in the first place so she purposely attended every chance she had — to get out of the house and to make her mother angry. A parent asked me how she could get her son out of his room. He gave his parents the silent treatment — hiding out in his room, reading, listening to music, or sleeping. It was his way of rebelling. Some young people will use whatever they can to satisfy their need to rebel. In most cases both parent and child are able to work the situation through satisfactorily; in other cases, this is not so and the generation gap turns into a great gulf fixed.

When a young person reveals his feelings of resentment, bitterness and rebellion to the counselor, an effort should be made to see if he is rebelling against known truth or against unknown or misunderstood truth. The concept some young people have of Christianity and the church may be based on half-truths or "hobbyhorse" truths. They may have come from a church that majored in minor aspects of denominationalism. They may have seen only the negative side of Christianity and not the positive side. They may have seen real hypocrisy in the church. When young people throw out the hypocrisy bit, it may be only a cop-out, but again there can be substance to it. Find out if they are talking about general or specific hypocrisy, and what concept they have of the church and of biblical truth. It will not take long to determine if the rebel is rebelling because of a wrong concept of Christianity, or because of his rejection of real Christianity.

Why do young people rebel against conditions in the home? How do parents contribute to their rebellion? Here are some points to consider:

1. *The "regeneration" gap.* Young people want their parents to have a deep commitment to Christ. They are disappointed and feel let down when they cannot reconcile the behavior of their parents at home with their profession of faith. One fellow said to me, "I have two dads — a church dad and a house dad." Young people set high ideals for their parents. They can excuse and understand mistakes and human frustrations, but they will not accept outright hypocrisy. When they see the gap between a fruit-bearing, godly Christian and a carnal one, they are likely to rebel, possibly against both parents and God. Communication will not be effective in the home if there is a regeneration gap.

2. *Life in a "pressure cooker" home.* A home that is full of tension, strife, marital conflict, office troubles and church gossip is like a pressure cooker. Young people need the right conditions in the home so they can grow up with a feeling of security. A pressure-packed home will soon produce "boiling over" in the child. One young man told us, "I can't remember one day in our house when there wasn't someone fighting, arguing, or hollering. The only peace and quiet I got was out on the streets with my friends."

3. *Constantly squashing doubts.* Young people naturally express doubts about God. In addition, they have doubts and questions about Christianity, the church and family traditions. If they are not allowed to express their feelings

about such things, rebellion may result. It is better to have doubts discussed in the home, when children are younger, than it is to push them off until later. Then their minds will be fed other doubts, and doubt will be piled upon doubt. Questions should be asked and answered in the home where a sound, biblical explanation can eliminate some of the perplexities. It is wrong to tell teenagers, "You shouldn't feel that way; you have no right to question such things." We work with many young people who are sincere doubters. Their doubts are based on sincere, legitimate questions and misunderstandings. If the doubts of young people are handled properly, and if their faith is fed, their doubts and fears will starve to death.

4. *"Forced feeding."* Honest answers should be given to honest questions, but young people must not be forced to accept the answers. The forcing of parents' Christian ideals and beliefs on their children is likely to result in rebellion in later years. Parents cannot jam religion down their children's throats. They can, however, put on the table such a delicious spiritual spread that their children will want to "taste and see that the Lord is good." I will never forget the first time I challenged my mother and said, "I'm not going to church." She looked at me sternly and said, "All right, son, but you know what is right and what is wrong." A few hours later, while watching a basketball game, such conviction struck me that I literally ran back to church. Arriving as the preacher began his message, I dropped into the pew and sat down. What a feeling of comfort came over me! I knew that's where I should be. It was my decision, and my mother gave *me* the opportunity to make it. I thank God I was never force-fed Christianity.

5. *Demands of the "11th through the 20th" commandments.* In some homes parents add to the Ten Commandments by enforcing home-made rules as gospel truth. These rules, traditions and personal convictions can be set up as if they were the eleventh, twelfth or thirteenth commandments of Scripture. Rules on such things as hair length, clothing styles, extracurricular activities and so on are often forced on young people as if they were commandments right out of the Bible. Infractions of these rules should not be treated as sins, but as matters of obedience

and discipline in the home. My parents taught me to love and fear God. Such teaching did not make it necessary for them to post on the board a list of do's and don'ts. Through my relationship with Christ there were certain things I did not want to do. My parents did not tell me; it was the Lord's revelation. If some family rules are passed off as Bible commandments, and if young people are made to think they will go to hell if they disobey them, they will develop a negative outlook toward Christianity.

6. *Handling questions properly.* Some young people express doubts, but most of the time they ask simple, ordinary questions. Taking time to answer them is important. Many questions may seem trivial to adults, but they are very important to young people. It is not so much finding answers as it is taking the time and showing the concern. However, if parents can't answer a question, they should say so and not try to fool their teenager with an answer they know is not right or is shallow.

7. *Attitude toward the world youth scene.* Young people are sympathetic with their peers in the nation and around the world. Parents must show understanding and tolerance toward the world youth scene. Comments about youth movements, fads and ideals must be given carefully and judiciously, not critically. Consistently putting down young people as the "bad guys" will create a serious gap between parents and children.

THE RUNAWAYS

Rebellion can lead in several directions. Some rebels may end up establishing a lifetime pattern of lashing out against parents, teachers, authority, society in general, and religion, church and God. Some rebels are antisocial, but within the law; others, outside the law. Some become successful in life because they manage to suppress their rebellion. Most, however, are not smart enough to do that — their rebellious actions constantly get them into trouble. But while some rebels attack, others retreat. They hide, cop out, or get rid of their anger, resentment and bitterness by retreating. They are the runaways.

In 1968 some 150,000 young people ran away from home and subsequently were arrested. But most of those who run away do not get arrested. These figures would be conservative in terms of estimating the total number of run-aways. Some speculate that there were 500,000 runaways during the years 1968-69.

Running away is nothing new. In previous years children and teens ran away, but they ran around the neighborhood or the town and when night came or they grew hungry, they went back home. My mother always said "good" when I announced I was "leaving and never coming back." She would ask me, "Do you want me to make you egg, ham or cheese sandwiches to take with you?" It was never any fun running away; my mother took all the threat out of it. But nowadays young people are not just running around the town; they're running around the nation and the world, and they're not returning home. About 70 percent of the young people who come into our Greenwich Village coffee houses are runaways. Innocent teens who come to Greenwich Village on a whim or looking for excitement often get hooked on the way of life. When they run out of money they are forced to accept invitations to stay with addicts, way-out hippies, gangsters, and even psychopaths.

Runaways are not limited to the younger set. One young housewife in her mid-twenties came to Teen Challenge after having left her baby in a doctor's office. She had walked out of the office, made her way across the Canadian border, and ended up late one night in our chapel. When asked why she did it, she said, "I just felt an urge to go away." Further study showed she had begun a runaway pattern at the age of fourteen.

Running away is a form of addiction to some. One young man said, "I've been running away since I was nine years old. I can't stay anywhere more than a month. Something comes over me and I just want to run, run, run. I guess I'll never stop." He walked out of Teen Challenge and I have not seen him since.

Types of Runaways

1. *The full-time hippie runaways.* They live in city or country communes. There are an estimated 500 hippie communes across the country. Their speech, dress, drug-taking and political and social ideals are all hippie. Long hair, beards, beads, sandals or bare feet (boots in winter) are all part of their lifestyle. Some are high school or college

dropouts. They come from a wide range of academic and socio-economic backgrounds. The average hippie runaway is 21, white, middle-class suburbanite, and Protestant. His parents earn between twelve and fifteen thousand dollars a year.

2. *The part-time runaways.* They cannot rightfully be classified as hippies, since they work and function in the "straight" society. But they are thought of as hippies by adults. Not all are long-haired. Most still live at home, but for the most part they run their own lives and "do their own thing." There often is open conflict between parents and part-time runaways because their life patterns and attitudes are in direct opposition to each other.

3. *Holiday runaways.* These are the summer and school vacation beachcombers. Some do drop out permanently, either during a summer vacation or even during a school holiday.

4. *The "wheelaways."* They are the motorcycle gang members who run away on wheels. They usually have a headquarters, but they travel most of the time. They are known for their violence, sex orgies and the terror they sometimes cause in small towns. Not all "wheelaways" are members of organized gangs. Some go in small groups, alone, or in pairs. These are usually not the rough, sex-hungry types.

5. *The "rockaways."* Since Woodstock (1969) there are groups of young people who go from one rock festival to another. They are the "rockaways." They run away whenever there is a rock music festival. There they find others who share their interests in rock music, drugs and sex. Some of the rockaways are devout lovers of rock music; others go simply because there is a crowd there. Many go because the music, sex, and drugs fill a spiritual void in their lives.

The book, *Purple Violet Squish* (Zondervan), lists three types of hippies. Since many runaways become hippies, I include the list here.

Types of Hippies

1. *Hope-to-be hippies.* These are teenagers between fifteen and eighteen. They are attracted primarily by the glamor and the mystique of the abandoned free life, with-

out the restrictions of parents and the pressures of having to produce in the "straight" world.

2. *Tribal hippies.* They simply want to try something new and experiment with life. In a kind of tribal togetherness they seek to shake off their terrible guilt feelings and their emptiness, and to satisfy an inner craving for love and understanding.

3. *Synthetic hippies.* Among these are the city hippies, suburban hippies, political hippies, week-end hippies, musical hippies and tourists. They want the world to think they're hippies, but in their hearts they don't have the courage to go all the way. Most of them are under thirty, but some are in their sixties. Among them are business people who get a great kick out of rubbing shoulders with hippies.

The Runaway's "Bags"

To understand the behavior of runaways the counselor needs to know something about their interests, or "bags." "Bag" is a term the runaways use to describe their "thing." It is their main interest and concern in life. They consider the Christian who witnesses to them as having a Christian "bag." One fellow said to us, "Don't come out with that religious bag to me." What are the runaway's bags?

1. *The drug bag.* Many actively seek out runaway or hippie havens because they know they can easily find drugs there. Most young people turn to drugs later, after getting involved in the scene and making friends. Some do not fully realize what they are getting into with respect to drugs. But once turned on, they find drugs relieve their anxieties built up because of leaving home. Drug-taking comes from group pressure and from sharing "pads" (living quarters, apartments, or just a room) with others. To be socially acceptable, drug-taking becomes necessary in such an environment.

2. *The sex bag.* Teenage boys sometimes are forced into homosexuality and girls into prostitution. Most, however, get involved in sex vices by choice. Often there are group sex perversions and the sharing of many lovers. "Make love, not war" is one of the hippie slogans. They regard any and all sexual involvement with another partner as being a manifestation of that love. Under the guise of love they

give themselves license to do whatever they want, sexually.

3. *The political bag.* Almost all runaways are politically and socially active. Many decided to drop out because of political and social views. Some are dedicated to peace movements, while others mainly participate in protest rallies or riots.

The Reasons for Running Away

Why do young people run away? Capt. James Lynch, head of the Missing Persons Unit, New York City Police Department, says, "Running away from home has become a fad, a tragic, almost spontaneous answer to problems in either school or the home."

A National Institute of Mental Health study concludes: "Running away may be any number of things, ranging from a cry of despair to a victory yell."

One young girl told me, "My parents threw me out of the house." When I asked her why, she admitted, "They said, 'Live by our rules or get out.' I refused to live by their rules, so I got out."

Some young people run away on impulse, a reaction to a fight with their parents. Most of these return home. Others leave because of a series of conflicts with parents built up over a period of time. A sixteen-year-old girl who showed up at our center told me of constant conflicts with her mother over church and a boy friend. I learned her trouble was caused by a combination of the mother's paying more attention to her own desires, and the subsequent reaction of the daughter doing whatever she could to excite or anger her mother. When I asked her to call home, she did. The girl said, "Hello, mom, I'm at Teen Challenge in New York City." Her mother quickly shot back, "Well, you just stay there," and hung up. Capt. Lynch asserts, "Our runaway cases involve almost as much adult delinquency as they do juvenile delinquency."

Another contributing factor, often overlooked, is the glamorized publicity given to the runaway havens and the hippie style of living. Such vivid portrayals in the news media often are the trigger that ignites the action. Young people read about the exploits of runaways so much that running away appears to be "in" and fashionable. They begin looking around for a reason to run.

Almost every major newspaper and magazine, when the hippie culture began to emerge, gave it front page coverage. There is no evil of course in such coverage itself — but it was the manner in which it was presented. It all looked like an innocent lark or a cute teenage fad. Thus, teens were lured by the thousands partly by the kind of publicity given such psychedelic havens. Television programs pictured it also as a refreshing development in our society. As one San Francisco hippie drop-out in Haight Ashbury stated, "You can't find love in Haight (hate). They didn't tell us the other side of the story. This is a bad scene." Only when LSD began to blow a few minds did another picture emerge in print, and thus in a positive way did this help warn young people that drugs and the hippie culture were not all so pure and innocent.

Many runaways have provoked their parents to anger and to arguments, to find a reason to justify their leaving home. Others just walk off, hoping to shock their parents and gain attention from family, friends, and church associates. They run away mainly to punish their parents. They usually try to get in touch with someone near home, hoping the parents will somehow find out and try to get them back.

A *Christian Herald* article, May, 1970, about runaways states: "Apart from a few incorrigible delinquents who run away as soon as they are returned to their homes, most runaways are either worried, confused, or indulged children who are convinced that they have little dialogue with their parents, no matter how permissive they may be. Recalling that often busy parents showed little visible concern for their smaller difficulties, runaways contend that they anticipated serious complications over dates, hair styles, bedtimes, marijuana, or social values; or, that there were crises triggered by damage done to expensive furniture or the family automobile; or, most often, by their receiving poorer grades in school than their parents expected of them."

THE REVOLUTIONARIES

It is hard to prove a definite link between rebels, runaways and revolutionaries. There is always movement up or down the scale. Some rebels are not politically motivated or politically rebellious. Some become so because a political issue gives them a new target for their anger. But many radicals and revolutionaries have had no past history of parental or social rebellion, at least not the kind that got them into trouble with the law. Most of those arrested for rioting and bombing had no previous record of arrest for any reason.

What factors in our society produce revolutionaries? Why does the campus boil? Following are some things that have happened during the 1960's that have tended to radicalize our young people:

1. The civil rights and racial issues started by sit-ins in the South and riots in the North.

2. The step-up of the war in Vietnam in 1965, which struck a note of deep concern among many youth. Peace groups sprang up all across the country.

3. The Students for a Democratic Society turned from protest "within" to protest "without," making the universities, the ghettos and the government their targets.

4. Haight Ashbury in San Francisco added hippie culture and style to the newly emerging youth movement. It gave youth a means of expressing its rebellion and rejection of adult lifestyles.

5. Eugene McCarthy's success gave the youth movement its first victory when President Johnson withdrew from the 1968 presidential race. Not getting their way in Chicago during the Democratic national convention gave the radical young people their first bitter defeat. Legal protest gave way to violent protest.

6. The continuation of the war, campus strikes and the death of four Kent State University students in Ohio turned many moderates into revolutionaries.

These are some of the reasons young people have turned from being moderates into being protesters, activists, radicals, and eventually revolutionaries. *His* magazine says students are either (a) inactivists, (b) law-abiding activists, or (c) radicals.

Jerry Rubin, one of the leading exponents of radicalism, says: "We have merged new left politics with a psychedelic lifestyle. Our lifestyle — acid, long hair, freaky clothes, pot, rock music, sex — is the revolution. Our very existence mocks America. The old order is dying. The Democratic

Party is dying. While it dies we will celebrate the festival of life. We are the politics of the future."

But the revolt is not confined to rebelling against the Vietnam war. One college student said, "When the war ends, something else will be the main target of the protesters and revolutionaries." Large numbers of young activists see the problems of American society — poverty, pollution, the war — as fundamentally the fault, not of the government, but of capitalism itself. The hard-core radicals and revolutionaries believe that reform is not possible through the normal political system. They consider revolutionary violence the only alternative.

Some of the attitudes of youth toward materialism and capitalism are close to what Christians believe. Said one: "So much of the business system depends on messing up people's minds so they'll buy what they're told. They convince women that they will look bad in the natural state so there will be a market for makeup. They've created a whole country full of people who are just too uptight about themselves to care about each other." They are saying what the Bible says: "A man's life consisteth not in the abundance of the things which he possesseth" (Luke 12:15).

Another student said: "The values we need are love instead of power, brotherhood instead of competition. That sounds corny, except that thousands of people are dying because we don't have them. So now I think of myself as a revolutionary and I'm turned off to capitalism, but it is just a question of economics. It's a question of how you teach people to love under a system that depends on teaching them power and competition."

What are the causes of the unrest, protest, violence and revolution in the high schools and on college and university campuses? To find the reasons we must once again look at the home backgrounds and society as a whole. This generation is a product of the past generation. What are some of the emotional, psychological and spiritual factors that are causing our youth to want to revolt and overthrow anything and everything?

1. *Childhood permissiveness.* This generation is a product of mothers and fathers who said, "Our children are not going to go through what we did when we were children." With their prosperity they are able to live up to

such a promise. They make the whole world revolve around their children. Their offspring can have anything, do anything. The children run the home. They challenge authority and are allowed to get away with it. Every wish is gratified. Because mom and dad have money, or credit, they never have to wait long to have their wishes fulfilled. These young people come to the university with the same desire for painless, no-waiting gratification. They ran their homes, why can't they run the university?

The result, as suggested by John W. Aldridge in his excellent book, *In the Country of the Young,* is that young people are "paralyzed with indecision." He writes:

"But if the pressure of economic necessity is missing, not only is motivation reduced to a minimum, but one is confronted by such a plethora of possibilties for using one's energies that one may become paralyzed with indecision and end up deciding nothing at all — or, like mice, in an overly complicated maze, turn psychotic and simply sit down and goggle at the wall."[1]

Eventually youth get tired of "goggling at the wall" and they are then ready to tear down, burn, or bulldoze over the wall — either to get into the university and get some meaning out of it, or to get out of the university and find a solution to their paralysis.

2. *The absence of discipline in childhood and adolescence.* A lack of discipline follows material gratification and permissiveness. As children they got whatever they wanted; they had to pay no price for it, in terms of obedience to house rules and regulations. Aldridge states:

"No restrictions were placed on the child, and parents habitually made it a point, in moments of choice, to let the child cast the deciding vote." The result, he says, is that they became "drunk with the glory of their incontestable omnipotence. They entered the university convinced that whatever is required of them is wrong. Any exercise of authority, any imposition of laws, is a violation of their civil liberties, as well as their divine rights as members of the new world family of adolescents. It is also a violation of the rules of the game that they have been playing all their lives, the particular variety of checkers in which they

[1] John W. Aldridge, *In the Country of the Young* (New York, Harper & Row, Publishers, 1970) p. 97.

were always allowed to jump backward or forward on the board long before they earned any kings. They are convinced they are right, and where there is not an existing issue to prove it, they will make one. They seem to have a constant need to be right."[2]

3. *The need for identity through opposition.* A child who has never been disciplined, and who rebels but is never resisted, grows up with a feeling of guilt for not having been punished and opposed. The result is an identity vacuum or identity crisis. A child will challenge parents to see how far he can go, secretly hoping to be resisted.

Aldridge states:

> The young come to the universities with little or no respect for their parents, hence little or no respect for adults in general, and very little experience with organized authority. At the same time, their life-long exposure to parental over-protectiveness and permissiveness has given them a mass respect for themselves and an absolute faith in their own authority. But the trouble with their own authority is that since it has never been opposed, it has never actually been tested. It has evolved in a vacuum of nonresistance in which wants were satisfied by negotiations rather than through a direct or violent contest of wills.[3]

He goes on to say: "If adults can be made to resist rather than equivocate or compromise, the young will at last have achieved a condition they have never known in their lives before, and that is vital" to them. Aldridge says the school is an extension of the home, the administrators are the equivalent of parents, and rebellion is transferred from one setting to another.

But it is often too late and too much to ask the schools to solve problems that should have been taken care of in adolescence. The conflict the revolutionaries seek and need comes too late in life. This is why only a surrender to a higher authority (a divine one) will remove the deep-seated rebellion of today's youth.

4. *Boredom.* Aldridge puts boredom in its proper perspective. It has become the by-product of confrontation and revolution. He writes:

> This is the first student generation to be admitted to the

---

[2] *Ibid.,* p. 66.
[3] *Ibid.,* pp. 62, 63.

university on the principle that higher education is a right that should be available to all and, at the same time, a necessity for anyone who hopes to achieve some measure of success in middle-class society. The result is that for the first time in history the universities have had to accept large masses of students who may have the proper credentials from the secondary schools, but who possess neither the cultural interest nor the intellectual incentive to benefit from higher education. Such students when confronted with complex ideas tend to sink into a protective lethargy, or to become resentful because demands are being made on them which they are not equipped to meet and have no particular desire to meet. Most of them did not want to come to the universities in the first place, but did so for reasons of practical expediency: parental pressure, fear of the draft, or the promise of a better job after graduation. Hence their natural impulse is to try to compensate for their failure of ability or interest by involving themselves in some extra-curricular activity, which happens to be today political activism.[4]

This generation which has more advantages than any previous generation turns out to be bored. Boredom not only leads to drugs, but it can lead to revolution, just to give young people something to do.

How to Counsel Rebels, Runaways and Revolutionaries

It must be understood that some of the basic guidelines suggested for helping addicts, alcoholics and other people can also be applied to the rebels, runaways and revolutionaries. However, the following suggestions will be useful in relating to the needs of these young people.

1. *Break the "bag" barrier.* The counselor must get into the young person's "bag," spend some time with him in it, and then try to lead him out of it. This does not mean literally to participate in drug-taking, sex, or political protest. Breaking the bag barrier is getting beyond the drugs, the sex and the political questions to the underlying causes and needs. But before this "getting beyond" can be accomplished, a certain amount of interest must be expressed in the "bag" of the rebel, runaway or revolutionary. They will want to talk about their bag.

Don't try to put a pin in their balloon or bag; don't ridicule, condemn, or scoff. It is the only thing they have in life to call their own. It is precious to them. Try to

[4] *Ibid.,* p. 77.

break them out of their bag and get them into the Christian bag. Some ministers and Christian workers are going around preaching about bags — they are practicing bag-breaking — without demonstrating that they have something more meaningful and satisfying. When Jesus spoke to the woman at the well (John 4), He did not condemn her for coming to fill her water pot, but He told her about some better water. The idea is to present an alternative, a better way of life, so the young person will want to break out of his bag.

2. *Don't meddle in politics.* The counselor must be careful lest he meddle too deeply into political questions. Some well-meaning Christians get hung up on political issues and never get to spiritual issues. It is best not to be dogmatic on political questions, while at the same time expressing an interest in political and social affairs. The counselor might say, for example, "I have strong feelings about the war myself. I agree it's an ugly thing and I wish it would stop. But let's talk about the war that goes on inside a man." It is best to use political and social questions as leads to matters pertaining to the soul. The counselor who is alert and determined not to meddle will pick out the opportune moment to get to more important issues. The radical, revolutionary student will feel that preservation of human life and the earth itself are the most important issues facing society. Don't downgrade his interest in such; commend him instead. Then try to take him on to the larger spiritual perspectives on such matters.

3. *Don't get hung up on externals.* My wife and I visited a hippie coffee house in Sydney, Australia. As soon as we walked in, one of the young men looked at us, then looked at his friend and formed a square with his fingers and pointed to us. Later he said, "No one is going to listen to you here if you're dressed square."

"Listen," I said, "you are always complaining that adults will not accept you for what you are, and that they are always judging you by the length of your hair, your clothes, and other things. Why do you turn around and do the very same thing to me? Your long hair doesn't bother me; why should my short hair bother you? I'm not going to turn you off because of the way you're dressed. Please do the same for me."

Clothing styles mean a lot to most young people. For some they are only fads, but for many they are an outward expression of an inward attitude, rebellion, or search. One writer has suggested that the clothing of youth has "social and psychological implications" that are "depressing in the extreme." "The World War I uniform," he says, "is cherished as a sacred relic for drama, individuality, and romance of war fought according to principles of a now debased idealism."[5]

The Western outfit with the sideburns is worn because the plainsman "enjoyed the distinction of being in honorable contest with the primitive forces of nature, a kind of contest no longer possible."[6]

Wearing Indian garb is an effort "to remind the establisment of its ancestral guilt. The Indian was the original American frontier Negro, the first victim of our corrupt bureaucratic system. It is to suggest that the young, too, were once happy and free like the Indian, and might have remained so if only they had been left alone by adults to do as they pleased."[7]

Regardless of what the externals symbolize, they are very much a part of youth's personality. To criticize such trimmings is to slur him personally. Clothes and hair styles are part of their identity. This is why it is fruitless for parents to go around trying to get their children to dress "right" and to get their hair cut. Unless the inward emptiness and crisis of the soul is solved, cutting away the trimmings will be of no value. Let no Christian worker and counselor say, "I can't see your need and your soul for your hair or your dress." "Man looketh on the outward appearance, but the Lord looketh on the heart" (I Sam 16:7). Beneath the beards, beads, and hair is a person — don't get hung up on the externals.

4. *Magnify the personal experience, or "happening,"* *aspect of Christianity.* Most young people have an institutional view of Christianity. They see it simply as a dead system. They must be made to see the personal experience aspect of the Christian faith. A counselor should dwell on his own personal experience and relationship to Christ.

[5] *Ibid.,* p. 84.
[6] *Ibid.,* p. 85.
[7] *Ibid.*

Talk about answered prayer, the Holy Spirit's ability to lead in decision-making, the overcoming of habits, and other aspects that are relevant to everyday living. Rebels, runaways and revolutionaries need to see that Christ is "the real thing" and that "life goes better with Jesus Christ."

Most of them know what a personal experience with drugs is. They have had the experience of mystical, spiritual feelings. Their use of LSD is evidence of their search for something that will affect their spirits and expand their minds. One LSD user told me that when he was on a trip he "felt a oneness with the universe." Another said, "I took an end run around Jesus Christ and went right to the source — God." Here are a few more descriptions of how LSD users feel on trips:

> I cannot recall whether the revelation came gradually or suddenly; I only remember finding myself in the very midst of those wonderful moments, beholding life for the first time in all of its young intoxication and loveliness, in its unspeakable joy, beauty, and importance. I cannot say exactly what the mysterious change was. I saw no new things. I saw all the usual things in a new miraculous light — in what I believe is their true light. I saw for the first time how beautiful and joyous, beyond any words of mine to describe, is the whole of life. Every human being moving across that porch, every sparrow that flew, every branch tossing in the wind, was caught in and was part of a whole mad ecstasy of loveliness, of joy, of importance, of intoxication of life.
>
> A feeling of great peace and contentment seemed to flow through my entire body. All sounds ceased and I seemed to be flowing in a great, very very still void or hemisphere. It is impossible to describe the overpowering feeling of peace, contentment, and being a part of goodness itself that I felt. I could feel my body dissolving and actually becoming a part of the goodness and peace that was all around me. Words can't describe this. I feel an awe and wonder that such a feeling could have occurred.[8]

These descriptions in some ways could also pass as Christian testimonies of what it means to have experienced crucifixion of the sinful life and the resurrection of the Christ-life. To the child of God who has experienced his power, an LSD trip, or a drug experience, is a counterfeit.

Our mother once remarked: "Make no mistake about it.

[8] David Solomon, *LSD: The Consciousness-Expanding Drug* (New York, Berkley Publishing Corp., 1966) pp. 165, 166.

Most of these kids are seekers and searchers after the supernatural. Why else has the world gone mad over the occult, the mysterious, and the ouija board? They recognize a world beyond and they dare delve into it. The fact that it's evil and leads them on to further destruction is not taken into account by them.

"One of our workers was asked to speak to a group of hippie searchers. She was asked to tell what her evangelistic church believed. After going down the line of salvation, separation and the Second Coming, she told how she got 'high.' She said, 'God created you with a hunger for highs. I admire you for going all out for what you believe in — no matter what your trip might cost you, your mind, or even your life. I would to God that all Christians were as sincere as you are. But God has provided His own way of a Christian high. That is the baptism of the Holy Spirit, wherein one is anointed by God's Spirit and worships Him in spirit and in truth in a heavenly language. This is real communion with the supernatural.' As one person, they all rose in unison and said, 'That's what we're looking for. That's what we want.' They hoped the speaker had a bagful to distribute. But when she told them that they must receive this experience by believing on Christ as Savior, that was just too high a price to pay."

The counselor should magnify his own "trip" to the cross of Calvary and show that what people are seeking in narcotics and in revolution is found through Christ. When a former hippie and LSD-user was asked if he thought he would ever go back to using the drug, he said, "No, because now I have found the ultimate thing. I have no need for the old ways."

5. *Reveal Christ as a "revolutionary" in the proper sense.* Militants and revolutionaries like to point out, "Jesus Christ wore long hair and He also was a revolutionary." They are right on both counts, but they are wrong in their understanding of what kind of revolution Jesus promoted. The counselor must make clear the type of revolution Christ advocated. He worked within the system. "Think not that I am come to destroy the law, or the prophets: I am not come to destroy, but to fulfil" (Matt. 5:17). His was a revolution of ideals, of principles, and of truth. True, He did reverse the whole concept of religious and

social progress, but He did not riot, or sit-in, throw bricks, or burn down synagogues, or lead marches through Jerusalem. When He was asked about taxes, He said they were to be paid. In spite of the fact that the Roman government was corrupt, Christ did not spend His time trying to lead a campaign to abolish it. He came to conquer the human heart, not Rome. His methods were not revolutionary (though they were supernatural), but His message was.

When a long-haired youth said to me, "What's wrong with long hair — didn't Jesus wear long hair?" I replied, "Yes, and Hitler wore a mustache. Does this mean that I should fear or hate everyone who wears a mustache?" The fact that Jesus wore long hair was a sign of conformity. Long hair was the custom of the day. The Pharisees, Sadducees, politicians and tax collectors — the squares — all wore long hair. To be a revolutionary in Christ's day you had to shave off your hair. When the revolutionaries identify themselves with Jesus, pin them down to the true meaning of His revolutionary message.

6. *Expose them to an evangelistic atmosphere and a Holy Spirit presence.* A hippie walked into one of our rallies and said, "Wow, the vibrations in this place are terrific!" He was caught by the presence of the Holy Spirit. He sensed God was there. Most young people are sensitive to other people. They can pick up adult feelings of hatred, anger and fear. They also know how to pick out the "vibrations" of their hippie life which they call peace and love. Therefore, it is not difficult for them to sense the "vibrations" of the Holy Spirit.

For soul-winning to take place with this type of person, they must be brought into an evangelistic atmosphere, but not too soon. Many churches have made a mistake by promoting a big rally without laying any groundwork of seed-sowing. The response is usually a disappointment — young people walk out, mock, or just sit indifferently. Big rallies should not be a substitute for real Christian witnessing. No evangelistic rally can be successful until preliminary preparations have been made.

Often those who run the Christian coffee house ministries and do on-the-street witnessing make the mistake of not following through by not introducing the young people to a Christian "vibration" rally. Often at a service where Christians come together to worship the Lord, the young person can sense the personal presence of Christ and the Holy Spirit. One young lady told us how she felt as she sat in a rally where I preached. She said, "My mind told me this was garbage, but my emotions and my spirit told me something else. When the altar call was given, I accepted Christ. Now my mind and my emotions are in one accord with Christ."

The now famous Woodstock festival, and other similar rock festivals, have certain similarities to an evangelistic, revival crusade. Woodstock was a place for them to sing and hear their message, to feel the presence of others with similar feelings — a place to sense the unholy spirit of the music, as well as to trip out with the aid of drugs. What the Woodstock generation sought is a substitute for a personal experience of Christ. What young people are finding in the church through Christ is what the Woodstockers were seeking at their revival festival.

7. *Use attractive, thought-provoking literature.* Most of the runaways, especially the radicals, represent youth of high intelligence. While many of them may not have control of their emotions, they are nevertheless deep thinkers. Give them literature dealing with the particular subject that is their bag. Literature written by sound biblical scholars has a tremendous appeal for students we have worked with. After the counselor has gained his attention and confidence, the young person usually will accept a Bible and promise to read it. Most of them claim to know the Bible, but in reality they only know *about* the Bible and have never studied it. They will say they are going to read it as literature. But whatever their reason (some accept the Bible to read and try to refute it), if they read it, it is bound to have a powerful and profound impact on them.

Dealing with rebels, runaways and revolutionaries — like dealing with addicts — entails a long counseling process.

8. *Aim for the heart, not the head.* Many counselors make the mistake of trying to reach a student only on an intellectual level. It is not possible to win an argument with a young person and then expect to lead him to Christ. The counselor who aims for the head — to defend God, the Bible, Jesus Christ — may win a debate but lose a soul. Remember, "the natural man receiveth not the things of

the Spirit of God: ... because they are spiritually discerned" (I Cor. 2:14). This does not mean the counselor should ignore the mind and the head. Isaiah did say, "Come now, and let us reason together" (1:18). To reach the bright, smart young person, the counselor must know how — to a certain degree — to communicate on his level. This does not mean the Christian worker needs a college degree to reach the bright young person. It does mean he must be knowledgeable and able to hold his own in discussions and conversations.

But reasoning can go only so far. The danger is to go too far and try to prove a point without letting the Holy Spirit "prove" it. There are some young people who reason out the truth before making a commitment to Christ. They make an intelligent decision to accept that "without faith it is impossible to please him (God); for he that cometh to God must believe that he is..." (Heb. 11:6). If they agree to the premise, then they must be willing to lay reason and man's knowledge aside and take the step of faith and accept Christ. Faith is the bridge between human reason and spiritual reality.

9. *Love, love, love.* Loving the drug addict may come easier to the Christian worker than loving the rebel, runaway or revolutionary. The addict most often responds to love. He may hate, but his hatred can be understood and accepted because of his condition. The addict, alcoholic or delinquent has a low melting point. They respond quickly to the "bug with love" process. Many younger, part-time runaways will, too, but not the hard-core rebels, radicals and revolutionaries. They view the Christian as part of the "system" and look upon the counselors as part of religious, capitalist manipulation. The counselor must prove he is not "plastic." He must prove he is "for real."

The addict will display his anger with deeds, the radical with words. His words, like knives, will cut deeply into the Christian counselor. He will challenge the counselor's sincerity, intelligence, motives, morals, faith — almost anything. Many workers leave our coffee houses feeling like they want to "shake the dust" off their feet. To say the least, it takes love, love and more love to reach and win the rebels, runaways and revolutionaries for Christ. They must be tapped with the drill of love.

9

THE SEXUAL GENERATION

A girl drug addict strolls the streets waiting to "turn a trick" (sell her body) to the highest, even the lowest, bidder.

A girl, an employee of a "madam," waits in an apartment house for her next customer.

A twenty-five-year-old woman, dressed in a fur coat, diamonds, and other expensive clothing, drives her Cadillac to Long Island to meet Mr. Businessman — husband of someone else — in a motel.

A fifteen-year-old girl and a seventeen-year-old boy, alone in her house, let their passions run too far; they engage in sexual intercourse; she gets pregnant.

A young lawyer dates his office secretary, ending the evening in bed with her.

Eight married couples eat, drink, joke together. They finish the night by tossing their car keys into a bowl; the women pick out a set of keys and go to bed with the man who owns them.

What do these actions have in common? Fornication? Adultery? Prostitution? Promiscuity? Yes, but they also reveal: (1) sexual hunger, (2) a distortion of the difference between sex and love, (3) a search for spiritual fulfillment, and (4) the effects of the "new morality."

We live in a society that condemns the street-walking prostitute but condones wife-swapping and "playboy" exploits. But the two are one and the same. Each of the above persons, to one degree or another, and in his or her own way, is expressing the same need.

The sexual generation poses three different, but in some ways similar, problems: (1) premarital sex, (2) pregnancy, and (3) prostitution. There are young people who engage in premarital sexual intercourse (the "premaritals"), those who become pregnant, and those who get hooked (prostitutes). The premaritals may remain sex-users, or they may get married and never violate their marital vows. But they may become sex abusers, and prostitutes themselves — either by the less-accepted manner (on the streets), or by the more-accepted manner (dating, sharing apartments, motels, or living in common-law relationships). We will look at these three problem areas and the people involved and discuss how these problems develop. Then we will suggest some helpful guidelines for the counselor who deals with such problems.

The Premarital Generation

Many young people who pride themselves on not being drug users or addicts have fallen into their own kind of addiction — premarital sex. They have taken the church's silence and lack of courage in facing the problem as either a license to practice premarital sex, or as a sign that no one cares or would understand if they wanted to talk about it. Some church-going young people feel the same way. Their thinking is changing drastically on the matter of premarital sex indulgence. If they are not reached, they may face a lifetime of misery from a mistake, or even get hooked into a sex trap and never get out.

The subject of sex must be handled properly from the pulpit, the dining room table, the classroom and the living room. Sex must not simply be condemned, it must be understood. A young person's ignorance can only lead to experimentation — and trouble. Ann Landers said it well when she stated: "Only a fool would tell a teenager to stop thinking about sex. They are thinking about sex and will continue to think about it. What they need is sound information so they will know *how* to think about it."

Moral pronouncements against sexual sin are simply not in vogue with many of today's clergy, religious leaders, and youth counselors. Too many, I fear, are not courageous enough to urge students and other youth to live by the biblical standards. Also behind this silence is the fear of being unpopular among the so-called secular-minded youth who take nothing on faith but must have scientific proof and what they term a rational approach to sexual mores.

We are reaping the effects of muting the biblical code on premarital sex. In one college 92 percent of those questioned approved of sex relations if the couples felt they were in love, even though they did not intend to become husband and wife. In *The Sexual Wilderness* Vance Packard writes about the results of his survey among young people ages 21 to 23. "To the question asked, whether regardless of age or stage, full intimacy would be considered 'appropriate' if both persons desired it and had a 'sense of trust, loyalty, protectiveness, and love.' "

U. S. Male Students . . . . . 70 percent
U. S. Female Students . . 60 percent[1]

Playboy's own national student survey showed only 18 percent of the males, and 49 percent of the females, who reported they had not had premarital sexual relations. Stated another way, 82 percent of the males reported to have practiced premarital sex, and 51 percent of the females said they indulge. In an identical survey of 1,030 secular college students the result showed 66 percent holding that sex relations before marriage were not wrong and twenty-nine percent said such relations were wrong. I think the comment of one girl in a university in New York City, as quoted by Vance Packard, sums up the attitude of the premaritals, "A girl doesn't have to be madly in love with every boy she sleeps with." She thinks that sometimes intimacy with a boy to whom she is only "casually attracted" could be "very important to her development."[2]

What is behind the premarital sex problem? To find answers we must look at the problems and needs of young

[1] Vance Packard, *The Sexual Wilderness* (New York, David McKay Co., 1968) pp. 163, 164.
[2] *Ibid.*

people themselves. Our search for answers must take us to the Scriptures, to the lessons of history, to the testimony of psychiatrists, psychologists and professional counselors. The following are some of the factors to be considered.

1. *The reaction against Puritanism.* One of the favorite arguments used to justify immorality is the so-called suppression of sex by our forefathers — our Puritan heritage. In an effort to get away from the "under the rug" approach to sex, the pendulum has swung to the opposite extreme. True, many young people do have hang-ups about sex because of the hush-hush attitude of days gone by. Children did grow up with the idea that sex was dirty, a part of the curse, or something to be endured but not enjoyed — a means of producing children and nothing else. Those who came from such restricted or repressive sexual backgrounds often suffered unhealthy guilt when their biological urges started to develop.

On the other hand, proponents of the "new morality" have gone too far in breaking away from "old-fashioned" morality. They are now using the old restrictions as a license to do whatever they want. Young people need a wholesome, healthy, balanced approach to sex. But we are not going to right any past wrongs by making sex a game, a toy, a cure-all, or a liberation from past sexual misinformation.

The moral revolution has come about not only because of a reaction to Puritan ideals, but also because there is a rebellion against any and all morality. When we speak of morality, we think immediately of matters of sex, but morality has to do with all matters of behavior and conduct. In throwing off standards of righteousness and holiness, our society has created a spiritual vacuum. Values which seemed absolute have been desacralized; decisions once clear-cut have been relativized; and simple ethical certainty, of the sort available to the average man, has gone. To a few, such bottomless freedom may be exhilarating, but to the ordinary man the impact is devastating.

> When men lose their sense of established standards, they tend to fall victim to an urge for pleasure or a lust for power. And when the loss of standards occurs during a period of peril, men seem to prefer pleasure to power.

The old morality was in need of renovation, but it had its

better side, and we have discarded the total fabric too in-discriminately.

Because of the spiritual vacuum, it has been easy for playboyism to come forward as the new authority — the new cult or religion.

But what has happened is that he (the playboy) is emancipated from past prejudices only to be victimized by contemporary ones.[3]

The moral revolutionists in seeking to rid themselves and us of one set of problems have fixed another rope in which they are hanging themselves slowly but surely. The new morality is the old immorality turned inside out — or painted with another coat of paint. They may have done society a favor in pointing out some of the falsehoods of past inconsistencies; however this does not qualify them to move in with their own set of rules. A new kind of wrong does not right past wrongs. "There is no liberation in escaping from one bondage only to be signed up as a devout believer and practicing member of the pleasure establishment."

Hugh Hefner, editorializing in one of his special magazine publications entitled *The Sexual Revolution* takes great pains to justify premarital and extra-marital sex by blaming God, the Bible, and Christianity. He states: "But what sort of God would have man deny his God-given sexual nature?" However, he fails to quote any biblical source in which God states such denial.

He further writes, "As much as religion has done for the development and growth of society, sex has done more." Again, he fails to state just how or in what way sex has helped our society.

His conclusion to the sexual problem, and his solution to his belief that religiously-inspired sexual suppression is harmful to society is summed up in these words: "To some these views represent a decline in moral standards — a turning away from the divinely revealed Word of God, as expressed in the Bible, the Ten Commandments and Judeo-Christian heritage that a majority of Christians share; to others they represent a facing up to 'facts of life,' an enlightened search for a new morality more in keeping with

[3] William S. Banowsky, *It's a Playboy World*, p. 20. Copyright © 1969 by Fleming H. Revell Company, Old Tappan, N.J.

modern man's greater understanding of both himself and the world in which he lives — a quest for a new code of conduct consistent with our conduct itself based upon reason rather than superstition.

"But whatever viewpoint one espouses, there is common agreement that a sexual revolution is taking place and that the old religious restrictions have little or no influence on the sexual behavior of a sizeable segment of our society. For these citizens, at least, a new, more acceptable moral code must be found."[4]

We must not surrender to some of our intellectuals, writers, thinkers, philosophers, Hefnerites and clergymen who succumbed to the notion that if people cannot live up to the biblical standards, there must be something wrong with the standards.

Norman Vincent Peale in his book, *Sin, Sex and Self-Control,* writes about freedom from all authority and all restraints. "This trend began some fifty years ago as a revolt against Victorian prudery, and no one denies today that Victorian attitudes toward sex were rigid, repressive, and unrealistic. But the curious thing was that the revolt was led, more often than not, by individuals whose attitudes toward sex were hardly normal to begin with. . . . Gradually, and perhaps inevitably, the revolt against repressiveness in sex became a revolt against conventional morals. It was Hemingway, idol of a whole generation, who could write that 'What is moral is what you feel good after, and what is immoral is what you feel bad after.' What nonsense. Under this weird code of ethics Hitler could have told himself that slaughtering the Jews was a moral act because it made him feel happy. Millions of people gladly accepted his dictum as some kind of gospel."[5]

2. *A love-sex conflict and misunderstanding.* The reasoning of some young people is: "If we love each other, why can't we have sexual relations? We are going to get married anyway, so why not?" Others take a more liberal approach and state: "How can we know we will be compatible if we do not know each other sexually before we are mar-

[4] *The Sexual Revolution* (HMH Publishing House, Chicago, 1970).

[5] Norman Vincent Peale, *Sin, Sex and Self-Control,* p. 62. Copyright © 1965 by Norman Vincent Peale. Reprinted by permission of Doubleday & Company, Inc.

ried?" A young man will say to his girlfriend, "If you love me, you'll show it by going all the way with me." The young lady on the other hand reasons: "I'll lose him if I don't give him what he wants."

The tragic notion has been inflicted on today's youth that sex is love, and that if you love someone you should express it through sex. They think that to indulge in premarital intercourse is to prove love. The wildest concept of all is that by sharing the privileges of intimacy before marriage the couple will find out if they are meant for each other. Research reveals, however, that premarital sex is no guarantee against marriage break-up. Divorce records show that there is a greater rate of divorce where there was premarital sex. If sex were love, then perhaps the trial marriage, or "shop around" approach would work. Love may result in sexual intimacy, but sexual intimacy does not always, or necessarily, end or begin with love. Most often sexual intimacy is lust, under the guise of love. *Love requires neither sex nor marriage for satisfaction.* People who are in love want to marry, but love does not necessarily need sex to prove itself.

Premarital sex creates more problems and more marriage failures because the people who were enjoying sex thought they were also growing to love each other. Later they discovered that sex blocked the development and maturing of true love. Young people who come together in body only do not allow themselves to come together in mind, spirit and personality. They do not see each other for what they really are. This is comparable to drug usage. While the addict is shooting dope, his emotional and mental growth are stunted and stopped. So it is with those who get high on sex. To build a marriage on such a relationship is to build on quicksand. Eventually one or both partners wakes up; they see each other and themselves as they really are and the sex or marriage balloon bursts. Both suffer a shattering experience. Neither one may be able, from that point on, to determine what is love and what is sex.

"Love" that is sex alone is a barrier that keeps real love from being expressed in so many other important ways that are absolutely vital for any lasting relationship or marriage.

Being one in flesh before being one in spirit ruins any relationship.

> Too early sexual involvement can blind the pair to the other important aspects of their relationship that they should be building as a foundation for their marriage. All too often they fall into bed together rather than talk out the many things that need to be shared and discussed. Once sexual intercourse starts, their interpersonal communication slackens in many a case. Thus in their coming together the couple may lose the very thing they sought to ensure — intimacy and companionship.
>
> The danger of premarital sexual relations between lovers is a weakening of their feelings for one another on the one hand, and the possibility of too great involvement on the other hand.[6]

Those that meet together, flesh to flesh, will not meet together heart to heart, spirit to spirit, and eye to eye. It is the non-physical communication that reinforces the sex act. The former is essential for the fullest enjoyment of the latter. No marriage can last on sex alone. Premarital sex is a marriage blocker, not a marriage mender or maker.

> The evidence of antiquity and the findings of modern psychology concur in the conclusion that sexual intercourse is not one act among many; it is an act without comparison, a possibility for achieving and expressing human fulfillment unique unto itself. Thus the abuse of sexuality is a serious assault upon man's very nature. Sexual intercourse involves more than the body; it involves the whole person, or, more accurately, two persons. Whether they give themselves wholly to each other is one thing, but that they are wholly involved is beyond doubt. No act of sexual union may ever be regarded as recreational or as one person's private business, for someone else is always profoundly implicated and the participants will never again be the same towards one another as they were before coming together. Once done, the experience will never be undone, and its effect, though imperceptible, is indelible. If they are husband and wife, the embrace should be the source and symbol of the common life they are building together. But if they are not husband and wife, the sexual act is of such significance that its unitive power is frustrated. Intercourse without obligation depersonalizes the parties involved, uniting them in an act of mutual exploitation. It is not because it is temporary, but because, in a sense, casual

[6] Evelyn Millis Duvall, *Why Wait Till Marriage* (New York, Association Press, 1965) p. 43.

sex always involves permanent consequences, that it is intrinsically wrong.[7]

If sex were love, and if premarital sex guaranteed a successful marriage, then the best thing a couple could do is to learn all they can about the techniques of love-making and sexual intercourse. Clinics could be set up to teach such methods, and the result would be that everyone would live happily ever after. But young people are finding out that although they may be "making out" more, they are coming out with less in the end, in terms of loving and caring for each other. If sex guaranteed a good marriage, then the best man or woman in bed would make the best kind of partner. But in many cases what one is in the sex act, and what one is apart from that, are often two different things. The how-to sex manuals cannot tell a couple how to survive outside the bedroom.

It is true that some marriages are hindered because of incompatibility in sexual matters. But this only adds further proof that sex is not love, and love does not guarantee successful sex. They are not always one and the same. Incompatibility in sex can be caused by tensions in the nonphysical or nonsexual relationships of the couple, or it can be caused by a misunderstanding about sex itself. Most marriages do not break up because of too little sex, but rather because of sex without love, and sex sharing without love sharing.

Many young women have been tragically disappointed by trying to use sex to sell their boyfriends on marriage. A girl explained: "I figured if I let him have me, I would have him. But the more we were intimate in sex, the less we were intimate as persons." Many young men, when dating a girl, will go all-out for sex, purely for physical gratification. But these same fellows want *their* brides to be virgins. If such a fellow tests his girlfriend to see if she will give in (really wanting her to keep her chastity), and the girl does give in, the fellow immediately will lose his respect for her and the relationship may go downhill from that point on.

3. *Sex as a pleasure and as a game.* Some persons are confused about sex and love, others are not confused —

[7] William Banowsky, *Ibid.,* p. 230.

they know just what they are doing; they go after sex for the sheer pleasure of it. For them sex is a matter-of-fact thing, casual and recreational — a game. A young high school student said, "Most of my friends do not consider sex to be a problem. It's just something we like to do and to have fun with." He was honest, yet self-deceived.

Others who want sex for sex alone sometimes cover up their desire by saying they are in love. Few people are honest enough to admit that they are breaking the seventh commandment for the simple and understandable reason that they enjoy sexual intercourse. They justify themselves by stating that they are in love with one another. For these people sex is a pastime to be indulged in, in the same way a person drinks, smokes, eats, goes to movies, and so on. The Russians once lived by this philosophy; they called it the "drink of water" approach to sex. Whenever you were hungry sexually — like being thirsty for a glass of water — you reached out and took someone to satisfy your sexual appetite. But they have since abandoned this attitude, because:

"Within a few years hordes of wild, homeless children became a real menace to the Soviet Union itself. Millions of lives, especially of young girls, were wrecked; divorce sky-rocketed, as did abortions. The hatreds and conflicts between polygamous and polyandrous mates rapidly mounted — so did psychoneuroses. Work in the national factories slackened. The total result was so appalling that the government was forced to reverse its policy."[8] The Russians found that the "no holds barred" approach to sex did not work. The unconscious sex drive plays havoc if it is not brought under conscious control; if sex drives are given free rein, civilized life is impossible.

American society, to an ever greater degree, is headed in the direction of casual sex. Novels, the lyrics of popular songs, movies, television, magazines and advertising all seem to be saying sex is fun, fun, fun: "If it feels good, do it. Because it's fun and no one should be denied it," the message seems to be. The conclusion of the sex advertising bombardment is that you have not lived until you have proven, and enjoyed yourself, sexually. "Teen-agers

[8] Norman Vincent Peale, *Ibid.*, pp. 78, 79.

are stimulated by advertisers to buy more and to want more. Advertisers suggest that the way to be popular is to rev up the sex appeal. Sex screams from the billboards. Everybody is lying down with someone."[9]

God intended the sex act to be pleasurable. The Puritans and Victorians implied it was evil. Some pious people refuse to admit to themselves and others that they derive pleasure from it. But sex for pleasure only — any time, any place, with anyone — is a gross distortion of what God intends the sex act to be. To treat something so pleasurable and beautiful, and divinely instituted, as a glass of wine, a game, or as you would a drug, is to cheapen it and rank it with the animal habits. Sex for the sake of sex alone debases both the one who plays the game and the one who is the object. The playboy implies: "I am a machine. I have been created purely as a physical being whose primary function is to enjoy himself and to satisfy his craving for food, water and sex." The person who plays the sexual game deceives himself into thinking he is proving his manhood, when in reality he is saying he is not a whole person made up of mind, spirit and body; he is saying, instead, that he is just body and flesh. "The paradox of the playboy philosophy is that, while seeming to glorify sex, it really depreciates it. . . . When one makes sex a plaything, he forfeits the real thing. Playboys grow old wondering why they are playing more but enjoying it less."[10]

We have found that with many drug addicts one of the factors (at least on the surface) which led them into drug usage was that they engaged in sex pleasure at such an early age that by the time they were in their late teens the thrill and kick of it had worn off, so they opened themselves to new searches for kicks. A fellow said, "I smoked at twelve, was drinking at thirteen, drinking more at fourteen, engaged in sex at will at fifteen, was in gigs (orgies) at sixteen. By the time I was seventeen I was ready to die. I had tried about everything the world and the devil had to offer; drugs became the next step."[11]

The result of sex as a game, or sheer pleasure, is "that

[9] Ann Landers, *Ann Landers Talks to Teen-Agers About Sex* (New York, Fawcett World Library, 1963) pp. 18, 19.

[10] William Banowsky, *Ibid.,* p. 90.

[11] Norman Vincent Peale, *Ibid.,* p. 80.

it becomes progressively less exciting, less thrilling, more barren and more sterile. That's why so many of these people turn eventually to alcohol, or drugs, or twisted versions of sex, anything that seems to offer new kicks."[12]

4. *Sex as an escape.* Fornication often is the result of trying to escape a problem. Long before drugs came along as the new way to escape life's realities, sex was number one on the escaper's hit parade. Before the drug crash pad there was the car pad, the teen-age motel on wheels where young people could park, pet, and play with the fires of sex. "More than any other single factor in the past thirty years, the automobile has exerted the strongest influence on teen-age behavior. . . . It is a status symbol and a passport to freedom. Six gallons of gasoline can propel a couple of teen-agers into another world. A car can be a portable bedroom — 'even with those crummy bucket seats,' as one teen stated."[13]

When mom and dad are away, the teens will play. If the home is a "pressure cooker," if mother and father fail in their responsibilities, if there is a moral and spiritual vacuum in the lives of young people, sex can become the most natural and the easiest form of escape.

Various studies have shown that school drop-outs are more likely to take sexual liberties and subsequently "get into trouble." Those who have high ideals, who are goal-conscious, have less need to turn to sex to prove themselves, to find love, and to have a sense of accomplishment. Those who drop out of school, or are failures at school, or in life, have a sense of worthlessness. They look to sex for the satisfaction they could and should be getting out of other fulfillments in life. Sex is one of the most convenient forms of escape, in that it requires no education, no talent, and no character to make an attempt at it.

A young woman related, "I couldn't wait to get out of my house and away from my parents. I decided that getting pregnant would be one easy way to get out." Those who use sex as a getaway, and to fulfill emotional or spiritual needs, are often the most lonely, disillusioned, distressed and disappointed with sex itself. "With each indul-

[12] *Ibid.*
[13] Ann Landers, *Ibid.,* p. 19.

gence the level of physical and emotional expectation gradually rises so that an increasingly greater thrill is required to satisfy the urge. Eventually the thrill begins to diminish, but the hunger for stimulation is ever present, now stronger than before. Without finding full satisfaction, the hunger need settles into the monotony of filling and emptying."[14]

As with taking drugs, in sex the pleasure and thrill can also build up tolerance. With each indulgence the need or expectation becomes greater, and thus the potential for disappointment is likewise greater. It is not that the sex act itself is perhaps less pleasurable; it is that the emotional need is greater. The effect, however, is that the sex act seems not to satisfy.

Sexual dissatisfaction leads in various directions, just as drug tolerance leads to more powerful doses, or to more of the same drug. Some seek heightened pleasure by playing the field; married couples by infidelity, divorce, wife-swapping; or more sexual power through smoking marijuana. More and more, so-called "respectables" are trying to turn on more and better sex with pot. A *Playboy* magazine national campus survey of students' attitudes on today's major issues (*Playboy* magazine, September 1970) revealed the following differences of sexual practices among non-marijuana smokers and marijuana smokers. The survey found that among the non-pot smokers 20 percent of the males and 62 percent of the females had never practiced premarital sex. However, among the pot smokers, only 6 percent of the males and 14 percent of the females had never been involved in premarital sexual activities. The increased sexual activity among pot smokers is significant.

One fellow told us, "I kept having sexual experiences to prove to myself I was a man. But the more I got involved the less pleasure I was getting. So I started needing alcohol or marijuana to loosen me up. The only trouble was, I found if I didn't mix sex with booze or pot, I couldn't get turned on."

Because under the influence of marijuana the smoker is less inhibited, feelings regarding sex become free and open. Marijuana not only expands the mind — it loosens the morals. Some doctors are now prescribing "pot" for sex-

[14] William Banowsky, *Ibid.*, p. 50.

ually incompatible couples. Such a prescription is felt to aid middle-aged or older couples who are "bored" sexually, or when one or the other partner cannot experience total sexual expression due to emotional conflicts. Some single girls and men are now carrying marijuana around to give to dates as a method of accomplishing seduction — just as alcohol and sex is mixed for the same purpose.

The danger of using "pot" as a cure-all for sexual release is that it can become a permanent tool in a couple's sex life. One fellow said, "I got to the place where I feared any sexual contact, even social contact, if I didn't have 'pot.' " But the most tragic outcome of those who look for sexual power in marijuana is that they may not be able to control unleashed lusts. Married couples who smoke together can end up in bed with their closest friend's wife or husband. It is now popular for married couples who are already practicing swapping partners (swingers) to use pot to assist them in their weird search for sexual fulfillment. However, even where such practices never took place, married couples who previously never for a moment entertained the thought of sharing sex with a friend — sadly end up doing so when stoned with pot.

Marijuana, in our estimation, supposedly helps those couples who have never known spiritual and emotional togetherness. The sex part of their marriage was no different than that of prostitute and client-partner — the only thing they really shared in life together was sex. Such physical relationships soon wear out. Any couple living together body with body, sex symbol with sex symbol, is going to end up sexually bored. For these couples "pot" provides a momentary new sex kick. Most, however, do not know the devil they may unleash in themselves. The eye is never satisfied with seeing — and the sex explorer may not be satisfied until he has experienced all — conquered neighbor's wife — or whoever.

Middle-class people now use "pot" to expand their shrinking sex lives. The users say that marijuana makes them less inhibited, helps them find fuller self-expression, helps them to relate easier, and blocks out external distortions. The use of marijuana to heighten sex satisfaction reinforces our argument that premarital and extramarital sex exploits lead only to sexual *dis*satisfaction, not to sexual satisfaction.

5. *Sex as a temptation.* We should not overlook the fact that sex is a natural part of the human make-up. Sexual desire and expression of affection are natural. Because of this and the external forces in society, sex is a temptation even to the dedicated Christian. Sex, like other forces in life, can be good or bad, right or wrong, natural or unnatural. The same act that brings pleasure can bring misery. "Other desires in life may be rather easily deterred or sublimated, but not so with sex. God has given men and women strong attraction toward one another. It is this intense force which, if not directed to honor God, surges like a mighty river, leaving untold problems in its wake."[15]

The beauty of sex has been marred by sin. Because of this we find ourselves in the inescapable position in which the apostle Paul found himself when he said, "The good which I want to do, I fail to do; but what I do is the wrong which is against my will" (Rom. 7:10, NEB). Sex is a temptation because the flesh wants to go in one direction and the Holy Spirit in another. The flesh is in conflict with the Spirit. Controlled sex can be a blessing; uncontrolled, it can be a fire that destroys. The enemy continually tries to use it against the Christian. He wants to take a thing of beauty and turn it into just a "thing" and to drag it into the gutter and outside the bounds of righteousness and holiness.

Another factor in sex temptation is the people who do the tempting. The tempter (Satan) has a bunch of little tempters helping him with his temptation business. They portray sex as America's favorite pastime. Advertisers seem to have an organized effort to extend and intensify desire. They have succeeded in brainwashing the American male into believing that the truly successful man is the truly sensual man. Even the federal government goes along with the sex stimulation process. A job corps center bought $10,000 worth of books with such titles as *Orgy at Madam Dracula's* and *Sex Turned On* as part of a reading program. An official of the center, now closed, described the books as "soul material."

Counseling About Premarital Sex

Counseling must begin with those in their early teens

[15] Clyde M. Narramore, *Psychology of Counseling* (Grand Rapids, Zondervan, 1960) p. 207.

and with preteens, when puberty begins in the female and sexual awareness begins in the male. While sex education courses are being recommended and conducted on the grade school level, this may only further complicate sex questions if personal counseling — either formally or informally — is not instituted as youngsters reach physical maturity. There is a difference between classroom sex education and personal and individual counseling with young people. The latter is a step beyond the textbook approach. It is the come-down-to-the-young-person's-level-and-talk-about-sex approach, for which there is no substitute.

Most of those we have dealt with who have been heavily involved in numerous sexual practices are actually ignorant about sex. One fellow said, "I learned everything I knew about sex on the street corner. Now I know the two-bit street corner sex counselor knew nothing. If only someone had sat me down and talked to me before I got married, I wouldn't have gone through so many difficulties."

One researcher dealing with prostitutes found that most of them were not fully and rightly informed about sex. Ministers and Christian workers should not assume that a young person who has been converted from a life of promiscuity is properly informed about sex. Most of the young people in Teen Challenge who have experimented sexually from an early age are confused, perverted, or unsure about proper sex information.

The best way to begin is with an honest, open discussion. Neither "beating around the bush" nor oversimplification, nor straight-laced prohibition are adequate approaches to sex counseling for today's young people. Ann Landers, who ought to know when it comes to youth's sex problems, says, "What they need is sound information so they will know how to think about it." Most of us would rather deal with any other problem than sex. But the counselor can be effective in counteracting some of the unhealthy, mysterious, gutter sources of information about sex. Rather than get his knowledge only from books, sex education courses, magazines, peers, or other adults who volunteer information, the young person needs to get it from a trustworthy resource person. Especially in need of counseling are the teens who haven't yet tried sex but who are on the verge of doing so. They are thinking about it and attention must particularly be given to those who are going steady.

In urgent need of the counselor's help are those who already decided to become members of the "premarital sexual relations club." Finding out who they are is the hardest task. Only a few counselors have the ability and the rapport with young people to obtain such information, either by careful probing or through the willing submission of information by the young person himself.

> I believe that sex attitudes are formed early in life and that it's important to reach young people at that critical point where they are ready to break away from traditional external authority and are groping for self-discovered standards of their own.
>
> Youngsters talk about sex a lot, but apparently they are ignorant about the general functions of the body. They do not discuss their concern about sex with adults very much, and when they do they are often given inadequate answers. We must also deal with the attitude of the high school girls who, in their bull sessions, instead of discussing how to turn a boy down, often talk instead about the danger of pregnancy and how they would break the news to their parents.
>
> We need ministers and Christian counselors who will take the time for straight, frank talk about sex and about the role of religion in sex. Some parents I have talked with feel they cannot instruct their children in sexual behavior because they don't feel capable of explaining it. They hem and haw and make excuses and act as though children have no right to ask about sex. One mother I know told her daughter, "Don't even mention sex to us again. You should respect your mother more than that. Don't embarrass me that way again." This breakdown of communication puts an unfair burden of responsibility on the child.[16]

Following are suggestions about how to counsel young people with sex problems:

1. *Provide a comfortable setting.* The counselor must ask himself, "Am I the kind of person others would feel comfortable talking with about something so personal and intimate as their sexual hang-ups?" The Christian counselor who hasn't solved his own sexual hang-ups will not be able to make others feel comfortable when discussing their problems. Young people complain that they just do not know anyone in whom they have enough confidence to approach.

[16] David Wilkerson, *Parents on Trial* (New York, Hawthorne, 1967), pp. 141, 142, 143, 144.

The counselor should not express shock, disappointment or disgust when the person comes with a confession of sin, or to talk about a problem. A young lady, twenty-eight years of age, came to us — she was pregnant. Her family were faithful members in a suburban evangelical church. Their daughter was actively faithful as well. When she found out she was going to have a baby from an unconverted man she had been dating, she came for help. "I made a mistake, and there was no one to turn to. I cannot tell my parents, they are along in years and would just not be able to understand. This would just shock them too much."

After discussing her case fully we accepted her at Teen Challenge as an office worker. This had been one of the first cases over the years of a Christian girl getting into trouble who has come to us for help and advice. My first reaction was to condemn and to sermonize, but it immediately became apparent that the situation called for compassion not for condemnation. She had already suffered waves of tremendous guilt, nothing more needed to be said to add to it. What she needed was someone to talk to and who would, as she said, "understand."

From our first talk together we did not moralize, condemn, or seek to punish her. Our task was to accept her just as she was and to provide words of comfort for her guilt, not to reinforce it.

Often adults and Christians develop the attitude that sex sin is different from all other sins — and that man is God's instrument to punish one who has fallen. Apparently, David, the psalmist, found a comfortable setting when he went to the Lord after his sex sin, for he wrote in Psalm 32:5: "I acknowledge my sin unto thee, and my iniquity have I not hid. I said, I will confess my transgressions unto the Lord; and thou forgavest the iniquity of my sin." He wrote as well in the opening verse of the same chapter, "Blessed is he whose transgression is forgiven, whose sin is covered." We might add to this our own translation, "Blessed is he who understands and forgives the one who has transgressed, who doesn't try to uncover the sin God has already covered."

Avoid such reactions as, "Oh, how could you do a thing like that!" or, "Don't you know that's wrong?" or, "God will punish you for this." That will only cause the person to go deeper into a shell of guilt or fear. The first reaction should be one of understanding and compassion, so the individual will open up and pour out the whole story.

A sex problem is often hidden behind other problems. In such cases the sex problem must be uncovered. "A person's problem may not be a sex problem as much as a life problem.... He will set up several sessions to look at his school life, his family life, his spiritual life and his social life."[17] By working at some of the surface problems and showing a genuine interest in the counselee's overall life situation, a relationship can be built upon which the sex problem will either come out naturally, or the counselor will be able to dig it out.

2. *Take a positive approach.* The counselor should not try to scare young people into chastity or out of promiscuity by painting a picture of sex that is only sinful, ugly or dirty. The young person will have already found out that sex can produce guilt and even be disappointing. Sex should be presented as something you step *up* into, at the right time and in the right way, not something you stumble or fall into.

Young people should be taught that sex surrounded by the sanctity of marriage is something that is wholly good. For example, share the fact that "the physical pleasures a man and woman find in each other amplify and confirm their sense of commitment and joy in each other. Outside of this relationship, sex is a distortion of the divine plan of God. Sex was designed as a means (not an end in itself) of assisting in the development of that most intimate of all human relationships between husband wife."[18]

"Married lovers come together free of guilt and shame. They have fewer qualms of conscience than those who are haunted by the ghostly reminders of previous affairs. Jealousies born of comparisons with former partners are avoided by a husband and wife who wait for marriage before being active sexually. It is a rare husband who is completely happy in the knowledge that his wife has slept with some other man before she married. Even the most sophisticated lover is proud to marry a virgin whom he alone possesses.

[17] Clyde Narramore, *Ibid.*, p. 231.
[18] Larry Richards, *How Far Can I Go* (Chicago, Moody Press, 1969).

The predominant reaction of wives discovering their husbands' premarital experience with previous girls is unfavorable. Sex reserved for marriage starts out with a clean slate upon which the marriage partners write their own love story in their own way from the beginning."[19]

If the sexual generation can be made to see the beauty of sex as God intended it to be, the counselor and parents do not have to dream up scare tactics. Young people must not fear sex, but rather respect it and wait to "step up" into it.

"Down through the ages, some of the most thunderous don'ts leveled at mankind have to do with sex. This is not surprising, because sex is just about the most powerful and explosive force that is built into us.

"Don't rely too heavily on 'don't.' While there are negative reasons for not doing something, there are often positive reasons for doing the reverse. Seek for them, find your motivation in them, and you will come much closer to your goal."[20]

3. *Exalt the authority of the Scriptures.* In the final analysis, whether young people keep themselves pure sexually will be determined by their acceptance of Jesus Christ as Savior from sin and Lord of their lives — including one's sex life. They must accept the Word of God as their final authority and the only authority in matters dealing with sex. He did not invent sex just to tempt people, but to add to their earthly and spiritual enjoyment. When God confined the sex act to the boundary lines of marriage, He gave man the ability to live within these regulations and He warned that violations of His commands in this regard would bring sorrow and misery. He knew what He was doing.

"The choice is inescapable, and I am convinced that in this confusing and complicated area of sex conduct self-discipline is the key. Not grim, authoritative, threatening rules from without, but patient, watchful, steady, intelligent responsibility from within."[21]

Young people need to be challenged to make the right choice for themselves, as they come to know and accept God's authority. It cannot be a case of the counselor's

[19] Evelyn Millis Duvall, *Ibid.,* p. 89.
[20] Norman Vincent Peale, *Ibid.,* p. 44.
[21] *Ibid.*

saying, "You must not do it because I said so," but rather a case of the young person's deciding, "I am going to abstain from premarital sex because I feel this is best for me and it is what God wants me to do."

"Make him see that there is one authority that he won't resent — and that authority is himself. If he gives the orders, if he demands the discipline, if he sets the standards high, then he won't resent the controls."[22]

4. *"Tell it like it is" about the backlash of promiscuity.* In addition to asserting the authority of Christ and the Scriptures in matters of sexual relations before marriage, the counselor must "tell it like it is" and give stern warning of the possible after-effects. "Sex outside marriage is a bad bargain when you measure what you stand to gain against what you stand to lose. It's just not worth it," says Ann Landers.[23] It may be helpful if another young person who has gone through some of the sorrows of an affair, or an unwed mother, can be brought into the discussion.

One of the most serious aftereffects, especially for a young person who has had high moral teachings instilled in him, is the feeling of guilt. One college student has theorized that one of the reasons for the unrest among today's campus youth is that they are trying to overcome their feelings of unconscious guilt from their immorality. This is one of the bad bargains that must be weighed against the momentary thrill that sexual intercourse provides. Here is part of a letter we received from a girl:

"For the past three months I have prayed and prayed. I have asked the Lord to forgive me and to take my sin away. I prayed that he would help me. I even went to church in the afternoon alone sometimes and sat there and cried, but sometimes I only felt half forgiven. I knew God was there watching me, but I was afraid He wanted to kick me out of His kingdom forever."

Another after-effect of premarital sex is the feeling of having been exploited. A girl told me, "At first I really thought it was true love; he said sweet nothings to me, but then I discovered he was just using me; I was just a body."

In the letter quoted above, the girl wrote: "The boys are

[22] *Ibid.*, p. 77.
[23] Ann Landers, *Ibid.*, p. 43.

all out to 'get the girls.' They are cool if they do, and the girls have to fight it. The trouble is, the boys plan and scheme every possible way to break a girl down. Some use the rape method, some are more subtle. Some will lie, and make you think they can be trusted, and all along they are just waiting for a weak spot. Some talk their way through. I have been out with all of them and until Billy came along I held up. But girls are weak, too. It is hard sometimes to say no. A person can stand only so much. Boys want to marry 'nice girls' and yet they are all-out to break every 'nice girl' down. It doesn't seem fair."

5. *Forgive the fallen.* The young lady whose letter is quoted above is typical of many who write with similar problems. Whether such letters come because it is easier for the guilt-ridden person to write to someone they do not have to encounter personally, or whether they come because they do not have anyone in the church or the community to turn to for help — we do not know. We fear it is the latter reason that prompts many such letters.

Many are forceful in preaching against petting, promiscuity, and fornication — but few know how to handle the sinners. And so some sin the more.

Whether it is a problem of petting, promiscuity, or premarital or extra-marital sex, the guilt may be the same. Many young ladies have felt like one teenage girl who spoke to me about her petting. "I feel like a slut," she said. It was as though she had committed the full sexual act as far as the guilt that followed. For such guilty persons the counselor is the bridge from condemnation, shame, guilt, and depression, to forgiveness, cleansing, and freedom. If the counselor is the parent of the fallen, or pastor, Sunday school teacher, youth leader, or close friend, the guilty will also feel they have personally offended the counselor. This presents another problem in counselor-counselee relationships.

The counselor must watch for the fallen client, especially the Christian who has failed, who has a need to do penance. Guilty persons — psychologically, emotionally, and spiritually — feel a need to do something for their wrong doings. They want to punish themselves in payment and penalty for their sin. One young convert at Teen Challenge returned from a weekend at home and became sick. "God is punishing me," he told me. He then confessed he had committed fornication. Perhaps he became psychologically ill to punish himself. Rather than accept the chastisement of spirit and soul the guilty want physical or emotional chastisement to pay the penalty for their sin.

The guilty may also feel a need to be punished by the counselor. They may be saying to themselves, "He (the counselor) is disgusted with me," "He doesn't want anything to do with me anymore," "I won't be accepted any longer." This feeling of self-rejection is projected to the counselor to satisfy the client's punishment need. Avoid being caught by such a punishment complex and of being manipulated by the fallen person into a position as a whipping lash against them.

Those who have fallen into sexual sin need patience and pity, not punishment. The counselor's role is to be an agent to bring healing, not to haunt the client. The most serious crisis the church faces today is the need for leaders who know how to forgive the sensuous and the sexual generation. When the fallen can see forgiveness coming through a human instrument, then perhaps they can find assurance in Christ that "as far as the east is from the west" so far has He removed their sexual sin from God's remembrance. The counselor's attitude should be, "Neither do I condemn thee."

6. *Other tips.* The counselor should not forget other problem areas in addition to the sex problem. One factor in sex problems is the person's inability to accept himself as he is. Many of the young men who come to Teen Challenge as drug addicts have hang-ups about their physical make-up; they are too short, too fat, too skinny, too ugly, or whatever. They have an identity crisis. This often affects their sense of manhood and sexuality. This dissatisfaction with self leads them to emulate others, or to seek acceptance with their bodies. A person who sees himself in the "image of God" and as the "temple of the Holy Spirit" will not put a cheap price tag on himself and will think twice about giving his or her body to anyone, without regard for God's will.

Other helpful suggestions have to do with keeping the right company, having a large circle of wholesome friends, and avoiding the dangers of going steady. Those who do go steady can avoid temptation if they double and triple date. Going steady in isolation puts the couple in a position of sexual temptation; it also stunts the development of a well-rounded outlook on life. Young people who develop a wide circle and variety of friends are better prepared for life later on, have a greater opportunity to find the right partner, and most of all, will find themselves less frequently in compromising, tempting situations in regard to sexual matters.

Young people must also be instructed to avoid petting and borderline promiscuity. Warnings of the dangers of "arousements" should be made firm and clear. Too many play the "see how far we can go" game and do everything but commit the final climactic sex act. Jesus said those who practiced mental or 'thought' adultery are guilty of the actual deed. No one ever wins in such a game of promiscuity. Those who spend too much time alone, who keep the wrong company, who expose themselves to risque movies, and who go to sensuous parties or gatherings, or who read novels, magazines, or literature that is sexually stimulating — are moving out of the sexual safety zone and into the "passion pit." Norman Vincent Peale's advice to young people should be offered by all Christian counselors. He advises, "Make a commitment. This is the key, I think, to sanity in sex. You have to use your intelligence to discern the values of self-restraint."

Unwed Mothers

Let us look at the why, what and how of the problem of counseling those involved in the unfortunate tragedy of pregnancy and out-of-wedlock childbirth. Why does it happen? What courses of action can be taken by the mother-to-be, the young man involved, and the families and friends? What should be done before and after the child arrives? Should the baby be kept? What should be said, what not said? What should be done, and not done?

Why do girls get into trouble? Pregnancy may be the result of rebellion. It may be a way to get even with parents for wrongs inflicted, or a way to get attention.

Pregnancy often occurs just because a couple fell into temptation and made a sorry mistake. Young people are open to temptation, they play with fire, and have no one but themselves to blame for the outcome. In spite of the pill, this still happens. There are those who had never previously indulged in sex relations, but who suddenly found themselves in a compromising situation. In the heat of passion they let the barriers down and pregnancy resulted. Pregnancy often happens in cases like this because no spiritual or moral precautions were taken. The couple did not plan or intend to have sexual intercourse.

Young people who determine, through the help and strength of the Lord, not to engage in premarital sex have the best and only protection. Those who say, "I couldn't help it," or, "It just happened," or, "I made a sad mistake" could have avoided trouble if they had made spiritual and practical disciplinary preparations. The fires of passion must be fought with fire — the fire of God's power. This letter shows what can happen when a young person is indifferent about the fires of sexual passion:

"I am known as a well-respected girl by my friends and family. I held a secretarial job after graduating from high school, and I attended junior college for two quarters. A good friend got me a date with a boy whom I knew about but had never actually met. . . . I dated him about one month and he told me he cared for me. He had a good personality and tried to be a little too cool sometimes about wine, women and song — and he was part of the crowd. We went to the show one night and afterward he told me we were going to his home. Well, I didn't like that. It didn't look right and I was afraid — of me and him. We argued but he got his way. . . . I went inside but I wouldn't go near the bedrooms. I stayed in the den. Then things began to happen. It kept getting worse and worse until sin took over completely."

She could have avoided trouble, but her moral restraint was very weak; she put up only a shallow fight. There were no spiritual forces behind her to help in the fight.

In cases when, in spite of sincerity and Christian commitment, the young person fails, the road back is long and difficult. But the trip must be made. The fact that restoration is possible is seen in the life of David in the Old Testament and in the example of Mary Magdalene who many feel was the woman Jesus forgave for adultery and while her accusers sought to kill her wrote "love letters in the sand."

The difficulty in the case of the Christian girl who becomes pregnant — and cannot leave home — is that the evidence of her sin is paraded before herself and others for about six months. And if she keeps the child, for years later. The key is a counselor who will serve as a close friend to the girl during pregnancy and following the birth of the child.

We have seen too many in our street ministry who were condemned and cast out of the church by unforgiving and *unforgetting* church members who never let the unwed girl, or the young man involved — "live it down" — or should we say live it back up to a place of regular fellowship in the body of Christ. Even family members and relatives have been victims in such cases of Christian condemnation.

We must advise young people as forcefully as we possibly can to avoid sexual sin — but when it happens nothing is gained by a "Why did you do that," or "You shouldn't have done that," or "Get yourself out of this mess" attitude. We must honestly, practically, calmly, hopefully, positively face such situations. There is no way in ignoring the persons involved that the problem will go away or turn a wrong back to a right. The counselor's duty is to turn evil into good.

When a girl does get into trouble, what can she do? She has several choices: marriage, keep the baby without getting married, or terminate the pregnancy. These are not very good choices. Each one has its own built-in set of problems. If the unwed mother decides not to keep the child, one of three things is likely to happen: She can put the child up for adoption, get an abortion, or abandon the child.

Some girls try to terminate the pregnancy themselves. Some go to a state that has legalized abortion, if they can find a doctor who will perform the operation and if they have enough money. Some wealthy girls go to England or Mexico. There are underground "abortion rings" which pregnant girls can patronize, at the great risk of life or arrest. But terminating one's pregnancy is a drastic solution. A girl may have no ill effects physically, but she may suffer serious psychological after-effects: guilt, shame, nervousness, worry, depression, fear of exposure, etc.

If the girl, and especially her parents, will face the situation forthrightly, without becoming hysterical, and consider all sides of the problem, they may decide that putting the child up for adoption is the best course — for her, the family, and the baby. In this manner everyone can be assured that the child will grow up with a family ready, willing, and able to give him a good home. There are of course unavoidable psychological after-effects of this step, but it is the most practical and just action for the child.

1. *The pressure marriage.* A girl wrote to us, "Please pray that the fellow who made me pregnant will marry me." This "shotgun" approach is perhaps the worst solution. The girl, boy, or parents, who decide on this course of action are thinking only of themselves, of saving face for their family. The young people are rushed into a responsibility that neither wants or is prepared for. Many pressure marriages end up in divorce. The couple feels trapped. As soon as the child comes along, the father may leave.

2. *The diplomatic marriage.* The couple, again perhaps under the influence and pressure of parents, agrees that perhaps the best thing to do under the circumstances is to get married. Even though marriage had not been planned or intended, they feel this is the best way out. Such a marriage is built on a weak foundation; it is likely to crumble. Just as an older married couple might stay together only "for the sake of the children," a young couple might marry for the same reason, but that is not a strong enough bond to make the marriage last "till death do us part."

3. *The "let mom raise the baby" solution.* Some young men who have come into our Teen Challenge program as addicts have come from homes where they were raised by their grandmothers, who played the role of stand-in mothers. Sometimes this works, but often it causes serious problems. If there are other children in the family, they may resent the baby.

4. *The "do it yourself" solution.* The unwed mother may decide to keep the child and raise him herself. She may live with her family, go on welfare, or get a job and hire someone to take care of the baby while she works. This

rarely provides an adequate answer for either mother or child.

Our experience at Teen Challenge convinces us that adoption is the best direction to take. The counselor should never be a party to abortion, nor should he recommend a forced marriage. He should strive to help the girl face the problem head-on; bring all persons involved into the counseling; consult professional agencies; and help those involved return to normalcy as soon as possible.

Counseling the Prostitute

"Where's the red light district?" a friend asked me while I was showing him New York City. His question was based on the assumption that there was a place where young women paraded their wares. He came from a country where such districts exist and where many such lights shine brightly. However, in most U. S. cities the "red light" district has given way to the "white light" district. That is, prostitution is no longer confined to certain areas, nor is it conducted in certain rooming houses or apartments in one special section of the city. Most prostitution is carried on under the white lights of any city street. It is carried on under the white lights of motels and bachelor apartments. The absence of a red light district does not mean there is less prostitution; in fact, the opposite seems to be the case. Prostitution has become more integrated into the whole of society — so integrated that it is often difficult to distinguish prostitution as a trade or business.

It might be well to point out here that the definition of a prostitute is "common and venal lewdness among a class of women" who are "devoted to base or unworthy purposes." The popular and more familiar image of the prostitute is the street-walking harlot, or the high class prostitute, both of whom make a profession of it. I would like to expand this to include the unofficial hidden prostitute whose actions may not be lewd on a day-to-day hiring basis but nevertheless is "base" even if it is not as frequent.

Prostitution has existed since antiquity. The story of Rahab (Joshua 2, 6) is one of the first records of prostitution in Bible days — and interestingly enough — the first record of the conversion of a prostitute. Overall, the term "harlot" is mentioned forty-four times in the Bible and the word "whore" fifty-three times.

Many prostitutes claim to have chosen their profession purely for economical reasons. While this is true especially for the addict prostitute, it may not necessarily be the primary motivation behind the non-addict prostitute becoming involved in such a life.

Prostitution is a very easy way — from a labor standpoint — to make a lot of money, but there are always emotional and spiritual factors that set the stage for a young girl to entertain the thought of such money-making. But when the prostitute does have an opportunity to live well and secure without prostituting herself, she will usually turn it down. One high-class prostitute told me proudly, "I had all kinds of men ask me to marry them. Some were very rich."

"Why didn't you accept their offer?" I asked her.

"I just didn't want to," was her answer. The truth was that she was "hooked" on her way of life and probably would have still been in it if she were only getting half or less the amount of money for selling her wares. Therefore, it seems that more is involved than an immediate economic problem.

There is no special method of counseling prostitutes. The same guidelines mentioned in previous chapters should be followed in counseling the prostitute. The prostitute is no worse than the homosexual, the rebel, or the addict. The woman of "ill repute" needs the same compassion, understanding and faith for deliverance as anyone else does.

Where the Tricks Are No Treats

Rose had been standing on Winchester Boulevard for almost two hours and business was dead. Sal came by several times to see if she had "turned" one. His concern was only to sell a bag of heroin. Rose was a prostitute who needed a fix, but she also needed to sell herself to get enough money for her pain killer. Usually the cars would be lined up four or five deep along the street with customers ready, willing, and able to pay for their desired pleasure. But tonight was slow. Patrol cars were heavy in the area.

Rose knew if she waited long enough something would

turn up. She was used to the waiting game. The worst was when she was sick and business was poor. Then she would have to settle for some weirdo — and maybe have to perform some perverted form of the sex act to earn her money. She began to wonder if maybe this was going to be one of those nights.

About 10:30 Freddie, one of the neighborhood winos, came by. "Come on, Rosie," Freddie propositioned her.

"Get out of here, Freddie. Go find Marie, she likes your kind," Rose responded.

"Please, Rose. I like you," Freddie continued.

Rose knew she couldn't get rid of him so she walked on down the street. She spotted Elaine across the street, she had just turned her trick and was on her way to an apartment two blocks away to finish the deal. Rose wished it were her — and the anxiety mounted. Back in front of the Sunshine Cleaners she stood back at her post, eyeing each passer-by. Her eyes met the eyes of each man as he passed wondering if the next would be a client. It had been about four hours since her last shot of heroin and the effects had almost completely worn off. She still felt a little warm — and "straight" as addicts term the act of getting high — but by 11:00 or 11:30 she would really need an injection.

She spotted Sal. "Sal, Sal," she yelled running after him. "How about some credit please? I'm sick, I'm real sick," she begged and lied about being sick, thinking about the hour deadline she had to meet.

"Your credit's no good, Rose. You already owe me for six bags. I want cash," Sal said as he walked on.

Once again she walked back to the doorway of the cleaners. She thought about Henry, her partner, who was in jail. If only he were around she would be taken care of. Rose and Henry were co-owners of her body. She sold her body and Henry hustled around for the dope. He also pulled robbery jobs so he always had extra money and bags of dope. Usually when there were no tricks to turn she didn't have to worry. But Henry was doing nine months on a drug possession charge so things were tough for Rose.

A man in his early fifties finally approached Rose at about 11:45. "I've got ten dollars, honey. What have you got?" he asked.

"What I've got is worth more than a measly ten bucks,"

Rose snapped back at him faking her disinterest to see if she could get enough for two fixes.

"Look, it's late," the little fat man said. He was no newcomer to this kind of badgering. "Do you want ten dollars or don't you?"

"Don't," Rose said firmly trying to call his bluff. The little man started to walk away and she was just about to call him back when he turned around and said, "I'll make it twelve dollars and no more."

Slowly she walked toward him and gestured with her eyes and head that she would accept the offer and together they walked to the basement of an apartment dwelling. In five minutes her duties would be over — the $12.00 would be in her hand — and then she would be off to find Sal and fifteen minutes after that a needle would be in her arm. In her moments of bliss she would forget the fact that tricks are no treat — but tricks do finance her "highs" and that is the only treat in life she has ever known.

Types of Prostitutes

1. *"White slavery" prostitution.* Sally, a young girl in our Teen Challenge home for girls, got into a form of white slavery prostitution through her involvement with a motorcycle gang. To pass her initiation she had to prove that she could ride a bike and jump sixty feet in the air and land upright. What she did not know is that she also had to prove herself to the leader of the gang by committing sexual acts with him. She soon learned that the primary purpose of the gang was not to ride motorcycles, but to indulge in all kinds of sexual perversion. By becoming a member of the gang she became a sex slave to all of the male and female members of the gang.

The old form of white slavery, in which girls are recruited and captured to sell their bodies, is no longer widespread, but the above does describe another form of a partial and voluntary type of white slavery. Male drug addicts often manage to turn their wives or girlfriends to prostitution to help them make money to support their habit. This too is a form of white slavery.

2. *The street-walker prostitute.* She is the teen-age girl or young adult who has run away from home, or who has gone to the big city hoping to be a career girl. It is difficult

to get the job she wants and she finds life hard in the city. But there is always a young man, or a middle-aged man, who will help her out. He may rent a room or invite her to live with him. Of course, in return, she feels obligated to satisfy his sexual needs. If she is not careful, and if she finds herself financially and emotionally desperate, she may start a habit. She may meet another girl, who tells her how she can make some real money, and thus she is introduced to full-time prostitution.

3. *The drug addict prostitute.* With her, prostitution is a secondary problem. Her first problem is drugs; prostitution has come about as a result of the addiction. The easiest way for the female drug addict to get money to support her habit is by selling her body. Few female drug addicts were first prostitutes and then drug addicts. Almost all of them do their business by walking the streets. Often the drug addict prostitute not only supports her own habit but also that of a male drug addict partner. She makes the money and he does the "scoring" (purchasing the dope from the pusher). Some of these relationships are like small businesses. Each works for the other to obtain dope. In some cases they marry, in most cases not.

4. *The office prostitute.* If you were to ask the single men in an office if there are any prostitutes among the secretaries, they would probably say no. But a closer look reveals a form of unofficial, sophisticated prostitution. If you were to ask the same men which of the secretaries are promiscuous, they might tell you. This means you would have located what I call the office prostitute. This is the young woman who dates the young bachelor. They go to a movie, to dinner, then to his apartment for dancing, alcohol — and sex. No money is passed into her hands, but she is paid off for her services. The young man may have spent $50.00 during the evening on her. At Christmas or other occasions she may be showered with gifts. All the attention he pays to her, all the generosities extended to her, are intended for one purpose — sex. The young woman is always available. A prostitute? Certainly she would never consider herself such. Neither would her male partner. She dresses nicely, comes from a good family, is socially concerned — and no one would compare her with the prostitute who walks the streets. But there are many similarities.

The above situation represents the most widespread kind of habit of selling one's body. It is not prostitution as most people think of prostitution. But it does exist in almost any office in any American city. Another name for the office or "white light" prostitute is a "party girl." Again she does not ask for a set fee — this is a matter simply understood with her date. The party girl will also refuse occasionally to keep her status, in her own eyes, of being a non-prostitute. This form of "white light" prostitution makes it unnecessary for there to be a "red light" district. The men who need to buy their sex don't have to drive downtown to some dark street. All they have to do is walk across the office floor. They don't have to go through the degrading process of handing over $25.00, $50.00 or $100.00 in hard cash for "services rendered." All they have to do is show a girl a good time and dish out the money in other forms, and they have accomplished the same thing.

5. *The "credit card" prostitute.* She is sometimes referred to as a "call girl." From a social or economic standpoint she is the high class prostitute. She makes most of her arrangements with customers over the telephone. She has contacts through business associations. She usually does business with the executives. In some cases they are able to pay the prostitute with their credit cards. There are even call girl prostitutes who have printed business cards referring to their work under the heading of public relations. The call girls are the money-makers. Some call girls have been known to make up to $50,000.00 or $75,000.00 a year. But such girls have big overhead expenses: expensive clothes, a good apartment, and money for such occupational hazards as abortions, court fees, doctor bills, and even answering devices. If she drives a car, she must maintain her image — and Lincolns and Cadillacs are her style.

How and Why Does a Girl Become a Prostitute?

Why the female drug addict turns to prostitution to support her habit is understandable. One habit becomes necessary to support the other. But why a teenage girl, or a young working woman, becomes a prostitute is hard to understand. Even harder to comprehend is the housewife who "moonlights," that is, prostitutes to make extra cash for the home. In some cases the husband may know of and even condone her practice. When this is the case, then of course both of them are sick spiritually and emotionally.

The teenager who gets involved in prostitution often starts on the road through promiscuous sexual activity. This is a way of rebelling against parents who don't pay any attention to her, or who are overly strict. She is promiscuous to fill the emptiness within her. Such rebellion through sex is never intended to lead to prostitution. Usually that happens unexpectedly. Slowly the habit creeps up on her and she finds herself hooked.

Eventually, every prostitute is in it because she wants to be. Many find it glamorous, exciting, and strangely gratifying. Dr. David Reuben, M.D., in his book, *Everything You Always Wanted to Know About Sex,* quotes a prostitute:

"I know some people think it's terrible to be in the racket, but they don't understand what it's really like. Always knowing that men are running after you, knowing that they leave their own wives just to make it with you, controlling them just with your sex — there's nothing else that can make a girl feel so powerful."

Dr. Reuben goes on to say, "All prostitutes have at least one thing in common — they hate men. Why is that? The full answer is a complicated one related to the deep underlying emotional problems that drove them into the game. Basically, prostitution is an ironic form of revenge against all men."[24]

More light is thrown on the prostitutes' emotional and psychological make-up by Dr. Harold Greenwald in his book entitled *The Elegant Prostitute.* He found among a group of twenty call girl prostitutes, some who took therapy from him, and others whom he interviewed, that not one of them had come from a family where there was a well-adjusted marital relationship between the parents. He stated:

> Not one of these girls reported growing up in a happy home where her parents got along well together.
> The attitude of the parents towards the children seemed to be one of complete rejection. . . . The open rejection caused them to feel unwanted and unloved and unworthy of being wanted or loved.

[24] David Reuben, M.D., *Everything You Always Wanted to Know About Sex* (David McKay, New York, 1969) p. 209.

The Sexual Generation

213

They discovered at an early age that they could get some measure of affection, of interest, by giving sexual gratification. ... In giving this sexual gratification they were rewarded by overcoming, no matter how temporarily, their feelings of loneliness and unworthiness, and at the same time expressed hostility towards the parents.[25]

How to Counsel the Prostitute

1. *Don't probe into her prostitution habits.* In one of our Teen Challenge centers a prostitute went to the director about an evangelist who was holding services at the center. She requested, "Please keep that evangelist away from me." The director wanted to know why. She said, "When he counsels me he has an unhealthy curiosity about my past. He has a sensual spirit; I can spot his kind." The prostitute can pick out those who are interested only in her body and in her habits.

As in dealing with the alcoholic, the addict, the homosexual, and other habit-bound persons, the counselor must find out if she is thirsting for "living water." This is the kind of probe that Christ made with the woman of Samaria, a type of prostitute. The question in dealing with a prostitute is, does she want to be clean?

2. *Give the prostitute a father image.* Because most prostitutes either hate men or have a bitter attitude toward them, they need someone — after conversion — to relate to them who is strong yet tender and understanding. They do not necessarily need a male counselor, but they do need either to live with or be associated with a family or group in which the love of Christ is manifested through a father, a husband, or other men. They may find it difficult to relate to men. Dr. Greenwald says "Because they had such a poor sense of self, it is very difficult for them to achieve any kind of satisfactory relationships with other people. The individuals with whom they tended to establish relations were apt to be equally unstable. In addition, since these girls feared and mistrusted other people, they were shy and awkward in any relationship except a commercial one."[26] They will be reluctant at first to become socially involved or even to date. But in time it is possible

[25] Harold Greenwald, *The Elegant Prostitute* (New York, Ballantine Books, 1958, 1970) pp. 165, 167.
[26] *Ibid.*, pp. 179, 180.

for them to fall in love, to marry, and to have a happy and normal marital and sexual relationship.

3. *Help the converted prostitute through her times of discouragement.* Like anyone else who has had a severe emotional problem, prostitutes are subject to great periods of loneliness. This may come in the form of guilt and a feeling that she is not a person of worth. The memory of her life as a prostitute may come back to haunt her and sink her into the depths of depression. The counselor must understand that this is to be expected, and help her to come out of it. Such discouragements seem to be necessary to prepare her for a Christian walk. In fact, discouragements can serve as a strengthening process.

The prostitute must learn to forgive. She must forgive those whom she may have blamed for leading her into such a life. Be it parents, a bad marriage, or whatever, she must come to the point of saying, "I forgive you." She may not have to say this in the presence of the person or persons involved. In fact, to mention it to these people may do more harm than good. But she does need to forgive them in the presence of God and the counselor. She also needs to forgive herself. Can she forgive herself for not fulfilling her role as a daughter, a mother, or a wife? Can she forgive herself for not fulfilling her role as a woman? The counselor should confront her with such questions, especially during her times of depression. Such forgiveness is essential to her recovery from her life of prostitution and for her growth as a Christian.

4. *Counsel her about dress and mannerisms.* Sometimes the ex-prostitute can make it hard for herself, in terms of recovery, by dressing or using her body in such a way that she attracts attention to herself. Because she has gained attention in the past by selling her body, she may unconsciously continue to seek attention by revealing her body or by sensual body movements. In seeking this attention she may fall into a trap. Through Christian teaching and by her relationship to Jesus Christ she will develop inward beauty. She will learn to be accepted on the basis of her inner qualities, not on the basis of what men see on the outside. When she learns this, she will realize that she does not need the other means of getting attention.

10

THE TRAPPED GENERATION

"Hey, George, are you coming with us Saturday? We're goin' ta downtown Brooklyn," a fourteen-year-old from the Coney Island section of Brooklyn asked. As they talked about their upcoming venture, it came as a surprise — and a shock — to me that this would be their first trip to downtown Brooklyn, a trip of about ten miles.

Where Trouble Is a Fifteen-Year-Old Boy

"Usually it was the little things that triggered big things. I mean, another rival gang member would make fun of one of our gang members' debs or dolls (gang girlfriend) and we would build it up as a big thing and use it as an excuse to fight." Sundown, the vice president of the Roman Lords, was speaking. We were standing on Chester Street, one block away from Stone Avenue, the dividing line between the Roman Lords gang and the Egyptian Kings. The two represented two of Brooklyn's most notorious gangs. Across Stone Avenue a huge mound of dirt created an artificial turf battleground where the Roman Lords and Egyptian Kings rumbled (gang fighting).

"Sometimes one of their dudes shoots a zip gun from off that hill down on our street," Sundown complained. "This can start an all-out war. I don't like it when they do that."

"You never do the same?" I asked. Smiling, Sundown said, "Well, yeah man. I guess we do."

"What else starts a rumble?" I asked.

"Well, we go around I guess you could say — we look for trouble. If things are dull we make up a situation and build it up as a reason for getting at them. For instance, one of our gang members will come to us all excited saying the Egyptian Kings are going to grab one of our fellows and stick a knife in him. Or he'll say, 'They're out to get blood.' But it will just be somebody making up a story — just to get something going. Then we'll start getting prepared to rumble. Their president will hear about it and get his gang ready to fight back. Only he'll be thinking we're starting it — and we're thinking he's starting it. But it really doesn't matter who starts it; the important thing is who finishes it — alive."

"What weapons do you use?" I asked.

"Zips (a homemade pistol), blades, pipes, homemade brass knuckles, clubs, and sometimes a sawed off shotgun." Sundown ran down the list.

*   *   *

The above interview took place seven years ago. It could not happen today. The sun has gone down on Sundown. He no longer carries a knife. Now it's a needle. He, like thousands of other gang members — such as the ones we came to New York City to reach in 1959 — are no longer in existence. Why? A white horse came riding into the teen gang turf and rode off with its members. In other words, "horse" or better known as heroin and the addiction that resulted broke up New York City's teenage gangs which was the reason the Teen Challenge ministry began in the first place. While other cities do have some gang activity, for the most part drugs is the thing in the inner city. Rumbles have given way to robbing for a fix.

But there is still fighting, shooting, and other problems that once characterized the typical gang rivalries. Only now it is not organized. The gang presidents, vice presidents, war lords, sergeant-of-arms, and the whole gang organization is gone. Today the style is small groups and cliques of fellows — or every man out to defend himself.

When I went to New York City to take part in the ministry of Teen Challenge, I was told there were young people in the ghettos who had never been out of the slums until they were teenagers. I couldn't believe it, but now

I was hearing it for myself. These teenagers are victims of the inner city, which is a nice way of saying ghetto or slum. They are, along with so many others, part of the trapped generation.

It is estimated that in the next ten years, because of population shifts, 75 percent of all Americans will be living in urban or suburban communities. Millions will be "walled in" and trapped by a ghetto, without the common blessings of green grass and fresh air. In addition, there will be overcrowded streets, limited school and recreational facilities, and worse, deplorable housing, plus such problems as drug addiction, crime, poverty, unemployment and juvenile delinquency.

This generation of trapped children, teen-agers, and young adults stands as a challenge to the church, as well as to all America.

One of our Teen Challenge workers describes the ghetto as "the electric atmosphere of Coney Island mixed with the suspicion of the jungle." But no description does justice to the ghetto, nor does any description adequately portray the injustice of it all. The ghetto produces some of the most terrible blights in American society. The ghetto spawns notorious gangs, militants and revolutionaries. Worst of all, the ghetto gives birth to drug addicts, alcoholics, prostitutes, and petty as well as professional criminals. That's no surprise when you consider that in New York City alone 800,000 people live in buildings that the state legislature declared unfit for human habitation — in 1901! Bad housing is one of the chief causes of the discontent, embitterment, and low morale among low income families. The average rent a ghetto dweller pays is about $60.00 a month. However, *The New York Times* reported, January 28, 1969, the case of a woman who was paying $106.00 a month for an apartment — the walls had been torn down and only three-foot high barriers separated her four "rooms." "The bathtub has been stopped up for weeks," she complained, "and the refrigerator doesn't work."

Simple problems become so complex. Living in the ghetto we found that in order to get anything done, you can't be too nice. We here at Teen Challenge had to threaten to hold back the rent money many times before we got action. It took almost three months to get an apartment cleared.

In the bleak existence of ghetto life babies become the sole purpose for living. They are the only dependable source of happiness. A ghetto mother must have a cuddly, understanding infant to accept her devotion. As babies grow up, however, they bring problems, so the mother must have another baby. In the book, *The Little People,* the condition of slum children is described this way: "Neglected, filthy and miserable, they are shut and locked in lonely tenement rooms; they are cast out to roam the city streets, early learning the ways of crime and violence — these are the little people. Born without warmth or love, subject to the lusts that govern those who give them birth — the muggers, prostitutes, alcoholics, addicts, and pushers — these little ones face a world they hate from their beginning. Robbed of their childhood, of love and care and attention, they exist just as their procreators exist — and the vicious circle grows wider."[1]

I have been writing about people who are hooked, who are addicted to drugs, alcohol and sex, or to hatred and rebellion. This chapter is about those who are hooked or "addicted" to a geographical location. Almost like a drug, the ghetto way of life is drilled into their minds from childhood. Again, like heroin addicts, they find it difficult to kick this "drug" for which they are not responsible.

In his book, *Riots in the Street,* Richard Wolff states: "Often the Negro is trappped in a vicious cycle from which he cannot extricate himself. Little in his environment is likely to give a Negro child a sense of aspiration and direction. There is no male model to imitate, and slight reason to assume that education offers a way out of the slums. A lack of education and aspiration makes it virtually impossible to find a job with dignity and status, even where discrimination sets in, and the conviction that it is pointless to try, resulting in a diminishing capacity to take advantage of opportunities as they do arise. In the technical language of the sociologist, such a person develops a self-

[1] David Wilkerson and P. Murphy, *The Little People* (Old Tappan, New Jersey, Revell, 1968).

defeating mode of living, which keeps him trapped in the slum condition."[2]

What can the Christian worker do to help reach the trapped generation?

A black minister and several other men from his committee sat in my office. They represented a newly-formed group in one of New York City's ghettos that had been organized to try to help drug addicts in their community. They had come to discuss the possibility of Teen Challenge's conducting on-the-street rallies for addicts in their area. The purpose was to introduce the work of Teen Challenge, and to tell addicts and their families how they could enter our rehabilitation program. As I offered suggestions about the kind of help we could give, I sensed that they were suspicious of my motives; they frankly discouraged the project. I could not figure out why. They wanted to help addicts. They had asked me how we could help them. After awhile it dawned on me why they were refusing to go along. They did not want Teen Challenge, and, more particularly, white people coming into their neighborhood to carry on a project *for* them. They really wanted us to come in and work *with* them.

In the past white churches have gone to the black communities with the attitude of doing something for "these unfortunate people." But black communities will not accept this attitude any longer — and it is to their credit that they won't. The various minority groups in the ghettos no longer are willing to sit by and let others do things for them — even against them — whether they be acts of charity or whatever. They want community control. The blacks I was talking with were trying to tell me, "Don't come without first coordinating your efforts through us and with us."

In previous years it did not occur to us to approach individuals in a black or ghetto community for the purpose of mutual cooperation. But now any work undertaken by the church, a Christian organization, or even by an individual Christian counselor must be done on the basis of community control and cooperation. The result of our not hav-

[2] Richard Wolff, *Riots in the Streets* (Wheaton, Tyndale, 1970), p. 26. Used by permission.

ing done this in the past is that the blacks feel that they have been exploited by whites and by the churches. Now, when white Christians want to go into black communities, often they are told to stay out, or they find it hard to be accepted and taken seriously.

"The role of the white Christian will not be heroic, glamorous, or directive," Richard Wolff explains in *Riots in the Streets*. "The day of the missionary is not over — the day of mission control is. The same holds true in the Negro (ghetto) community. White Christians can have an effective ministry if they go to serve humbly and with love, as Jesus did."[3]

The counselor must never give the appearance that he is better than those he is working with, or that he is doing them a favor by coming "down" into their environment. If the Christian worker gets the reputation for being a "white knight in shining Christian armor," he will soon be shot down — verbally. He must never show the attitude, "I'm doing you a favor by being here." Such an attitude means the counselor is not accepting the ghetto residents on equal terms with himself, not accepting them as persons of worth, as being on the same level with those of his own race, color, or economic status. He must avoid distinguishing ghetto dwellers as "them" and white, middle-class Christian workers as "us."

How then can Christians have an effective ministry in the ghetto?

1. *Gain community confidence.* The first step in going into the ghetto, either to establish a community-based ministry, or to go periodically to present a gospel witness, is to gain community confidence. Motives will be scrutinized carefully. Residents will watch to see if the Christian worker is a fly-by-night "do gooder" who is coming in to help himself, or if he is coming in sincerely and genuinely to help the community. Christians cannot go into the ghetto simply to ease their consciences from racial guilt by getting on some "do-gooder" bandwagon. The ghetto community will no longer stand for this.

An example of this took place when a group of suburbanites went into a ghetto street in New York City's

[3] *Ibid.,* p. 155.

Spanish Harlem to clean up the garbage, to paint and fix up the neighborhood with a one-day project. When the afternoon was over, they returned to their nice neighborhoods, feeling that they had made their commitment to the unfortunate people of the ghetto. Most of the people there, however, felt this was a "whitewash." While the suburbanites thought they could change the neighborhood with soap, water and paint and help alleviate the problems of the ghetto, the people of the ghetto community felt that they were doing this to ease their own consciences. They would have preferred some kind of long-term commitment to get rid of some of the root causes of ghetto problems.

The white person will be watched to see if he has come to "whitewash," to work out some middle-class white hang-up, to exploit, or if he has come to get involved in the total needs of the community. The counselor will have to prove himself. This may take weeks, months, or years. The people will ask, "Do you really want to help us? Do you really want to understand us? Have you come with your preconceived theories? Do you really care?" Only time and the counselor's nitty-gritty involvement will prove the genuineness of his commitment.

Teen Challenge CURE Corps workers in one of the worst areas in New York City, Fox Street in the Bronx, have gained over many months this necessary community confidence. The fact that the program has continued in the ghetto for more than two years in itself says something to the community about our commitment and motivation. The Federal government's domestic Peace Corps organization, VISTA, had tried to start a program on the very same street, but their workers were run off the block just before we arrived. Many white-sponsored, church-sponsored programs come and go. Because they do not get quick results, and because the people are not willing to make a long-term commitment, these programs fold. This breaks down the confidence of ghetto residents in church-sponsored programs. Our CURE Corps workers lived for a time on the block where they were working. They experienced the same frustrations and tensions the other people there do. Now some of the men on the block tell our girls, "You let us know if anyone mistreats you." Some blacks have protected them and stood up for them against other blacks. They can walk the streets at all hours of the day and night; they are accepted as a part of the community. Their motivation has been tested and proved, so they are able to relate to the members of the district. One black woman on the block commented, "You must really mean business about God. You live here with us and you really don't have to."

2. *Be open to change.* To become a worker in the ghetto, one must be open to change. Nice programs which sound successful on paper, and that may have worked in other areas, often do not work in the ghetto. Those who stick stubbornly to their preconceived ideas and programs often fail. One must remain flexible, ready to adopt new ideas and to make changes as a result of better understanding of the culture, the thinking, the attitudes, and the life-style of ghetto people.

One example of being open to change has to do with time consciousness. Those who are used to the simple middle-class habit of starting things on time soon learn that in the ghetto almost all functions start at least thirty minutes late. We have a little joke around Teen Challenge about American time and Puerto Rican time. The latter represents a difference of thirty minutes.

In the ghetto the counselor deals with people who operate essentially by feelings rather than by organization. They get up when they feel like it, eat when they feel like it, sleep when they feel like it. Their lack of organization is evident and real. One of our workers explained, "We had to adjust by not getting uptight because of some of their customs. In counseling, we find that much is done on an 'accidental' basis. We just happen to see them, or run into them on the street. We have tried many times to set up appointments, and many times our clients did not show. It takes time to orient them to schedules and to the seriousness of keeping their word."

A counselor must be ready to learn, to change his concepts, and to allow the people of the ghetto to teach him. It takes time to get white thoughts and suburban ideals washed out of the counselor's mind. A good example of this is what happened when we took a visiting pastor and his church's young people to one of the ghetto neighborhoods where we have a ministry. We were setting up sound equipment for an open air street rally. The pastor saw a little black boy, patted him on the head, and said, "How are you, little Sambo?" Immediately the little fellow looked up and said, "What did you call me? I'm no Sambo." Unfortunately, that exchange was broadcast to the neighborhood over our sound system. Soon people gathered and the crowd began to get hostile. "You'd better pack up and leave," one man suggested. However, one of our workers explained that the term the pastor had used was not a term of race prejudice, but rather one of affection. After further apologies, our team was able to stay and conduct the meeting. But that slip of a white tongue was almost enough to trigger some angry reactions against our whole group, which included whites, blacks, and other ghetto Christians.

Those who continue to think white in the ghetto sooner or later will find themselves out of a job and a ministry. Even one's theories about the causes of drug addiction, poverty, prejudice, and other problems in the ghetto must be kept to oneself. All those who enter a ministry in the ghetto must first learn the culture from the people before they can teach others.

3. *Have a vision but don't be a visionary.* A worker told me, "At first I was so stirred up with my vision I really thought I was going to save all of New York City." This young man had come from a midwestern college and was full of enthusiasm and zeal. Then he learned some of the hard realities of urban life, and the problems of reaching the ghetto. But unlike many visionaries, he had come to try to understand the tremendous obstacles that must be overcome and the limitations that these hard realities place upon one's vision. In the process he did not lose sight of his goal. He still had vision. But he did lose some of his lofty, visionary ideals.

Many who undertake the challenge of the ghetto have great visions that go up in a puff of smoke when they face the cold, hard facts of inner city life and the people with their problems. This is especially true when they are faced with rebellion and rejection of the Gospel on one hand, and the struggles of new converts on the other. One must learn to understand such problems, and be prepared to accept them, but still have faith, hope and vision.

The soil upon which the gospel seed is planted in the ghetto is extremely rocky. The seed-sower must have patience and longsuffering. One of my teachers in college said, "Every pastor who goes into a city to build a church needs to have a ten-year vision. You may not remain there for ten years, but you should undertake your ministry as if you were going to stay that long." The same may be said for the counselor's ministry in the ghetto. He must make a long-term commitment to it. Progress cannot be measured by the same standards you would use in middle-class America, or in a regular church program. There are results, of course, but until one learns to measure them by different standards, he may have a sense of failure.

Our CURE Corps workers dealt with one young man for about a year and a half before he went to Teen Challenge. He did everything he could to "drive us mad," as one worker said, "from pop guns to stealing our car radio antenna." Even after his conversion progress came quite slowly. An indication of his rate of progress was his comment, "Hey, I only cursed three times today." A counselor must learn not to judge or condemn in such a situation, but to wait for the Holy Spirit to do His work.

4. *Understand the environmental hazards.* The next thing the counselor must do is understand the environmental hazards of the ghetto and the pressures those who live in the ghetto must contend with: problems of housing, unemployment, poverty, family and home conditions, prejudice, etc. These obstacles often make it difficult for new converts in the ghetto to grow in their Christian faith. It is not easy to serve the Lord in these conditions. And yet many of them often are model Christians, lights in dark places. They live in situations that the average American and the average Christian never sees. The ghetto dweller is nourished in the sights, sounds, and smells of the inner city. These conditions drain him spiritually.

Many Earls, one of our CURE Corps workers, made this comment about life on a ghetto block: "My main impression from living in the ghetto is picking up the air of oppression — the atmosphere — which is so full of sin and evil that one can almost reach out and touch it. It is a combination of noise, frustration, street fights at all hours, the dogs barking, and the juke box playing until 5 a.m. All of this wears out your spiritual nerves."

I used to wonder why storefront churches in the ghetto held so many services during the week. I thought it was too much for them and that the saints were worn out. But I soon learned how important these services are in the life of the Christian in the ghetto. These meetings are his only escape from a rat-infested apartment, crying children, from drug addicts who parade up and down his apartment stairs, and from the tensions on the block. It is no wonder they go to church four, five, or six nights a week. It is no wonder they enjoy their own type of Christian soul music with its rhythm and beat. Their services are a wholesome escape, as well as spiritual and emotional therapy.

The Rev. Mr. Calvin B. Marshall, who pastors a Negro church in Brooklyn, feels that Christianity has a proper place in the ghetto and in the black revolution. In an article in *Time* magazine (April 6, 1970), he gives some insights into the value of the church and of the Christian message in the black community. He states, "If we were nothing here (in the white society), at least we were children of God. At some far-out point in time, all these things would be rectified and we would get our golden slippers. Our religion *had* to mean more to us. We had to emote, but we had to lose ourselves in it. We had to sing and shout, and after it was all over we had to have a big meal and have something going on Sunday afternoon. Because when Monday came, it was back out into the fields, or back to the janitor's job, or back in Miss Ann's kitchen scrubbing the floor." Another black minister, Atlantis Samuel W. Williams, in the same article said, "But because those churches are still the only institutions in the black community completely controlled by black people, they will continue to have an influence, however much the younger blacks may feel that the churches no longer speak to the black world's needs."

Those who identify themselves as Christians in the ghetto must make such a complete, drastic break from sin that their conversion sends vibrations through the whole neighborhood. Everyone seems to know when a ghetto sinner gets saved. Because the life of sin is what it is in such an environment, a conversion means a drastic change of life.

And because of the environment, ghetto churches have had to demand a complete separation from the old life. Most ghetto dwellers know that to identify themselves with the "hallelujah" church or the evangelical Bible-believing mission on the block means that such pleasures as drinking, dancing, going to gigs (wild parties), and gambling must cease. When he does become a Christian, he may pay the price of lost friendships, persecution, even the loss of relatives, and he loses his position as being part of the "in" people of the block. And when one's life revolves entirely around one city block, or within one tenement house dwelling, this can be a very severe price one pays to serve Christ in the ghetto. The approach of ghetto churches is often legalistic and turns many young people away, but essentially they are trying to protect their converts, especially the new and the young ones. Most of the unconverted know the separation that the born-again Christian experience demands, and therefore they are reluctant to accept Christ. The counselor must understand this factor in dealing with those in the ghetto. This often explains why those who accept Christ in the ghetto do not mature as quickly as new converts do elsewhere. The ghetto resident must pay a high price for being identified with a storefront church, or any church for that matter.

5. *Respect the possible dangers of ministry in the ghetto, but do not be fearful.* A young man bragged, "I'm not afraid. I go walking into those troubled areas anytime I want to. I know the Lord is with me." On the other hand, I have heard some say, "You'll never catch me going into Harlem." Some are bound by fears and others are reckless and proud. They don't respect the possible dangers. Neither extreme is good. However, danger barriers can be broken down. The Christian worker can overcome his fears and operate comfortably. It makes a difference in a Christian's witness if he feels at ease. If ghetto people sense that you fear or distrust them, they will distrust you in return.

The only way to start in the ghetto is to go first with a member of the community. If the area is controlled by a gang, or by some militant group, make yourself known to the leaders and gain their confidence. As I write this we are trying to hold open air street rallies in an area in Manhattan known as Spanish Harlem. This particular neighborhood is controlled by the Young Lords (the Spanish counterpart of the Black Panthers). As we always do when going into a Spanish neighborhood, we make sure we have the Spanish-speaking converts to head up the teams. One of our girls, Cookie, approached the leaders of the Young Lords and explained the work of Teen Challenge. She tried to show the Young Lords that we were concerned about the needs of the neighborhood, as they were. Because of the positive approach, they respected our work and said it would be all right for us to come into their neighborhood.

Once a contact has been made in the ghetto, or key individuals have become the worker's friends, they become the key to meeting others. After a number of visits, the worker often finds he can move freely throughout the neighborhood. Occasionally when we drive in some areas, drug addicts will walk away, thinking we are the police. Then someone will recognize us and give the word that we are all right. The addicts will stop walking away and allow us to talk with them. One addict said, "I thought all this God stuff was phony until I deliberately watched one of the workers for months, and he did not get angry or lose his cool. I decided God was for real."

When there is trouble in a community — a gang war, riot, or other disruption — the worker should be careful about going to or staying in the area at that time. Under riot or gang conditions, a person who under normal circumstances would be your friend can turn hostile. Unless a worker is absolutely sure of his position and influence, he should not try to be a mediator, or act like a hero. Some counselors command enough respect in a community to help prevent riots, gang wars, or street brawls, but one must definitely be sure he has such confidence before stepping in as a referee. In some past riots even black leaders were not able to stop the violence once it started. The Christian must remember that he is in the ghetto first of all to minister to the spiritual needs of an individual, and not to take on the role of a police officer, or a social worker.

Those who are afraid of the ghetto must get over it if they are going to be effective in ministering to minority groups. Too many Christians do not accept the challenge because they overreact to possible dangers. I have tried to get suburban Christians to come into the inner city for an evangelistic effort. Only a handful have enough assurance of their commitment to Christ to overcome their fears. They watch too many newscasts, read too many stories in the newspapers. We cannot allow the fear of militants to hold us back from ministry in the ghettos. We have proved in various neighborhoods in New York City, on hundreds of occasions, that "God hath not given us the spirit of fear; but of power, and of love, and of a sound mind" (2 Tim. 1:7). There are dangers and there are risks, but those who are committed to doing the Lord's work must accept them, while entrusting themselves into God's protective hand. To do less is to doubt the Lord who is "my shepherd, who leadeth me beside troubled tenement houses; yea, though I walk through the streets filled with robbers, muggers, militants and criminals, thou art with me, thy nightstick comforteth me; thou preparest a pulpit for me in the midst of would-be enemies. Surely trouble will not follow me, and I shall dwell in the ghetto safely" (author's paraphrase).

6. *Get involved but not entangled.* Another important factor in working in the ghetto is that the counselor should get involved but not entangled. The temptation is to get too involved, that is, to get into political and social matters while losing sight of one's call and Christian commitment. Those who minister in the ghetto must be prepared to get totally involved, but not at the sacrifice of not preaching the Gospel of Jesus Christ. The counselor should be well-informed about all social and community agencies available to help people. We have been able to get through to people spiritually because we helped them with a practical problem such as housing. Our CURE Corps teachers run a pre-school program, and they are able to talk to mothers about the problems of their children, then about their own personal problems. We first gained their trust as teachers of small children, and in time they saw our true concern and accepted our workers as people, not just teachers.

Many an evangelical has begun to meddle in the political, social and economic affairs of the community. These problems cannot be ignored, but they must not be allowed to divert us from the preaching of Christ and the ministry to the heart. There is the possibility of using the political and social structure of the community so as to gain a better hearing, which should be done. However, the Christian worker must remember that his power base is the Word of God and the Holy Spirit. He must try to erect a pulpit, not a soap box. He is to build faith, not seek new legislation. If a Christian counselor can work to improve social and economic conditions, he should do so, but not if it means he is no longer respected for his Christian commitment.

7. *The counselor must deal with his own prejudice.* In almost every conference I attend on ghetto ministries, the discussion turns to the matter of race prejudice. It's sad to listen to various pastors, Christian workers and laymen defend the fact that they are not prejudiced. They usually do this by telling about the colored lady or colored man who was or is their friend. The "I'm not prejudiced because I have a colored friend" line is phony. Many blacks are beginning to see through it. They wonder why the white Christian feels he has to prove he is not prejudiced.

William Pannell states: "Frequently we suffer while some brother tells us how glad he is to be with us. 'Us' being 'you dear folks.' From there we are likely to hear about the 'dear old colored lady' some place in his history, and how he loves us all 'in the Lord'. . . You see if you have to *tell* me you love me, I tend to suspect you immediately. I suppose this is why Jesus Christ never walked up to a man and said, 'Hey, I love you.' By going into all that rather syrupy introduction, you call attention to some difference among us. Because you didn't use the same words when speaking in your group. Be yourself. We can judge whether you like us or not. 'Blessed is the man who feels no need to tell us he loves us. He shall be invited again.' "[4]

The white Christian worker who goes into the ghetto must deal with his prejudice, and the best way to do so is to admit that he has it. I would not be honest with you if I said I was not prejudiced. We all are. It is part of human nature to prefer one's own culture, religion, nationality, and race.

Richard Wolff in *Riots in the Street* says, "The Christian is aware of the fact that prejudice is inherent in human nature. Not race prejudice specifically, or any other particular prejudice, but prejudice as such. This is part and

[4] William Pannell, *My Friend, the Enemy* (Waco, Texas, Word, 1969).

parcel of the innate disposition of man. . . . Ultimately it is sin against God. . . . The basic change has to take place in us and can only occur through a new relationship with God, where acceptance and forgiveness are experienced anew so that in turn it can be extended to others."[5]

Being prejudiced means you look differently upon a person of another race. It also means, to one degree or another, that you treat that person as being less of a human being than you consider yourself and your own kind to be. Such unconfessed, unsurrendered prejudice will show itself sooner or later in the counselor's ministry. When prejudice is dealt with, the counselor will come to the place where his reaction to people will be like that expressed by one of our workers who said, when asked if a certain convert were white, black, or Spanish, "I never noticed."

[5] Ibid., pp. 151, 152.

11

THE INTEGRATION PROBLEM

During one of my crusades in Sydney, Australia, a group of ministers and laymen, who were the sponsoring committee, met together in preparation for the rallies. They were discussing the matter of follow-up and what to do about those who would respond to the invitation. One man spoke up and said, "We can't send them to any of the churches. There isn't one good enough. I wouldn't recommend anyone to go to any of the churches in this city. We will have to start special meetings just for them."

After lengthy discussion the same layman rethought his position and stated, "Perhaps it would be a mistake to try to start our own church or another organization. This committee is only temporary, but the churches — no matter how we feel about them and what they lack — at least they will still be here tomorrow. Let's work through the churches and do our follow-up through them." Everyone agreed this would be the best procedure.

Never has the church been under so much attack — not only from without (that is to be expected and understood) — but also from those within its ranks. Many people feel that the church, any church, is a dead institution. Many recent converts from the college campus and out of the hippie lifestyle have carried over their rebellions into the Christian life. It is not easy for them to get free from the hang-up they have regarding the church. They often feel it is part of the "system" that needs to be changed, over-thrown, and revolutionized. No one would deny that there are some legitimate reasons for them to feel that way. There is, however, a radical element that wants to throw the baby out with the bath water. In an effort to change the system, or bureaucracy of the church, and to break away from programs too structured to meet the real needs of the people and the outsiders, they have developed an atti-tude which says regarding the church, "We don't need you. I am the church. The church is where a person is."

Even among some older, well-established Christians and those raised within the church there is a breaking away into small groups which become in some cases substitutes for the regular structured church program. These prayer groups, banquet-type meetings, and underground cells have been part of a great spiritual awakening among Christians, especially those from the old-line denominations where the Gospel has been too structured, institutionalized and for-malized. Many people in these small groups are finding new faith, or the new birth for the first time. They also are entering into the charismatic experience of speaking in other tongues as they are baptized in the Holy Spirit, as in the days of the book of Acts. This, I believe, is one of the greatest spiritual events in this century.

But in going out of the church to the small groups, these people have subtly reacted against the established, organ-ized, regular church. Some of those who for so long were dead in their churches have been so glad to be liberated from them that they fear going back, lest they become overly critical of them. Some openly refuse to accept the established church in any form. If and when they do attend, they go with a built-in set of criticisms. No matter how good the function of the church is, or the efforts of the pastor and the members, they are not prepared to accept it.

In one country I visited an organization that used coffee houses as a means of reaching the untapped generation. New converts were required to sign a pledge that they would not join any church. They would meet together for Bible study in their coffee house, have prayer meetings, and try to carry on the same functions of a church. The organization itself became a reactionary church, its members parading around saying, "We've got something better than the rest of you have." They snub their noses, as it were, at those who are the church "squares." In discussing plans for an evangelistic crusade, their director stated, "We don't want any of the churches sponsoring this crusade. There isn't one good enough for us to send any of our converts to."

We have learned through the years of our ministry in Teen Challenge that no evangelism or counseling ministry can be totally and lastingly effective if it does not associate itself with the church. I am convinced that many good evangelistic efforts fail in the end because of an anti-church attitude. They feel that the church is not doing its job, so they have to organize their own little group and get the job done themselves. They end up evangelizing but not nurturing anyone in the Kingdom of God. It's like bringing a baby into the world and then telling the doctor, "I don't need you any longer." Or it's like saying, "Let's get out of the hospital before it kills the baby." This is not to say that some churches have not spiritually "killed" new babes in Christ. They have. Others perhaps have not spiritually killed them, but they have stunted their growth, or raised them to walk as cripples, or kept them on the bottle, or did other spiritual damage.

Yet I say to those Christian organizations outside the main church body — and to those counseling and evangelizing independently of any church group — work in the system or your efforts may be in vain. Good, bad, or indifferent, the church is a divine institution. I do not mean to say that God is pleased with any and every church body or organization, but He is pleased with the concept of "assembling yourselves together." According to Hebrews 10:25, we are not to forsake the fellowship of the church.

Integrating the untapped generation into the mainstream of the church poses many problems. Some of them are seemingly insurmountable. But it can be done, and it is being done. Former drug addicts are finding their places in the church — even former alcoholics, prostitutes, criminals, and other sinners saved by grace. They are being accepted on the basis of the fact that "old things are passed away, and all things are become new" (II Cor. 5:17). Their pasts are not being held against them. Only congregations and churches that understand the untapped generation, and are willing to face the problems of integration, are able to have this kind of testimony.

The key to integration first of all is the counselor. If he develops the right attitude — a positive one rather than a negative one — the gap between the streets and the church can be overcome. The counselor must take the hand of the pastor and the hand of the new convert and bring them together. Then the pastor can take the right hand of fellowship he has extended to the new convert, and take his congregation, and bring them together. It is often a cold and reluctant hand that the congregation extends — but congregations can be won. The counselor must prepare the church for the convert and the convert for the church.

Many churches have ministered to only one type or class of people. A person from a different background, culture and lifestyle is made to feel strange. Or the new convert may feel strange by reason of his own fears of coming into a new environment. These barriers must be overcome. The church must widen its ministry to receive any and all. There must be the integration into the church of sinners saved by grace, who have come out of different segments of the world and who come from different levels of sin. The church must not be guilty of spiritual discrimination. Can he who was saved from the sin of pride say to him who was saved from the sin of homosexuality, "I want no part of you"? Or can he who was saved from the sin of indifference say to him who was saved from the sin of sexual promiscuity, "I want not part of you"? Can the church members say, "Find your own kind of sinners saved by grace and fellowship with them"? A church is unbalanced if it does not have a cross-section of converts. It needs saved businessmen, saved housewives, saved working men, and saved drug addicts, alcoholics, sexual perverts, and others.

There was a time during our Teen Challenge ministry in New York City that we would not work any church. Our theory was, "The only Christians who can adequately care for a new convert are those who helped bring him to birth." But we found that we could not evangelize and take care of their spiritual growth at the same time. We learned that God gave "some evangelists, and some pastors and teachers" (Eph. 4:11). Our calling was to sow the seed, and, up to a certain point, have Bible studies, prayer meetings, house visitation, and other methods of follow-up, but eventually our goal was to integrate converts into the church. We do realize our responsibility to help new converts get established, but since we are not functioning as a regular church body, we feel it is our duty to bring them into contact with churches. Our calling was to sow seed; others were called to help the growth of that seed and to develop the harvest into polished fruit. I am now convinced that lasting fruit can only result when the evangelist, the soul-winner, and the Christian counselor cooperate with the local church. They can do this either by officially coordinating their work with and through the church, or at least by affiliating with a church. If the Christian counselor takes the approach that "the church is no good," or "I am the only one doing the job," then those he helps bring to birth in Christ will have no respect for the church and will become a law unto themselves. These converts tend to become spiritual "freaks" — independent, spiritually aloof, proud, and lacking spiritual growth and maturity. Often they get sidetracked by some doctrinal quirk. Those converts who get started on the wrong foot often walk spiritually crooked the rest of their lives.

When we first began our rehabilitation program for addicts, alcoholics, delinquents and others, we held services right in our center on Sundays. When on occasion we did take them to a regular church to worship, they felt very strange and out of place. Sometimes they were critical. "Why isn't this place like Teen Challenge?" they asked. Or they said, "This church is dead. What's wrong with these people?" When they left Teen Challenge to go out on their own, they had a hard time fitting into a church. At Teen Challenge they were accustomed to worshiping the Lord informally. The new converts sang, prayed, and testified; the meetings were spirited and enthusiastic. They found it hard to adjust to more structured services. Because other Christians expressed their love and devotion to Christ in a more reserved manner, they thought their churches were dead.

Our Teen Challenge congregation was made up of people from similar backgrounds. It was not a normal church situation. We had to bridge the gap between the world of Teen Challenge and the outside world of the regular, established church. When we started to take our converts to various different kinds of churches, they soon learned the different forms of worship. They learned not to judge a church, its people, or its services by how loudly or softly they sang, by how they prayed and preached. They learned to judge a church by the quality of its worship. After participating in various forms of worship they were able to decide what kind of church they wanted for themselves after they left Teen Challenge. They met different pastors and church members, so they did not feel as strange as they might otherwise have felt, had they started going to church without any previous contact. During some of these services they made their decision to accept Christ, or other spiritual commitments. Because the church felt it had had a part in the birth of that soul, it took a responsibility toward helping the person in his Christian development.

The resistance of some pastors and congregations to members of the untapped generation is most often due to lack of contact. The less contact church folk have with the untapped generation, the more they fear them, or are prejudiced toward them. Most of what they know about young people comes from what they read in the newspaper, or from friends and neighbors. Once this barrier has been broken down, these preconceptions are alleviated. The pastor and people will see the grace of God in the lives of former habit-bound persons and accept them as they are. I have seen some churches and clergymen, once they begin to mingle with and relate to these young people, go out of their way to make up for past indifference. Whole churches have been revolutionized by the flow of "new blood" into their congregations. When they get their eyes away from a small circle of the same type of people attending their services week after week, and begin to get involved in the problems and needs of the untapped generation, a whole new ministry opens to them.

However, the sheltered, isolated church often becomes a stereotype church and its people are not prepared to accept those from a different side of town, a different side of the tracks, or from a different social or economic background. The silent majority shouts, "Why don't these people better themselves? Why don't they work and provide for their families like the rest of us?" The problem often is that these people are not welcome in some churches where they could hear a gospel message and receive a conversion experience that would motivate them to be the kind of citizens they should be. When they do seek to better themselves socially (and going to a nicer uptown church is a part of climbing the social-economic ladder, whether we like to admit or not), often they find that they are not welcome.

Middle-class protestant evangelicalism in America often is hard to break into. When outsiders try to break into the fellowship, they are frozen out, not trusted, or respected. So the new convert is forced back into his old culture, his old neighborhood, his old friends, and back to his old haunts. Even when he attends a church in the ghetto, or on the side of the tracks he came from, often he finds it is just as hard to break into the fellowship there.

I am not speaking of racial consideration alone; I am speaking about integrating the "vilest sinners" into the church, those from unpolished, uneducated backgrounds who might have severe growing pains in the church and upset the normal routine of its operation. This is not a racial problem alone. There are black congregations that find it hard to accept the untapped black generation. There are ghetto churches made up of poorer classes of people who discriminate against wealthy people. Integration and prejudice work both ways.

Why Churches Fear the Untapped Generation

Why does a church fear opening its doors to the untapped generation? First, there is a fear that former addicts, homosexuals and others like them might backslide and adversely influence other youth in the church. Of course, there is always this possibility and the chances of its happening are greater than for the "average" Christian. But this fear should not hold back the church from opening its heart and its doors to those who are "different" or who have been "different." If the church has strong leadership and a good sound program to hold its youth, and if the majority of the youth are mature in their faith, they will not be overcome by backsliders. However, we must face reality. Our Christian youth who come from a more sheltered background must not grow up in a spiritual hothouse.

Church youth who are never exposed to other types of young people, and to those from different or less stable backgrounds, are not adequately prepared for the world when they grow up. Christian young people, well-grounded in the faith, have made tremendous strides in their spiritual growth once they were exposed to the spiritual needs of the untapped generation.

When Teen Challenge converts give their testimonies in suburban and rural churches, often the young people are overly inquisitive about their backgrounds. Some have an unhealthy curiosity. Does the fault lie with our converts? Or does this happen because these youth have been overly protected, sheltered, and kept from any contact with the outside world to such an extent that they have suppressed desires that come out later?

A pastor complained to me, "One of your fellows took one of our young people away from the church." That happened because the so-called Christian youth was a ready target for such influence. The backsliding was already there, another backslider simply came along and happened to bring it out.

This leads to another great concern of churches and pastors. It is the question, "If former addicts, homosexuals and others start coming to our church, will they start marrying some of our young women?" This is a serious problem. The fear is understandable.

It is not good for a girl from a sheltered background to marry a man who comes from an extremely different culture and background. The solution seems to lie in the manner in which the parents, the pastor and the church leaders handle each particular case. For example, breaking up a couple who have been dating, primarily on racial grounds, can cause an adverse reaction and make them all the more determined to marry — in rebellion. When adults advise young people against marriage, they must have sound reasons. It is better to approach it from a cultural and social standpoint. Young people from two extremely different backgrounds, no matter what their race or color, have a high potential for trouble in their marriage. The pastor should caution young people who are developing such a relationship. If they persist, and if after prayer and consultation with all parties involved the pastor and family still feel the relationship should be broken up, such measures should be taken very carefully. There have been exceptional cases in which people from extremely different backgrounds have married and have been very happy. On the other hand, there are cases of difficult and shaky marriages because the two people had too much to overcome. Young people reason that "love can conquer all." They feel that the combination of their human love for each other, plus their Christian love, will make for an untroubled marriage. They must realize that when a person comes to Christ, all his problems are not automatically solved.

The church that has a good number of young people who socialize with others of similar backgrounds will not have such a serious problem in this regard. However, in churches where there are not many Christian youth, especially fellows, and where the young people are too sheltered, there is likely to be trouble. My father was a pastor and once he looked at two rows of young girls sitting in church and said to the adults, "There are not enough young men in this church, folks, let's pray them in and let's bring them in." They did — and it worked.

Another fear churches have in working with the untapped generation is that if a few of them come into the church, "we'll have a church full of them." They feel this will hinder them with others in the community who they are trying to reach. Converted addicts and others like them often are quite enthusiastic in wanting to help others like themselves. Converted hippies and runaways will want to bring their friends to church. However, if a large group comes together, they could disrupt the meeting. It is best to bring street people into the church singly or in pairs. If a person is addicted to drugs, he may need the kind of help that only a Teen Challenge-type program can provide. The pastor and those working with youth will have to make such a judgment. Because of the great number of young people now on drugs, and because of the limited number of people the rehabilitation centers can care for, the church must make every effort to reach the addicts and the drug abusers. If the regular church ministry cannot meet the spiritual needs of this person, then referral should be considered.

If a church is not willing, or is unprepared to try to work with those whom former addicts, rebels and others typical of the untapped generation will bring with them, counselors should help them to find another church that is in a better position to accept the responsibilities of such a ministry. No church should fear that it will lose new people because it becomes involved in reaching the untapped generation. Churches should not be built on the type of person who would not come because he feels the church is catering to the wrong kind of people. In most cases the outside will have more respect for a church that is making its presence felt among the unfortunate of this world.

How to Integrate the Untapped Generation Into the Church

1. *Develop a right attitude toward the church.* There are two types of Christians workers and counselors: those who are a part of the church and work through a particular church or a group of churches; those who work with an organization that is independent of any one church, but is supported by churches some distance away. Counselors working closely with a church will have no problem bringing about integration, unless the church has an "outside" ministry to the untapped generation so it will not have to work with them *in* the church. This is a subtle way of trying to avoid certain types of sinners.

Those who work independently often act this way. "No church will cooperate with me," the director of an evangelistic work told me. "Have you given them any reason to want to cooperate with you?" I asked. Those who feel that the church is not doing anything, or that "I am the only one with a burden," naturally find it hard to find churches that will cooperate. Those who indict the church for its lack of vision, and browbeat the people and beg for funds, understandably are turned off by the church. Those who are out to "get the church" and just take from it — rather than give to it — are going to be bitter toward it. Such an attitude works against the counselor. He will tend to gather his converts around himself. Such converts usually do not last, or they are weak and become embittered themselves.

The independent counselor must remember that he is dependent on the church for his support and for prayer backing. He must take the initiative in establishing a good relationship with a number of churches, or at least with one church with whom he is trying to work. Counselors should not become church "draft dodgers," that is, they should not go from one church to another, attend one special service after another. It is easy to go to the big meetings, to hear the best preachers, to go to the most publicized rallies, all the while keeping yourself from being drafted into a specific responsibility in the church. If the counselor is a full-time worker in a Christian organization, he perhaps will not be able to limit himself to one church, or to a specific work in that church. However, even if the counselor is in full-time Christian work, it is not a good idea for him to float from church to church, dodging the draft of regular weekly service, paying tithes, and other obligations. This certainly is not a good example to those he is trying to introduce to Jesus Christ.

In dealing with new converts the counselor need not defend the church. He can try to understand the accusations of those who feel the church has failed them or even done them an injustice. Some will be bitter because they turned to the church in time of spiritual need and were not satisfied. Find out if they rebelled against the church because it did not minister to them, or if they rebelled against the truth that was declared. The counselor should not add fuel to the bitterness, prejudice, or doubts that some people have toward the church. Often a new convert will try to get the counselor into a debate about the church. The most common argument is about hypocrites. This is a trap every Christian worker should avoid.

Argument may be avoided simply by admitting that the church does have hypocrites. This agreement usually will disarm the person. We suggest that Christian workers might use this approach, "Yes, the church does have hypocrites, but what better place is there for them to be? If you are going to drop out of any group that has hypocrites, then you will have to drop out of life. There are hypocrites in politics, in democracy, and communism, and in business and industry, and in almost any organization you can think of. Furthermore, the Bible does not cover up the fact that among God's people there were hypocrites. God deals with the problem openly and honestly — just read the history of Israel or Paul's letters to the early Christian churches. Hypocrites are very much in evidence and the problem is dealt with properly."

The client will no doubt cite specific incidents of a hypocritical parent, relative, neighbor, or friend. The counselor should agree that perhaps what this so-called Christian did was wrong but that vengeance belongs to God. The counselor should point out that he wants to show the client that there are Christians who really do care and back up what they believe.

It takes time, but the new convert must grow before he can see the true value of the church.

2. *Find the right church for each convert.* Some churches are better suited to meet the spiritual needs of one convert; another church is better for another convert. The counselor may need to take the convert to various types of churches until the convert learns which one is best suited for him. There are personal tastes in the kind of spiritual diet we feed our souls. Personality, education, and culture often determine the type of church in which the convert will feel most comfortable. Some prefer a large church, others a small one. Some prefer a more formal type of worship, others, the more informal and evangelistic type of service. The decision often is based on the kind of fellowship extended to the convert. His spiritual needs are important, but so are his emotional and social needs in the early days of his conversion. He needs to be surrounded by a strong fellowship of believers who are patient, loving and understanding. He also needs an active church. Converted addicts at first find it hard to know what to do with their spare time. They need a church which has a busy, yet meaningful variety of Christian activities.

3. *Work with the pastor and other officials of the church.* Gain the favor of the pastor, deacons, other church workers, and the congregation in general. If the pastor knows, trusts and respects the counselor's ministry, there will be no problem for the counselor to bring converts into the fellowship of that church. Pastors and their people are lukewarm toward couneslors who carry a chip on their shoulders, who seek to lord it over the pastor, and who give the impression

that they are making a greater sacrifice than anyone else.

Tell the pastor about the type of people with whom you are working. Invite him to visit the areas where you are working. Have him meet some of the people involved in your program. Many apprehensions about certain young people are based on the fact that Christians are not in a position to know how to relate to them. The counselor can overcome these fears. When the counselor gets active in a church, he should coordinate his activities with the pastor. After a new convert begins to attend church, and after he becomes a member, the counselor should not interfere with his duties in the church. He should not continue to counsel unless asked to do so by the pastor, or in cooperation with him.

4. *Do not integrate too soon — or too late.* Many members of the untapped generation are not able to find the help they need in the average church. They need special ministry in a special environment. A person hooked on drugs or alcohol can't walk into a church one day, accept Christ as his personal Savior, and walk back into society the next day. Those on the fringe areas of addiction may be able to get the help they need in the church, but hardcore cases need special attention.

It is a mistake to bring large groups of troubled, disturbed, distressed, rebellious youth into services that are primarily geared for other types of young people. This often causes trouble. The only time it should be done is when the service is promoted entirely for such kinds of youth. Young people who come into services in large groups act to please, or compete with, their own crowd. However, when they are alone, or in small groups, they are more themselves; the Spirit of the Lord has a greater opportunity to speak to them. The counselor should work with such youth on the streets, or through other means, before bringing them into the church.

During a service at which I was to speak in Great Britain, a young Christian worker brought a group of mods and rockers (English motorcycle gangs) into the service to see a film. They watched part of it, but when it got to the point where there was a Christian message, they began to carry on, started smoking, and one by one walked out. Finally the whole group was gone. After the service the young man who had brought them said to me, "Your film wasn't any good. My friends didn't like it."

The reaction of the mods and rockers was typical, but the counselor did not understand some of the basic principles in working with youth. He was hoping that in one service he could accomplish something with his friends that he had not been able to do in preparatory work. He was embarrassed and sought to blame his failure on the film or the church. The counselor must gain the respect of delinquent youth first before they can be controlled when they go to a regular church service.

However, there is a point when it is good to bring the untapped generation into a service. The counselor cannot produce the atmosphere of evangelism and the moving of the Holy Spirit in any other way. Such services and rallies turn the church into a "delivery room." We lose many potential converts by not bringing the lost into the church where the Spirit can travail upon the seed that has been planted in them. The counselor needs a church. He needs this evangelistic atmosphere, but he must not bring youth into it too soon or too late. Timing is important. Often the Christian worker is not aware of this principle. The Holy Spirit will direct the counselor as to the right time and place. The success of youth crusades is due to the fact that Christian workers and counselors have laid the proper groundwork of witnessing, prayer, preparatory counseling, or precounseling with the unsaved. Through proper timing the unsaved are brought to a crusade and the work of conversion takes place.

Guidelines for Churches

1. *Develop an open door policy.* Every church must take a long, hard look at itself to see if it is guilty of practicing what I call "catership." Is it a closed corporation? Does it shut out those who would change the composition of its congregation? Does it shut out certain types of people? This happens if the church gears its outreach to selected segments of the community. If there is not a large number of the untapped generation within the sphere of the church's outreach, it should not neglect those in the immediate community to look elsewhere. But if the church is

in a position to reach the untapped generation, it must not by-pass them for a different or better clientele.

Does the church allow former members of the untapped generation to take part in its various functions? Are they welcome at services but not in various groups within the church, at social functions, and at other special events? If these questions cannot be answered in the affirmative, the church does not have an open door.

Whatever types of people the church caters to eventually determines the composition of that church. A church that seeks only certain types of unconverted people soon takes on the characteristics of that class of people. If a church shows that it wants and welcomes the untapped generation, then integration is possible. It is not easy. It can upset, and it has upset, the normal and often smooth (too smooth in some cases) operation of the church. Not all members will go along with this broadened vision. Some pastors who have decided to broaden their outreach to all segments of the community have been frozen out of their churches, or they have lost key members. (I use the word "key" to describe the key financial supporters.) It takes great courage to face up to the integration problem. Those who decide to do so are likely to face opposition from those who are against such a ministry. The backlash of intolerance, prejudice and "closed corporationism" can make it difficult to accomplish a ministry of integration.

A church going through the throes of reaching the untapped generation must, with compassion and understanding, be taught, preached at, and prayed over to prepare for such a task. (Once again, I interject that I am not necessarily writing about racial integration; that may or may not be a factor in the integration of the untapped generation into the church. I am speaking of integrating those with a different religious, social and cultural life-style into the church. Some white churches would be more opposed to having long-haired youths coming in their doors than they would be to having blacks coming in.)

The pastor should not challenge the attitudes of his congregation without making the necessary preparation. The counselor, regardless of how negative the reaction of the church may be, should always maintain a positive attitude and do as much as he possibly can to bring about integration. The counselor should not purposely work against the church or buck the "closed corporation" congregation. If there is no welcome, go to another church. A new convert can get caught in the cross-fire of such a problem and become a victim of it. He should not have to go through such an experience so early in his Christian life. There are many other churches that do practice the open door policy. The counselor must find them and work out the integration problem through them.

A church in a small rural town where there are no slums or ghettos wanted us to send them some of our problem people. They wanted to import the needy. Evidently they felt guilty for not having helped the ghetto types, or like some they may have felt it fashionable to reach them. This is not necessary — we suggested to this group that they assess their most immediate needy problem and start at that point. Every community, to one degree or another, has members of the untapped generation. A vision must be developed to see them. The church does not need to import them. However, when a congregation begins to minister to such, the grapevine will buzz. The word will spread that Pastor Smith's church, or whatever the name, has put out the welcome mat to the "now" generation. The congregation must be prepared to handle the growing pains of such new converts. A church accustomed to doing "business as usual" stands a chance of getting upset when new people with new problems start coming in. Those young people from unstable, socially-maladjusted backgrounds may do a little bit of stumbling on the road to maturity.

During one of our staff meetings at Teen Challenge we were discussing some of the problems our new converts were going through. Some of the staff were reacting under the strain and pressure of these problems. A few felt that such problems were an indication of a lack of spiritual power, perhaps the personal failure — or even sin — of some of the workers. One of them said that if we were really "on fire for God" such problems would not exist. Then one of the other staff members spoke up and said, "We must remember, we are dealing with problem people. These are not the usual, run-of-the-mill problems. These cases have baffled doctors, social workers, psychiatrists, and ministers. In our situation we must expect these kinds of problems." Then my mother remarked, "Yes, and where there are no oxen, the crib is clean."

When a church decides to nurture the babes in Christ who come out of the juvenile jungles, the addiction centers, the ghettos, and the youth subculture, it must expect dirty diapers, spilt milk, and crying and whining. That is a part of growing up. The church that wants to enjoy only the peace and calmness of "the same old people and the same old services" should stay away from' the untapped, unwanted generation. At Teen Challenge we have a busy, dirty crib. But spiritual births are constantly taking place. And spiritual manhood and maturity do come.

2. *Don't baby the new babes in Christ.* The church need not spoil the newly-converted. It is possible to display a misguided attention and spoil new converts. One pastor, to bolster and encourage a converted drug addict, kept pushing him to the front. He magnified his testimony and set him on a pedestal. The young man couldn't take all the attention, became proud, and then stumbled and fell. The pastor thought he was doing the right thing for the young man, but in his sincerity, however, brought about his undoing.

There are other dangers in glorifying a convert's past. A preacher's son tried drugs so he "could have a bigger testimony." An evangelist, who had been in the drug scene in the past, began to overplay it and overstated his drug involvement. He felt pressured by others to talk about it, and his story grew more dramatic all the time. Finally, he fell under the pressure of guilt for having embellished the story. He fell back into his past and did what he had said he had done, but had never actually experienced. Counselors must avoid overexposure and exploitation of a convert's past.

Neither should converts be displayed to brag about one's success. Although the transformation of addicts, rebels and others is living proof of the grace and power of God, if it appears to a new convert that his conversion is being used to prove the validity of someone's ministry, he is going to feel manipulated. This does not mean churches and organizations should never use converts' testimonies. They can and should be used in the proper way. When chosen and screened by the pastor and counselor, their testimonies can be very effective.

Babying new converts keeps them from sprouting their own spiritual wings. Some churches are afraid to "let go" of converts. Behind this is a fear of losing them. It is also an admission that perhaps their faith is not strong enough. New converts must have breathing room.

I know of a young man who was converted at a particular church and became an instant spiritual "star" and trophy. He spoke at ministers' meetings, conferences, rallies and other special gatherings. He became an expression of the pastor's and the church's soul-winning ego. When he inquired about Bible college, he was told he didn't need it. What he really wanted was to get out from under the church's control. He wanted to prove himself elsewhere. But friends told him, "You'll never make it on your own." They refused to support his efforts to try out his own wings. They didn't want to lose their star. As a result, the young man became bitter. He had a disagreement with the pastor, left the church, and eventually backslid. Then they told him, "Didn't we say you weren't ready to go out on your own?" Given an opportunity to face testing and to "pilot his own ship," he no doubt would have grown quickly and would have returned to the church later to become a spiritual leader. He fell because he had no foundation. It happened because the church loved him too much.

3. *Trust new converts.* The opposite extreme of babying new converts is to keep them under suspicion. Certain types of new converts do need extra attention for a period of time. The pastor, counselors and members of the congregation must keep an eye on them during the early stages of their Christian development, but this must be done carefully and tactfully so as not to give them the impression that they are not trusted. Such converts will be very sensitive to this kind of treatment. Some of them have been under suspicion all their lives. Many have never been given an opportunity to accomplish anything they can be proud of. At the first sign of failure they were fired from their jobs or thrown out of their homes. Through Christ, for the first time they feel like "somebody." They need the chance to live on an equal basis with other Christians. They need to be trusted with responsibilities. When they struggle, give

them the benefit of the doubt. Those who work with them must have what we call a "third eye," the eye that watches over them without their knowing it.

In some cases there has been difficulty because wives — or parents and relatives — of new converts don't trust them. In such a situation the young man feels like he is on constant trial, and that if he makes one wrong move he will be pounced upon. A young man I am counseling is having difficulty with his marriage because his wife has every one of his moves under suspicion. He told me, "Brother Don, I have no breathing room."

The same kind of attitude can come from the church. I know of another young man who had difficulty with his pastor and with his wife because they would not let him go anywhere except with his wife or someone in the church. They told him it was for his own good, but he knew it was because they didn't trust him. "It's hard," he said to me. "What more do I have to do to prove myself, if they don't treat me like a man? Don't they believe I'm a new creature in Christ Jesus? I know my past is behind me, but they don't seem to think so." Finally, he gave up his membership in the church and told them, "I'm not going to be a dog on a leash anymore." He moved into a circle of fellowship where he felt trusted and respected.

New converts should not be kept from certain tasks in the church just because of their pasts. Of course, there are certain responsibilities the pastor and the church will not give to any new convert, regardless of his past. When a person comes from a troubled past and is denied the opportunity to participate in some Christian service, he tends to feel it is because of his past. This is where the counselor must make the situation entirely clear.

4. *Learn how to handle backsliders.* Often the immediate reaction, when a convert falls, is to cut him off completely from fellowship. This may have to be done, if it appears he has no sorrow or repentance and no desire to be restored to Christ and the fellowship of the church. But what about those who are interested in recovering? Should the counselor look for them? Should they be left alone until they are ready to return on their own? Should the burden and responsibility be placed entirely on the backslider, or should the counselor resume some of it?

When an addict, or others in that category, falls back into his old life, it is a shattering experience. Not only is he out of fellowship with the church and with God, but his whole life has fallen apart. If a person who has never been an addict, rebel, or runaway backslides, he can still usually function as a normal member of society. He can work, care for his family, and have social contacts. However, when an addict or alcoholic backslides, it is quite different. He has failed not only as a Christian, but as a parent, husband, or son. He loses his job, friends, and everything. Therefore, his discouragement is greater and it is harder for him to recover. He will feel that he has failed the church, the pastor, his counselor, and others who have worked with him. That's why he may run away.

Therefore, the counselor will have to go after the backslider. Tell him he is welcome back to the fellowship of the church, and that he can be restored in faith. It may take a number of visits on the streets or to his home, and much counseling and prayer, before there is victory over his sin and failure. If the backslider still does not respond, he should be left alone and dealt with through the prayers of the church. If the counselor knows where he is, he should visit him periodically just to show that he has not been forgotten, and that the church is still praying for him and is interested in his restoration.

The backslider's family will need special prayer, counseling and attention during this period of testing. In their frustration they must not do anything that would create a gap between themselves and the backslider. The family's immediate reaction often is to do something drastic. However, a patient and understanding spouse, parent, relative, pastor, or Christian worker can help to bring the backslider back to the Lord.

While walking along a New York City street, I spotted a former client approaching me approximately three quarters of a block away. We had come to know him quite well and had seen the grace of God revealed in some measure within his life. However, he reverted to drugs. There had been no contact with him for nearly a year. As soon as our eyes met, he quickly walked across the street to avoid me. Apparently, he was too ashamed to face me. Running after him I hollered, "Walt, Walt." But he kept on going. Finally catching up to him, I said, "Walt, it's good to see you. How are you doing?"

"Well, all right, I guess," he hesitatingly answered. As we chatted he finally admitted what I already knew — that he was back on drugs.

"Why don't you come back, Walt?" I asked. He seemed disinterested, but I knew this indifference came from his shame. Then with a strong sense that my words were being anointed by the Holy Spirit, I proceeded to tell him, "Walt, it was no accident that we met here tonight. This just didn't happen. God sent me out here right on this very street to meet you and to tell you that God is not finished with your life." He listened carefully.

"Do you know something, Brother Don," he said. "You're right. I do believe God sent you to find me. I'm usually never in this neighborhood, but I couldn't get drugs where I usually hang out so I came over here."

As a result of that meeting he did come back to Teen Challenge. It was not easy to face those who once knew him during his days of victory and deliverance. Walt was to leave and return once again before he finally matured and became rooted, grounded, and settled in the faith.

In another case it took a little hand-scribbled note to a drop-out client to get him back. He was living with a prostitute and would not come out to talk with me. I sent in to him the message of concern with another drug addict. The note read — "Dear Bob, if God is speaking to you, call me. You know where you belong. I hope to hear from you."

In a few days he did call and break the silence barrier. The little note helped him get up enough courage to come back. It is often such simple contacts that can trigger an interest that lies buried under fear, guilt, shame, and sin. Perhaps, the prodigal son decided to "arise and go" home because the father had sent out messengers with the word that a welcome mat was out on the doorstep.

The backslider's immediate need is not sermonizing, but comfort and food for his faith. Later, judgment can be made as to why he failed. However, he should not be cuddled and babied. In one case, a Christian family helped a backslider when he gave them a sad story of financial difficulties. He blamed his backsliding on his money problems. The family gave him money, which he used to support his drug habit. He was doing what in the drug world is called "working an angle." Instead of helping to restore him, this family aided in keeping him in sin.

The most important thing for the counselor is not to give up on backsliders from the untapped generation, especially the addicts. Often new converts become too proud of their new lives and they get spiritually lax. I have seen many who have fallen because of this, but in the end they were stronger because they learned through their experience that they must put on the whole armor of God and keep it on at all times. In the case of the addict, he never forgets what a shot of dope feels like, and this and temptation may present itself even many years after his conversion. Sometimes it is only through a relapse that an addict learns how important it is to walk in the Spirit. Converts from the untapped generation must live the Spirit-filled life to maintain their victory in Christ.

CONCLUSION

This has not been a happy, "inspirational" book to write. The people about whom it is written are not the leaders but often the dregs of society; still they are human beings and, most of all, they are people whom Jesus Christ loves. What we have tried to say is that Christ's love for these people must be shown through other human beings, Christian counselors, workers and pastors who can say with the apostle Paul, "For the love of Christ constraineth us" (II Cor. 5:14). No other motive will suffice.

This book is about serious human needs. All men have needs of one kind or another, but somehow the needs of the untapped generation seem to be worse than most. We have not tried to elevate or exalt the miseries of sin. We must keep ourselves from a morbid delving into iniquity. But Jesus told us to "look on the fields; for they are white already to harvest" (John 4:35).

We have tried to write confidently, however, that the enormous human needs can be met through the Gospel of Jesus Christ and by the power of the Holy Spirit. The cost is great, to be sure, in perseverance, faith, courage and hard work. In the end, we at Teen Challenge give ourselves to this ministry because we believe not only that the needs are great, but because we believe our job is a fulfillment of Christ's commission to all of His followers: "Go ye into all the world, and preach the gospel to every creature" (Mark 16:15).

We are going day by day into the world of the untapped generation. This book is an appeal for you, the reader, to follow us into that world. We have tried to tell you, without embellishment, what it is like, about the real people who live under the scourge of sin and addiction, and how Christians can be involved in reaching these people for Christ.

The things we have learned in our witness, our counseling and our rehabilitation work at Teen Challege we are glad to share with the churches and with all Christians, as the task is too great for any one church or organization. For whatever successes we have seen, we are truly grateful to the Lord. Our prayer is that as you come to the end of this book, you will sense something of our burden, something of our very strong feelings about reaching the untapped generation for Christ.